A Mind of My Own

memoir of recovery from Aphasia

By

Harrianne Mills

This book is a work of non-fiction. Names and places have been changed to protect the privacy of all individuals. The events and situations are true.

First published by AuthorHouse 10/11/04

ISBN: 1-4184-0656-2 (e-book)
ISBN: 1-4184-0655-4 (Paperback)

Library of Congress Control Number: 2004105286

This book is printed on acid free paper.

Printed in the United States of America
Bloomington, IN

"Did I ever tell you you're my hero(es)?

You're everything, everything, I wished I could be.

And I, I can fly higher than an eagle.

You are the wind beneath my wings."

(song "Wind Beneath My Wings," composer Joe Brooks)

To my extraordinary Mother, Bertha Mills,
a role-model impossible to follow,
and to the beloved memory of my Father,
Leonard J. Mills, whose memory never dies in me.

Contents

Introduction

There are 3 beginnings to this story.

1) I now know that it was May 1985 when I was taken to a hospital in Greece, declared dead, and put into the morgue. In examining my body, and realizing that I was only in a coma, they sent me to Evangelismos Hospital in Athens. My coma lasted only about 12 hours, but my recovery took a year, during which I first had to remember who I was, and then gradually re-learn how to walk, talk, read, and so on. I had suffered a brain injury from a motor scooter accident. The helmet had broken, and a piece gone into my brain between the parietal and occipital lobes on the right side of my brain.

2) I realized in June 1985, when I fell down while trying to walk to the bathroom, that my mind had it backwards. I had thought my

memories of recovery from an accident and being in pain were all in the past, and so part of my dreaming state while asleep. But when I fell down, and it really hurt (!) I realized that the pain was the present, and the rare moments of good health were all dreams. I had been sleeping 22 hours a day, so it makes sense that my dreams felt more real than being awake. It had taken my mind about a month to wake up.

3) Back in Greece in the summer of 1992, I decided that the time had come to gather up all the notes and tapes and journals kept by my family and friends and doctors, not to mention my own attempts to write about my recovery, and finally to do what the doctors had asked me to do while recovering from the accident 8 years earlier – to write a memoir of my recovery. The person experiencing such a recovery is rarely a college Classics professor, and they were certain that any notes kept during that recovery would be helpful to caregivers facing clients in a similar situation. I began writing this memoir in the Summer of 1992. I didn't touch the manuscript for about 10 years, then decided in the summer of 2003 to revive it, finish it, and get it published.

What follows, then, is both a narrative of my recovery from aphasia, and a series of meditations surrounding that experience, in an attempt to capture the essentials of the event. If nothing else, let this book be a testimony to the deceased Harrianne, a.k.a. Annie. For while my memory of the journey is no doubt full of inaccuracies and/or misinterpretations, my general <u>sense</u> of the event, like my transient memory, is quite clear, though again, perhaps only in my mind's eye…

Finally, the title of this creation was consciously chosen to refer at some level to <u>A Mind of Her Own: The Life of Karen Horney</u> (psychoanalyst who challenges Freud's conception of women) by Susan Quinn (NY, 1987). I also warn the reader: however unimaginable the following account may seem, it is a truthful exposition of the events, along with a few speculations as to their significance. None of the characters or events in this book are inventions of the author, though some names have been changed to allow them some privacy. Only the dreams are unreal.

Acknowledgements: Thank you, thank you, thank you, to my plethora of doctors, nurses, and caregivers, but most especially to my Mother Bert, brother Gene, sister Nancy and their families, and to my closest friends at the time, notably Wesley and Timothy.

But most of all at this point, I am especially grateful to my lifetime-companion Tom, the love of my life who, perhaps more than anything and anyone, believes in me. I have come to rely upon him for encouragement, advice, and moral support. Above all, he has taught me to recognize, to value, and to require, the essentials of life.

"There are many reasons…for writing a memoir about an illness: his friends have egged him on; he wants to reach other sufferers; he thinks his example may do something to change the climate within which life-threatening illnesses are treated. There is a kernel of truth for me in each. Yet my real reason is an experiential one. I passed through a searing experience that tested and changed me in ways I never foresaw. And like the Ancient Mariner I want to tell my story, to whatever listeners it finds." Max Lerner <u>Wrestling with an Angel: a Memoir of my Triumph over Illness</u> (NY, 1990), p.20

Harrianne,

a.k.a. Annie and Arianna

Chapter 1: The Start of the Journey

"The mind is such a fragile thing.

This curving whirr of crystal wing descending lightly on my brow,

Befuddles all that, up 'till now,

I thought I knew by reckoning.

Eyes shut, hands forward thrust, it leaps along,

Oblivious to my shattered song.

So now I sit and idly ponder dazzling dreams

That follow silver thread,

And weave a ring of fancy 'round my head."

Dolores E. McGuire

Falling victim to the historian's inclination to begin at an arbitrarily selected beginning, let me start with the event which precipitated the process of me first losing and then gradually regaining, a mind of my own.

It all happened like this.

It was 1985 and there I was, finishing up the school year in a bit of a rush, as usual, since I was not only getting ready to go to Greece (my ordinary summer habitat), but I was taking a group of college students for the first 3 weeks of my summer, as I had done many summers in the previous 5 years. Not only was I very busy, but I had been, well, tense, nervous, anxious, etc., due both to job uncertainty and to some personal lifestyle transitions. Basically, during the preceding month I had found myself exploring an immense assortment of various aspects of my life – my career, my family, my sexuality, my philosophy, my friends, even my likes and dislikes. I kept wishing for new ways either to entertain and please myself, or at least to avoid irritation, which had been frequent of late.

You need to understand that I previously had not been disposed to being self-absorbed. Nor did I have the late-20th century predilection for self-reflection. Rather, I had been schooled in the graduate study of Classical Antiquity, and not in the intricacies of personal therapy (say through self-talk), or the analysis of interpersonal relationships. During that month immediately prior to my accident, however, I had ventured into territory remarkably similar to that of a Harlequin Romance. At any rate, I know everything was alright when I arrived in Greece, reached Ancient Korinth, and (eventually) went to sleep.

A day later I was hospitalized. But the next thing I remember is falling down, hurting myself, and starting to laugh, which it turns out happened about 3 and 1/2 weeks later.

Now it's true that certain specific moments between those two events have since re-occurred to me. But I didn't remember them at the time or soon afterward. No, the first meaningful moment for me was when I fell down onto the floor and found myself laughing in the middle of the night in Boston.

I woke up the whole house, and tried to explain what had occurred and why I was laughing, but I didn't possess the tools with which to do so.

I had awoken in the middle of the night, and didn't wake up my brother Gene who was, as usual, asleep in the chair by the side of my bed, to help me to the bathroom. I must have decided to try it all by myself, and to let him sleep. (I certainly don't remember deciding any such thing, but I extrapolate such thoughts from the ensuing occurrence.)

I didn't get very far. I couldn't walk, so I fell down. What woke me up, and induced the laughter was, believe it or not, that it <u>hurt</u> me to fall down!

You see, I had been living in two very different worlds for the previous month. While asleep (which I later found out was approximately 22 hours a day), my world was 1988 and I was remembering, and often recounting for others, a time past when I had experienced a very bad accident, was in much pain all the time and could not take care of myself. I lived in that world recalling my healthy past most of the time.

In my other world when I was awake, on the other hand, those exact same things were actually happening, including the intense pain. Luckily for me, I was only awake for short periods of time. But (and here's the catch!), until I fell down in the middle of the night in Boston, I had it backwards. Until then, I was certain that being in pain was just a dream and the memory of it was real.

Now I know that sleep, when medicated, and especially in hospitals, can result in a blurring of the dividing line between reality and the imagination, but my experience was exactly the opposite. There was no blurring at all. I did not travel back and forth. I was either in one life or the other, and I was certain that the one with pain was definitely a recurring dream I was having. But when I fell down that night while trying to walk to the bathroom, AND IT HURT, I suddenly realized that THIS WAS REAL, that I must have been dreaming about the lack of pain, and that the supposed recollection of such an event was JUST A DREAM…(!) I had gotten it wrong as to which was reality and which was imaginings. And when I realized my mistake, needless to say, I burst out laughing. That is when I first woke up.

Woke up? Well, it felt like the beginning of the world. As if I had finally gotten a long-due new lease on life, or a transfusion from a blood bank. For me, the event gave new meaning to the expression "I must have been dreaming." I certainly didn't know at the time if something had just begun or something had just ended, but I knew that everything had just changed, and that I was most definitely alive, in spite of the pain.

Life had fallen on her once like a tree that had cracked and been blown over in a storm. She had crawled out from under a ton of broken branches, shocked, bleeding, traumatized; but after that, life had more or less let her be. A little crippled was fine with life. So long as you're wounded you know you're alive. (Bernard Malamud <u>Dubin's Lives</u> (NY, 1977) p.380)

From then on? Well, my recovery from the accident that caused all that pain is what this whole book is about, finally begun to be written

7 years later, and completed about 10 years after that. Mostly written in Greece in the summers – i.e. in the country (surrounded by mountains and animals), in the summer (with sun and heat), in the Mediterranean (with passion and vitality), when single (no sex or passion), and when working very hard (and so with a need for escape). Looking back over my journey of recovery 17 years later, when I have finally gotten around to completing this manuscript, it strikes me as both a scary and a fascinating process (both for myself and for others) to have survived. I certainly did not feel that way at the time. No, those words do not come even close to expressing my thoughts and feelings back in 1985, following the accident. To understand why not, you need to understand why I keep calling the process one of recovery.

It took me quite a while to understand from what I was recovering, but let me recount what I now know, based upon what I have read and been told. Feel free to take my rendition of both the event and my resulting recovery at face value, as it is intended. Others may view things differently, but what follows is how I <u>lived</u> it, and so have encoded it. I do not claim to represent a whole group of people who have had similar experiences, but my memories may help them too.

"So, where to begin?" as I got in the habit of starting virtually every journal entry during my recovery. Well, it may seem strange, but let me quote from my diary entry written just <u>before</u> the accident occurred:

> *Sun. May 19, 1985: Once again, I have high hopes of keeping at this diary business, hopefully encouraged by the immense pleasure I experienced while writing during the last month in America. Today was, as always with traveling to Greece, a <u>very</u> long day. All told, the trip took 28 hours, not including a stop in Amsterdam (on Monday) and a coffee frappe stop in Eleusis. The flight from Columbus to New York went fine, until we had to make an emergency landing in New York due to a failure in the hydraulic brakes. Scary! But, it turned out OK. The trip from New York to Athens on KLM was remarkably good, and included a wonderful 5 hour stopover in Amsterdam, which was long enough to walk around the city, and even take a boat tour through the canals. I only wish the weather had been better.*

It seems that I had arrived in Ancient Korinth rather late on Monday, May 20th, 1985, the same day on which my airplane had arrived in Greece. My arrival, already, is one of those moments to which I have returned again and again, like a dream, in the process of reclaiming my memory: I am standing at the gate to my then boyfriend

Timothy's house in Ancient Korinth, talking with his friend Marianne. Now I remember, but do not know exactly why, that I am standing outside the fence, on the path to his house, at the gate. I cannot remember what we were talking about, but I can well imagine. In fact, as is common for my memories of conversations with various people at the time, I cannot remember the substance of the conversation, but only its existence and especially the intensity of our emotions.

I must have experienced some jet-lag, for I was wide awake for quite a while, until I fell asleep around 2am, after telling Timothy not to wake me when they all left for work at the Isthmia Excavation (of which I was a member) at 8am. Instead, I slept considerably late. I know I had in my possession a <u>lot</u> of money, in the form of traveler's checks, which I needed to change into drachmas in order to pay for the students' study-tour, which would begin in a few days. So, for about the 200th time in my life, I mounted Playmate, my little Vespa motor scooter, and took off for the bank in New Korinth, my backpack filled with those traveler's checks.

I didn't make it. I didn't make it to the bank. I didn't even make it to New Korinth, which is only about 3 miles from Ancient Korinth. Rather, I apparently ended up unconscious in a ditch with a broken helmet.

Whether I somehow just veered off the road (which I doubt) or was forced off, perhaps even hit by a car, I will never know. There is, to this day, a major bump in the road where it happened. If I had been driving quickly, which I doubt, I presumably could have caused the accident myself. Who knows? In any case, some sort of accident happened, just after I crossed the bridge over the National Road, and I ended up in a ditch. Who knows how long I stayed there? Some people came and picked me up, unconscious, and took me to the New Korinth Hospital. They would not leave their name, which makes me think they may have had something to do with it, or perhaps only knew something about it, and did not want to tell the police. No matter. Still, I would like to know who these people were, in order to thank them! After all, I suppose I could still be lying there, unconscious, or dead, on the side of the road! Instead, they took me to the New Korinth hospital, where it was thought that I was dead. Or so I was told.

Sometime later, someone noticed that I wasn't dead at all, but only unconscious, from a head concussion resulting in a coma. Then, having realized from my ID cards in English that I was a foreigner, an American, they sent me, by ambulance, to Evangelismos Hospital in Athens, where I remained for about 3 weeks. Remember: I have no recollection of <u>any</u> of this narrative. Not yet. They say that I was only unconscious for about 12 hours, but I don't remember coming out of it at all, so I wouldn't call that moment my regaining consciousness.

My state was not exactly conscious, I assure you, which is why I don't remember.

Well, Timothy was notified, and he came to Athens with some of the OSU students who were on the study-tour <u>he</u> was leading. He found me in a bathing suit (!), unconscious, and covered with blood, with dirt and stones in my hair. He spoke with the doctors, who told him I was in a coma, but that all my signs were good, and I would be just fine, probably all better and allowed to leave the hospital in just a few days. They had stitched a bandage to the right side of my head.

When I did not get all better, but was still virtually "out of my mind" about 3 days later, he called my family in America, and aside from their shock and horror, they decided that my younger brother Gene (who had been to Greece before) would come and assume the responsibility for getting me back to America, and that Timothy would lead around the group of students who were arriving for <u>my</u> study-tour around Greece. Or so I later was told, though I'm sure I must have been told much earlier, when nothing spoken made any sense to me.

Since I can't tell you much about my time in the hospital in Athens, aside from what I was later told, let me take advantage of a letter written by Timothy to me and my family, explaining what happened that first week following the accident, before my brother Gene arrived to take care of me and bring me back to America.

Dear Annie,

You were unconscious most of the night, although you woke up unpredictable, shouted, thrashed around, and tore at your I.V. By the morning (22nd) you were more alert, but still by no means responsive. You couldn't really talk and didn't recognize anyone. You had a language of your own and made lots of strange noises. You spent most of the day asleep and were awake most of the night. The I.V. continued to occupy most of your attention and they finally fastened your right arm to the bed.

By the 23rd (Thursday) you had begun to eat a little, but you were still violent and made very few real words. The night were the worst since you were awake most of the time and you shouted much of the time.

By the 24th (Friday) you looked better, but your violence was at its worst. You tore off the covers, wouldn't keep your shirt on, and generally rolled around as naked as you could be. You shouted "no...no..." a lot. You were scheduled for a brain scan in the afternoon and we took an ambulance to the place where it's done, but you wouldn't sit still for it, so we had to come back.

These first four days were the hardest…You couldn't be left alone for a minute – also, there was very little sleep at night since that was your "busy" time…Lisa, Anya, and Becky came to visit you and you said I was the "magician" for bringing the 3 little girls to stare at you. You were beginning to use more English and the I.V. was out, but you had begun your habit of getting up and trying to escape out the end of the bed. At night you did this 10 or more times an hour! Every day, however, you seemed to be getting better.

By Sunday it was clear that you were going to need considerable time to get back to your old self. On Monday (27th) I again arranged to have the brain scan done. This time the doctor had arranged for an anesthesiologist although I'm not sure you needed it since you had calmed down considerably – but it was done under a general anesthetic. You had really begun to calm down by Monday, although you continued to get up and try to get out and your catheter came apart at least 3 times every day. You were beginning to eat all of your food and even helped feed yourself.

On Tuesday (28th) you continued to improved and we had a real conversation in the afternoon. You were much calmer during the night. You were restless and moved around a lot, but only tried to get up twice! The big news of the day, however, was the result of the brain scan, which [according to the Evangelismos doctors] showed absolutely no abnormality!

And I hope every day gets better and better. Love, T.

Now I'm sure I was told many things about the accident and my condition at the time, but I couldn't understand anything people were saying, I didn't remember anything I was told, and I didn't seem to understand that I didn't understand. Here, let me explain.

My helmet had broken in the accident, and a piece of the helmet had gone into my head, between the parietal lobe and the occipital lobe on the right side of my brain, severing the connections between those two lobes. As a result, in order for incoming information to be understood, it had to be processed using a brain whose connections were undergoing natural (no need for drugs or therapy) reconstruction. After all, since the connections had been broken between those two parts of the brain, the information kept getting lost traveling around my brain, looked for an open bridge to cross from one lobe to another.

In the Athens hospital, with my arms were tied down to the bed, I was mostly asleep, awoke for short periods, and then went right back to sleep. After the first week, when I did wake up, my Gene would usually be there, asking me all sorts of questions. Do you know who you are? Where you are? Who I am? etc. My answers varied considerably. I would often nod my head yes (that was what he wanted, wasn't it?), but when asked my name, for example, I could not answer. Then, when told the correct answer, say, that he was my brother Gene, I would reply something like: "Oh yea, I knew that." Then I would fall asleep, and when I woke up, I once again had no idea who he was or why he was there…This event occurred regularly. Over and over again I awoke completely confused.

In a sense, every time I woke up, I felt as though I knew who I was, except for a few biographical details in need of clearing up — such as my name and what I was doing there! "Little" things like that…It was as if I had to discover anew who the hell I was each time I woke up, and yet I was unaware that it was rediscovery, because I didn't recall it having happened before.

What were my thoughts doing, lying there with my arms strapped down, staring at the ceiling, when I wasn't asleep? I honestly have no idea, but I would guess very little. Based on my later thoughts, however, lying down staring at the ceiling for long stretches of time a month or two later in Virginia, my guess is that I was "studying" the situation — if the word "study" can be applied to the operation of my mind (i.e. lack of a working mind) at that point. I must have been taking account of the situation in which I found myself — assuming, that is, that I was aware of that situation,…which I honestly doubt.

Gene became my guardian and my shield. With only a bare smattering of Greek, he made phone calls, wrote notes, made arrangements for our return to the U.S., etc. Not wanting to leave me unattended in a Greek hospital, Gene mostly slept on the floor next to my bed, or under my bed, but sometimes another bed in the wing would be empty, and he learned to use it to sleep. I didn't notice. And he noticed that I didn't notice – one of the many things bothered him. Once, for example, when I woke up, Gene told me he had found the bed right next to me empty, whereas someone had previously been in it. Gene had come to know the patient and their family pretty well. He asked after them and was told "she died." He was sad, and sorry to hear that, but when he told me, I said: "Oh," or "So?" or something like that. I just didn't care. It wasn't me, and I hurt all over and didn't even know who or where the hell I was…Gene was considerably bothered, wondering if it was something I would grow out of, or a new personality I was developing as a result of the accident.

Another thing about being in the hospital in Athens. I had brought with me many, many, travelers checks, both of my own money, and for the study-tour which I had planned to lead. While in the hospital, that money was needed - in part to pay for the new return trip ticket Gene was buying for me, and in part for Timothy to use in leading the study-tour in my place. Unfortunately, in order to get the money, I had to sign all those traveler's checks. And there were so many of them. And I didn't know how to write.

Almost every time I woke up for a few minutes, Gene would hand me some traveler's checks and help me sign my name, guiding my hand with the pen, in order for me to copy my name as he had written it out on a piece of paper. Of course, I don't remember any of this.

Oddly enough, I can recall two specific moments toward the end of my 3 week stay in the Athens hospital with immense clarity, though I have no idea which one happened first, or even if they really happened! In one such moment, I remember riding in an elevator, I believe while still strapped down onto the bed. The other thing I remember is Gene wheeling me out into the hall, in a wheelchair, and looking out the window onto the grounds of the American School of Classical Studies, which I apparently recognized.

Well, realizing the futility of these attempts to give you a good sense of my Greek hospital existence for those first 3 weeks following the accident, let me quote from the start of the narrative written by Gene, beginning my second week after the accident. Gene recorded the events as follows:

5/29/85:

2pm: I arrived at the Hospital with Timothy, and I see Annie just ending lunch. She greets me warmly but a little oddly. I'm not sure she really knows who I am or is only pretending to. I give her regards from Mom and Nancy; she smiles and says "that's nice," but gets confused when I say she's her sister. She does spontaneously take my hand. I ask if she knows where she is: what country? She says yes, but when I ask her to <u>name</u> the country, she gets confused, says "it's like an event that…" and then trails off. I say it's Greece; she's nonplussed. She says she's sleepy, goes into a mildly fitful sleep. I see her open her eyes pretty often, and then close them again. Also, she says she wants to leave "this place" tomorrow. I say it will be soon. Now and then she opens her eyes, smiles weakly at me, and closes them again.

8pm: Annie slept for 1 1/2 - 2 hours. When she awakened, she greeted me cheerfully, but didn't remember our earlier conversation at all. I asked her a lot of questions to see what she remembered. She said she didn't mind my asking. This time she remembered Nancy easily; I showed her a snapshot of Mom and 2 other women (Esther and Diane), and she picked out Mom without any prompting. She knew that Dad is dead and that's he's buried "near Washington," but couldn't remember his name. Said she could remember Nancy's

17

husband, but not his name. A lot of things she got right, but only after a lot of thought. I could see her trying to remember. "Nancy lives in…Boston!" ("She doesn't live in Virginia, does she?") I asked her what she did for a living. She thought awhile, and said "I go to school." (I laughed: she hit <u>that</u> one on the head!) She also decided that she studied Ancient History.

5/30/85: The inefficiency (incompetence?) of the Greeks is driving me crazy. When I was touristing, I cultivated a "Greek attitude" about such things: no use getting upset about what can't be helped. It's <u>still</u> no use – but in the present situation it's making me furious. The medical records are a fiasco. When I asked for them (copies), the doctor sat down and "wrote" a short paragraph saying when she was admitted, no external injuries, 8mg x 3 dexamethasone, negative x-rays [ha!] and CAT scan. That's all! He was very offended when I insisted on getting a copy of the CAT scan. He finally said I could take the originals myself out to the copy shop and xerox them. I tried, but they didn't come out, being negatives. I would have just kept the originals, once I had them in hand, but I figured that might make it hard to get Annie out! I stopped by the institute where the CAT scan was done to see if they could get me a copy. Needless to say, I was told to call back in a few hours. I'm going to try again in a few minutes. We'll see.

6/1/85:

4pm: Moderately encouraging developments. Annie's bandage finally came off yesterday morning, and her catheter came out just an hour ago. She's very sleepy now – still under sedation – but the plan is to get her up in an hour for her first walk. The Doctor says that she'll have no trouble traveling in a week, but I'm going to try for Friday the 7th to go back. Still no word on Annie's passport.

And how is Annie? She seems to be making some progress, but it's very slow. The most moving sign was on Thursday night. She had been very foggy about Mom and Nancy. She seemed to remember them, knew a little about them, etc., but not much interest expressed, couldn't remember Mom's name, etc. Anyway, I played, at her request, the taped letter from Mom, and when she heard Mom's voice, she grimaced and began to shed tears (so did I!). I asked her if she remembered them, and she nodded yes. I stroked her hair for awhile, and she stopped crying.

Today she seemed to be recovering more of her lost memories, and wasn't quite as confused as she has been. She asked about her students – said she remembered coming to Greece with them – and asked why she had to go back to the U.S. A good sign. Until now, she hasn't known she's in Greece.

6pm (written in a café in Syntagma Square): Annie couldn't stand unsupported, but with the help of the nurses and myself, she managed to "walk" (i.e. move her feet) from her bed to a chair, 6-8 feet away. Trouble controlling her left leg, but she does have sensation and limited control of it. Her left arm seems fine. (She was hit on the right side of her head.) When she got back to bed, after sitting in the chair for about 10 minutes, she was exhausted and wanted to sleep.

Back to her mental state. She has a hard time finding words. She asked this afternoon for her "wine," while pointing at her wrist; then she tried "oil;" I suggested "watch" and that was it. When she can't think of the word for something, she generally calls it either an "evidence," an "example," or an "event." But she's doing better today than yesterday – a wider variety of words used, and more complicated sentences. She still tends to use stock phrases a lot in response to comments: mainly "that's true" and "that would be nice." Her use of these phrases would not seem inappropriate out of context, but after awhile, when these are (nearly) her only replies, one realizes that she has only a limited understanding of what she's responding to. But she clearly does have <u>some</u> understanding. She never uses one phrase where the other would be more appropriate. An example:

Gene: It looks like you got rid of that scab.
Annie: That's true.

Gene: I think we'll have you out of here in a few days.
Annie: That would be nice.

But even these stock answers were fewer today than yesterday. She can almost sustain a "real conversation," for a very short time. A few minutes at most.

She is aware, at least usually, that she's not quite herself, and remarks on it frequently: "It's odd," "It's strange," "It's very unusual." Once, she did say (matter of factly) "It's sort of scary," but aside from that, there's been no indication that she's frightened (thank God!). That may have to do with the sedation; <u>all</u> of her emotions seem depressed. She told me a couple of days ago that she knows <u>who I am</u> (i.e. Gene, her brother), but she doesn't really <u>know me</u>. I just seem "sort of familiar." That's changed since, I think. She still doesn't show much emotion, but she doesn't treat me so distantly anymore; sometimes her manner towards me is almost normal, and she seems genuinely glad (at least sometimes) to have me around now.

Her memory of very recent events has improved a lot in the last two days. When I first got here, almost every conversation had to start almost from scratch. I.e., every time she awoke, she had forgotten what country she's in, what year it was, whether she had been in the hospital before that moment, etc. No more. Now she seems to have a least a dim recall of the last 2 or 3 days. This may have its bad side: almost every time we've talked, she's said that she could stand saying "here" (in the hospital, though I'm not sure she's always known that it _is_ a hospital) for one more day at most. I always tell her that it might be a _little_ longer than that, but it hasn't been a problem, since she never remembered from one time to the next that she'd been there before. Now she does, and that might make her more restless to get out. We'll see.

Other newly-recovered memories: she remembered today that she taught 3 classes last year: "Greek, Italian (???) and Ancient History." I assume the Italian is a close approximation to Latin. She wanted to know why she had to go back to the U.S. Why not stay in Greece? "Everything I have to do is here." I explained, she acquiesced, "...I suppose."

She was surprised by her weakness when she tried to walk, and especially her trouble with her left leg.

Her attitude is also improving. Two days ago, she said that she wasn't interested (her word) in getting her old self back. For that matter, she said "There's nothing at all that interests me." Now, she's a little more interested in getting better. I told her she <u>would</u> get all better, and she said "eventually!"

6/2/85:

10:45am: …Annie woke up for a few minutes, and we talked, but she wasn't at her best.

Annie: It's very unusual…

Gene: What is?

Annie: To be so unusual.

Gene: It's unusual to be unusual?

Annie: It's unusual to be an example.

Gene: An example of what?

Annie: It's unusual to be an example of an idea.

    - End of Conversation -

She also repeated her earlier claim that she's not interested in getting to be herself.

She seems to have no trouble controlling her bladder. She tried to get up twice during the night to go, but was too weak. I ended up bringing her the bedpan.

6/4/85:

9am: I talked to Mom and Nancy this morning. It looks like Annie will go to a hospital in Boston for tests, and then we'll see. The problem is that each of us wants her nearby! The perils of a close family.

Annie left her room for the first time this morning. She walked (with help) across the hall, to go to the bathroom, and back. Her left leg is still extremely weak and out of control, but it seems slightly better to me than it has been. (Wishful thinking?) She was exhausted when she got back to bed.

She spent a pretty uneventful night, though she was awake a lot until about midnight. For the first time, she did not have to go during the night. About her left leg: last night I asked to move just her foot (unable) and to wiggle her toes (no luck). But she can move the leg.

Her favorite topic of conversation is still the oddity of her situation. She keeps commenting, "It's strange," "It's odd," "It's unusual," though when I ask her <u>what's</u> strange, etc., she generally can't find the words to describe it. (But sometimes she does.) Her favorite word is still "example." If anything, she's using it more now. I think that's because she's trying to talk about a wider variety of things, but doesn't have the words at hand. Example:

> Annie: "I have to finish my example."
> (But then, without any prompting)
> "I have to finish my dissertation."

She understands that we're going back to the U.S. soon. She said yesterday that she'd like to go a few places in Greece first to get some things (Korinth, I assume), but she didn't seem too disappointed when I told her we probably wouldn't' be able to.

She's still under sedation. I'll talk to the doctor about that this morning.

1:45pm: Annie's asleep. She just finished lunch. We talked while she ate, and she was more lucid than she's been yet. Almost normal, though not quite. She's still searching for words. She was concerned about money, wanted to know how I was paying for everything, offered to sign some traveler's checks. Wanted to know if I was doing anything fun in

Athens. (I said not yet, but would before I left.) She brought up Mom and Nancy, unprompted, for the first time: I said I might buy some trinkets, and she said, "Mom and Nancy would like that." Again expressed a desire to get her things from Korinth. She asked where Timothy is (though it took her awhile to remember his name), and wanted to know whether she would see him before we leave. (Doubtful.) Most interestingly:

Annie: It's strange. Sometimes I'm a full person and sometimes I'm…(She made a face as if to say "out of it" – rolled her eyes, stuck out her tongue.)

Gene: Out of it?

Annie: Yeah, out of it.

Gene: You sure seem like a full person right now.

Annie: Yeah, but what's strange is that I can see it finishing.

Gene: You mean you can tell when you're starting to lose it again?

Annie: Yeah.

Gene: Are you starting to lose it now?

Annie: Yeah.

She actually didn't lose it right away. We chatted for a few more minutes, and then she said she wanted to sleep.

6/5/85:

9:45am: I think Annie had X-rays of her left leg yesterday afternoon while I was at Aradou. I say "I think" because the report came from her, and she's not very reliable right now. She didn't say "X-ray," of course; she told me she went "downstairs." I asked if it was the nurse. "No, it was for a male photo."

Gene: You mean some men took you downstairs for photos?

Annie: That's right.

Gene: Photos of what?

Annie: Of my leg (tapping her left one).

Gene: You mean X-rays?

Annie: Yeah. They took…four (holding up 4 fingers).

Gene: It's probably just because you have photographic legs!

Annie: No, I don't think so.

Gene: How does your leg feel?

Annie: Well, it really doesn't work at all.

Gene: Oh, c'mon, I know it works <u>some</u>. Is it at all better than yesterday?

Annie: Not really.

I don't know about these doctors and their X-rays. Layman that I am, it's clear to me that it's a neurological problem, not a skeletal one. I hope they're competent enough that the CAT scan was really negative, as they say. She's controlling her bladder fine, and the bladder is very close to the leg in the brain. And of course she can move her leg, though without fine control. So, if there is any brain damage, it must be highly localized – which is good.

Annie's very concerned about her leg, and about her right shoulder. The shoulder has a hell of a bruise. Even now, after more than 2 weeks, it's very ugly – all black and blue, and yellow around the edges. But I think it's just a bruise.

I got the approval from TWA this morning for the flight back. I sure hope we can go on Friday, though I'm a little worried about whether Annie will be able to sit up so long.

One more thing. I've been writing mostly about Annie's cognitive mental problems; that's because her personality hasn't been noticeably changed aside from the general lack of emotional intensity (though I guess that's a big change). But there's another exception that's becoming more and more evident: selfishness. I guess it's to be expected from someone who's trying desperately to recover her self, but it's disconcerting to see her so completely unsympathetic to the plight of her fellow patients, some of whom are quite seriously injured or ill. They brought in a badly hurt woman late last night – her head swathed in bloody bandages – the only thing Annie was concerned about was when they're turning off the light! When I made some comment about the poor woman being in a bad way, Annie just shrugged her eyebrows and said, "I guess so." I'm sure – at least I <u>hope</u> that this trait will fade out as the rest fades in.

THE END

Otherwise? Well, I remember that I was regularly bothered by a lot of what I would have described, had I been vocal, as noise. I am now certain that it was not noise at all, but words which I could not understand, whether in Greek or English. I could not differentiate between words, laughter, car horns, and engines. They all sounded much the same, and as such, obscured my attempts to understand my noisy environment. Comparing my notes with the experiences of previously deaf people equipped with hearing aids, I find their descriptions of the overwhelming noise remarkably similar to my early aphasia.

I have also been told that while in the hospital in Athens I was being prayed for, at the Greek Orthodox Church in the village of Ancient Korinth (see below, Chapter 3). And I do know that the motor scooter Playmate still exists, and runs, though no one seems to ride it.

After the Athens hospital, came the airplane trip back to the United States. I remember nothing about it. I must have slept a lot. The plane landed in New York, and we took another plane to Boston, where my sister Nancy then lived with her family. I don't remember that plane ride either. In Boston, the first thing they did was take me to the hospital. I recall some of that, because it was <u>very</u> painful.

They had to hurt me a great deal. And I screamed a lot. Repeatedly. But I didn't cry. Only screamed. I had become very infected while in the Athens hospital, and the Boston doctors had to break open the sores to drain them of the infection and to allow the sores to re-heal correctly. Put another way, I had been transferred from a Greek hospital to an American hospital with an abundance of subcutaneous septic lesions – all of which had to be lanced.

I was given another CAT Scan, since the Greek hospital would not allow their version to be removed from the country, and submitted to a series of X-rays, by which it was discovered that the Athens hospital had completely missed noticing a very broken (in 3 places) bone (clavicle fracture) in my right shoulder. The doctors asked my family if they should break it again, or just let it continue to heal the way it had re-shaped itself while lying in bed in the Athens hospital. They decided to let it heal itself, since I would still be able to move my right arm just fine. I didn't want them to break anything, knowing that would just cause me more pain. I was issued a padded clavicle sling to brace my right shoulder for support. My right knee was so infected that I had to return for a second lancing (incision and drainage) of the contusions.

While in the Boston hospital I experienced no apprehension of the unknown, which now strikes me as surprising, given the abundance of medical technology, hospital smells and uniforms. Rather, I recall being remarkably passive and accepting of whatever the various medical practitioners prescribed. After all – I was only barely there myself!

As for my week spent in Boston? Well, I do not remember being a recalcitrant patient, but am certain that I was. It suits both the circumstances in which I found myself and my (very independent) personality. I honestly do not remember anything, really, until I fell down onto the floor that one night and it hurt.

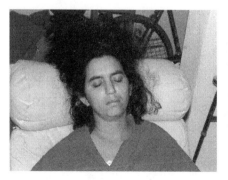 

I have been told that I slept a great deal (photo inserted, above), and have seen (and inserted, below) photographs of me getting my hair cut. As an adult I was in the habit of never cutting the length of my hair, but only keeping it trimmed. However they had shaved one side of my head in one of the 2 hospitals (Greece? Boston?), so my family (Nancy mostly) decided to cut my hair short while the shaven side was growing out. I must have looked strange with one side in part shaven and one side short, but better than otherwise, I'm sure!

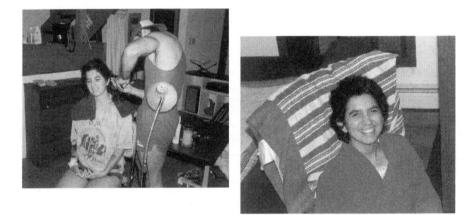

I also remember that Gene was, once again, regularly at my side before he returned to Charlottesville, Virginia, to prepare the way for my first months of recovery there with our Mom. He did not pester or confuse me, but was almost always close at hand. What I most remember is us (me and my Mom) leaving Boston on a sleeper train, and going to Charlottesville, where Gene and his wife Gayla had found me and my Mom an apartment very close to the University of Virginia Hospital, so I could easily be seen by the specialist doctors.

When we first arrived in Charlottesville I had been recovering from the accident for almost exactly a month, and I still was not understanding (or even aware of) most of what was going on around me. A month. A complete month. Completely lost. Now, 17 years later, that month seems like an eternity. But I know I didn't miss the month at the time…

In the hospital in Charlottesville, I remember that I kept being asked an enormous number of questions about what had happened, and how I felt, and where it hurt, and so on, most of which I simply could not answer. I did try. Really I did. I also kept being asked to <u>do</u> various things, such as "raise your left arm," or "move your right foot," or "touch your nose" and so on. At the time I guessed that the doctors could not believe or accept that I was still unable to walk on my own. Only later did I come to understand that they were testing my neurological as well as physical abilities.

The doctors also kept asking me to do such things as explain proverbs. When I did, I always explained them either inaccurately, or with overwhelming concreteness. One example of my literal (instead of symbolic) description of a proverb: To me "People who live in glass houses shouldn't throw stones" meant that in throwing the stones, the walls of their house would shatter, so they just shouldn't do that.

I also experienced a mass of headaches. Always. Now the medical world is excellent at making bad things (such as wounds) heal, and pain go away, but I must have wondered in some way at the time: could they likewise figure out a way to get my mind back in working order? I always felt like I was missing something. Nothing made much sense. Not that it bothered me, exactly. I certainly didn't feel confused. I just grasped only the simplest things in life. The rest was all noise.

Dr. James Miller, Univ. of Virginia Neurologist, 6/19/85:

Ms. Mills is a 32 year old Classics professor at Kenyon [College] who was injured in a motor vehicle accident in Greece on May 21. She was unconscious for approximately eight hours with significant laceration of the right parietal scalp and assorted bruises and fractures. She was seen today for neurological evaluation after immediate care in Athens, and a neurological evaluation by Dr. K. Taylor at the Chelsea Clinic of Massachusetts General Hospital on June 10.

She was amnesic for several hours prior to her injury and approximately two weeks after the injury. During this latter period, she was receiving analgesics [pain relievers] as well as Dexamethasone [an anti-inflammatory agent]. Upon evaluation in Boston on June 10, she had evidence of significant nonfluent [little speech produced, uttered slowly, with great effort and poor articulation] aphasia, decreased long and short term memory, left dominant parietal lobe dysfunction, and weakness of her left leg thought to represent right frontal deficits. An x-ray demonstrated a fracture of the right clavicle with displacement.

The patient has subsequently come to Charlottesville where her brother and mother are caring for her. They report significant recent improvement.

Upon examination today, the patient is alert and oriented for place, person, and date except for year. She felt it was 1984. She has excellent short term memory but could not remember three objects for five minutes on two separate occasions. Insight is excellent. There is some concreteness in proper interpretations. For example, she states that people living in glass houses should not throw stones because there would be jagged edges. She could abstract the similarity between a cat, a dog, and a snake, but had significant difficulty with erethismic [exaggerated response to stimulation] concepts.

There were occasional lapses in repetition of phrases such as "Mary had a little lamb" and occasional word substitutions.

She has considerable difficulty naming objects and expressed frustration. There was no evidence of any receptive difficulty and she could make all of her thoughts clearly known.

Parietal lobe function was essentially intact to the extent that there were no problems with stereognosis [form and nature of objects by touch] or graphesthesia [figures or numbers written on the skin]. She drew figures correctly and copies figures correctly. There was hesitancy in identifying appropriate fingers but she could carry out complex tasks without difficulty. There was no neglect of bilaterally simultaneous stimuli.

The eye grounds were normal and pupillary responses are intact. The visual fields were full to confrontation. There was no deficit of any cranial sensory or motor function.

There was no drift of the outstretched upper extremities and movement of the upper extremities were normal within the limits of the fractured right clavicle. Strength and tone in the upper extremities was normal. Deep tendon reflexes were equally hyperactive in the upper extremities. Abdominal reflexes were present and normal bilaterally in all four quadrants. Strength and tone in the lower extremity was normal except for weakness of left ankle dorsi flexion [bending] without involvement of plantar [sole of foot] flexion [bending]. Deep tendon reflexes were hyperactive at both knees, and hypoactive [diminishes activity] in both ankles. There was no Babinski response [bending of the big toe toward the ankle joint on stimulating the sole of the foot] today and no ankle clonus [alternate muscular contraction and relaxation in rapid succession].

Gait was possible without aid although she had difficulty arising from a chair due, I think, to weakness of left ankle and the residuals of right superficial skin knee infection.

Cerebellar functions in upper and lower extremities were normal.

Impression: Status following severe head injury associated with loss of consciousness anterograde [for events occurring after the onset of amnesia, i.e. inability to form new memories] and posterograde amnesia and residual improving nonfluent aphasia [little speech produced, uttered slowly, with great effort and poor articulation], dominant parietal lobe deficits [right-left confusion, finger agnosia, agraphia and acalculia: inability to perform simple mathematical problems], and left ankle weakness due either to previously detected right frontal lobe lesion or possibly left anterior tibial [skin] nerve contusion.

The patient is making such steady recoveries that no further steps are taken at this time. She is advised in methods of rehabilitation at home with her family's help and will contact me if she does not enjoy steady progress. She will return to see me in one month.

Finally, it's worth noting my memory of that same day in the University of Virginia hospital. After being asked to move various body parts, I was told to walk down the hall…and I just did it! Barely, badly, and yet bravely and boldly, almost to the point of brazen, I wobbled, I stumbled, I almost fell, and I remember seeing some fear in my brother's eyes. But I did walk, on my own, which I then knew would improve with practice, and that I would eventually re-learn how to walk. And how to talk. And how to read. And how to write. Just like other people.

Chapter 2: The Recovery Process Begins

Καί ψυχή
ε ι μέλλε ι γνώσεσθαι αυτήν,
ε ις ψυχήν
αυτη βλέπτεον
τον ξένο και τον έχθρο τον ε ίδαμε στον καθρέφτη.

And the soul

if one is to know oneself,

into the mirror

must gaze.

The stranger and the enemy; we have seen them in the mirror.

    Seferis "The Argonauts" <u>Mythistorima IV</u> (my trans.)

"When I stole a look at my chart and saw "Uneventful Recovery," I thought: "They're mad. Recovery is events, or rather advents – the advent of new and unimaginable powers – events, advents, which are births or re-births…"uneventful recovery." What damned utter nonsense! Recovery (as the good Registrar said) was a "pilgrimage," a journey, in which one moved, stage by stage, or by situations. Every stage, every station, was a completely new advent, requiring a new start, a new birth or beginning. One had to begin, to be born, again and again. Recovery was an exercise in nothing short of birth, for as mortal man grows sick, and dies, by stages, so natal man grows well, and is quickening, by stages – radical stages, existence stages, absolute and new: unexpected, unexpectable, incalculable and surprising. Recovery uneventful? It consists of events!"

- Oliver Sacks <u>A Leg to Stand ON</u> pp.154; 160-161

I was determined to be just like other people. Ay, there's the rub.

Immediately following the accident, other people seemed terribly insignificant compared with what I was experiencing, as they had no affect (that I could tell) on my pain. Events in Boston altered that opinion. Though people were inflicting <u>more</u> pain, clearly the result would be less pain, and that was good.

By the time I arrived in Charlottesville, I had begun to feel that perhaps people (I could not really yet differentiate between people in general and doctors in particular) could even make me hurt less. The word understand is still inappropriate to describe the bewildering and apprehensive mental process I was experiencing. I felt things.

My mind did not yet totally function.

Ever.

Oh, I would have moments when I'm sure I appeared to be fairly sentient, but only because I had become fairly skilled at pleasing people. I had learned the benefit of doing just what people wanted — especially when they asked me outright — and I willingly obliged. After all, in exchange for my doing or being what or how they wanted, I received not just a smile, but more importantly, often actual assistance, especially in getting my bandages changed, food to eat, and so on. Also while in Charlottesville I finally began engaging in some tasks all by myself, and trying to do a few things for others –- for my family, basically, who seemed to want me to fare better. Only much, much later, months later, did I engage in activities of my own inclination, once I was able to get a sense of who I was. In the meantime, I did as I was told.

Or at least I tried to.

My recovery had improved considerably not long after moving to Charlottesville, in that I soon was able to stop spending the day (when I wasn't asleep) just lying in bed mostly looking at the ceiling. Left to myself, I would no doubt have spent all my days in that room, on that bed, staring at the ceiling. That was certainly how our (Mom and my) 2 month stay in Charlottesville began, but once I had been instructed to walk, and <u>did</u> walk, my life improved dramatically.

For one thing, my family was advised to take me to a swimming pool every day. Not to swim, mind you, but to hold on to the edge with my hands and kick my feet. I guess the doctors figured that my legs were out of practice moving, due to my having been bed-ridden for so long. Well, I not only kicked along the side of the pool, but I even grew to enjoy it — mostly due no doubt to my being driven to the pool by Gene, who swam laps while I kicked.

In addition, I went for a walk every day. It wasn't easy, as I had a very difficult time at first keeping my balance. I kept tending to tip over ever so slightly, being unable to judge distances and what others called spatial relations. I found that I was unable to gracefully coordinate the movements of my body in general, and especially my hands and feet. I kept bumping into things, which often left me black and blue. Over the months, my bumping into things did not seem to decrease very much, with the result that I always seemed to have a black-and-blue mark somewhere on my body that first year. I stopped noticing, as my bumping into things became the norm, rather than the exception.

After a week or so of walking, I tried to run, but it didn't work. Having recovered my ability to write at that point, what follows is how I described the attempt.

> *Sat. June 20: A mostly typical day. Except the morning's running attempt. While Gayla and Gene made breakfast (pancakes), I walked to buy a paper, and decided to try running a little on the way back. Mistake! It hurt a lot on my behind (right side) every time the skin moved and pulled against the inside hurt place. Ouch. Most of the day was spent much as usual – exercises, reading, walking, writing, eating, etc.*

I persisted in attempting to jog as the pain decreased, but I simply could not master it. Then one day Gene accompanied me on a run, during which he discovered I had obviously (to him) not yet figured out <u>how</u> to run. He burst out laughing.

"Annie, look at the way you're moving your feet! You're trying to run heel first!"

"Well, isn't that the way you walk?"

"Yes, but not run!"

Gene showed me how to land flat on my feet, and as I practiced running that way, jogging was much easier and felt <u>much</u> better. It even became an excellent form of therapy. The steady tone of my footsteps would lull me into a trance-like state. I relaxed running, and gradually, no doubt as a result, my standing and walking became more comfortable and more normal. In fact, running became so pleasurable that I developed the habit of running around the neighborhood not just when jogging for exercise, but on my way to visiting places in general.

I would emerge from the apartment several times a day. Though being a thousand miles from home (Gambier, Ohio), everyone I encountered in Charlottesville was very kind. I liked walking around Charlottesville, and I did it often, though not so much around the city in general as the section of the city around and including the University of Virginia campus, near where we lived. I walked around the neighborhood a <u>lot</u>, looking at things. I had a great deal to learn, to see, to notice, and to file away, but certainly nothing to think about at this point. Not yet. Never in a hurry, I just walked around the neighborhood.

While both running and walking around Charlottesville, I developed the habit of returning to clearly recognizable environments, in which I collected information – words, ideas, sights, sounds – whatever was available. Virtually all the bits and pieces collected yielded considerable intellectual stimulation. I devised a map for my jaunts around the University of Virginia campus neighborhood, all of which gradually became quite familiar to me in those first few months.

What I did not do was explore. I seemed to have lost, or at least misplaced, my sense of discovery – something which I have otherwise been known for, and which did eventually return. During those first months however, I returned to familiar places, did the customary things, and didn't worry about not having usual, or for that matter unusual, thoughts. I had no regular thoughts anymore, and I didn't know how to miss them…

My process of learning (remembering really) once familiar habits occurred in much the same way as my recovering how to run. I had to be shown. And opportunities abounded, since absolutely every activity I tried to accomplish was painstaking at first. I took nothing for granted. Everything required an explanation. Even getting dressed. Nothing, not even clothes, got tossed off quickly or easily. Let me give you some examples, beginning with taking a shower.

45

I had been washed and kept clean by my family for over a month, when my Mom decided it was time for me to learn how to bathe myself. At first, I tried to simply go into the bathroom, turn on the water and take a shower. That didn't work. There were too many unknowns. So with her help, I finally took my first shower virtually alone, since the accident. Mom was there in the bathroom to help me understand how to do it, believe it or not!

"Understand?" (I can hear you say). "What's to understand?"

Well, quite a bit, I assure you! You are handed not just soap, but a washcloth. Does the soap go on the body and get pushed around with the washcloth, or do you put soap onto the washcloth, and then distribute it all over your body somehow. And how do you arrange for the soap to stick to the washcloth? It doesn't just get there all by itself. Water helps. Once you figure out that the soap will stick to the washcloth by rubbing the soap and washcloth together, then you have to figure out where to begin washing. What part of the body gets washed first? Do you start at the bottom and work your way up? Start at the top and work your way down? And how? Do you put the soapy washcloth on the dirty places and let the soap soak in? Do you pat it on? Move it around in circles? Back and forth? Do you press it hard? Soft? Fast? Slow? And what about the temperature of the water? How do you obtain hotter water, and how to get it cooler? I could feel heat and cold, but I could almost never figure out which side of the shower faucet got which. Then, moments later, while standing at the sink, I would have to figure it out all over again. I know it sounds crazy (it now does to me as well), but there simply are no givens, nothing is automatic, when your mind is not quite connected. Imagine life as an infant, for whom nothing can be assumed. Rather, each activity must be shown, explained, consumed, assimilated, and fully understood. And usually not just once. They also have to be remembered.

Another example of my re-learning: cooking an egg. After about a month in Virginia, having my meals cooked for me by my Mom, I decided to try and make my own breakfast, of scrambled eggs. I took an egg, tapped it on the side of the frying pan to break its shell, as I had seen her do it, and the egg broke into two pieces. I held the two halves, and saw that one half contained the clear stuff and the other half the yellow stuff. What to do? I did not want to ask, so I dumped the yolk into the fry pan (without having turned on the flame of course), at which point I remembered that I had seen my Mom use a fork when she made scrambled eggs. So I picked up a fork, stirred up the egg white still in its half of the shell and dumped it into the fry pan. It still didn't look quite right…At that point Mom came in and helped me scramble the yolk and egg white together in the pan, so I would get something to eat for breakfast.

"Concreteness, or inflexibility of thinking may manifest during ADL [activities of daily living] activities in a patient's inability to generalize from one situation to another. A patient may ask what time of day it is while eating breakfast. When asked how to wet a dried-out roll-on deodorant, the patient will put it under running water instead of turning it upside down. Thus, she is not able to think of simple solutions that require some thought, The patient will wash the body with ice-cold water without liking cold water, rather than turning on the hot water, too." (Gudrun Arnadottir The Brain and Behavior: Assessing cortical dysfunction through activities of daily living (ADL), St. Louis, 1990, p.134)

Activities of Daily Living for me? Well, for those first few months, it took me about the same amount of mental effort to recall basic math, say the times tables, as how to brush my teeth or to play solitaire. I had played solitaire now and them before my accident, but during my recovery I wanted to play it often, and managed over time to play it with remarkably little frustration. At first, of course, I could not grasp there being not just 2 colors, but 4 suits! Gene showed me, and I discovered a great deal of satisfaction in manipulating the cards correctly, even though I usually lost the game…

Sigh. I hope you are getting the idea of my life during those first months following my accident. I suppose my preference for alluding to particular events, rather than generalizing about them, is in part due to generalizations being very difficult for me. My brain no longer operates the way it did (or rather didn't!) back then, so I don't recall exactly how everything seemed to me. The other problem in my generalizing about the process is that my life during those first few months of recovery was not really a process, certainly not a thoughtful process, at all. What I experienced was more like a series of specific moments. I was out of my element, and my life felt like an assemblage of bits and pieces, with neither rhyme or reason.

And while I now know that each activity I engaged in (brushing teeth, bathing, eating, going to the bathroom, etc.) took me a longer duration of time than most people, it did not seem so to me at the time. My poor brain was always very, very occupied. I had to figure out what every object was, and why so, and how so, and what movement (maneuver, really) came next, and why, and how. All of this was very time-consuming.

Bits and pieces. The world around me seemed to consist of bazillions of bits and pieces. And the bits and pieces did not seem to fit. And I

49

never knew what would be my best bet to put my chips on, in terms of facilitating my recovery so the pieces would fit: Walking? Talking? Watching TV? Trying to read? Write?

I tried watching some TV. Now that was very strange.

I believe my watching TV was one of my doctor's ideas. My family had bought a small Black and White TV for our apartment and I watched it, regularly. And just as I couldn't dial the telephone, because I punched in the numbers too slowly, I was unable to change the TV channels according to their numbers. Rather, I would turn the dial and watch whatever was showing.

Now when I say I watched TV, I do mean I watched it – literally, not figuratively. I did not understand most of what I saw on TV. I just watched it.

I saw a great many different people, engaging in all kinds of actions and emotions, which was very educational, especially for stirring up my memories. And all these people on TV were talking a great deal, using all kinds of words, many of which I had not heard since the accident. Some people spoke their words, while others seemed to almost sing them. The people on TV spoke constantly. Rarely were there moments of silence. As a result I re-learned from watching TV how to speak a lot of words without saying very much! I even began to sound a bit like soap operas and talk shows.

In terms of re-learning how to both talk and <u>say</u> something, on the other hand, I learned more from our meals together, in different combinations. Most often, meals were just my Mom and myself. But Gene and his wife Gayla often joined us, and I remember small disagreements would break out from time to time, usually between Mom and Gayla, or between Mom and my sister Nancy over the telephone. Their arguments were usually about what to do with, or say to, me. I could not follow them, so I let them work it out themselves.

In addition, our meals now and then included visiting guests. In either case, no matter who the people at the table were, or what the occasion, I constantly re-learned words, behaviors, gestures and facial expressions.

Early in my recovery I was asked not only an abundance of simplistic questions, answerable with a Yes or No, but also questions which made explicit the expected answer, and so were relatively easy for me to respond to.

"You're probably hungry, aren't you?" I would be asked.

Gradually, each meal became a type of cross-examination, to facilitate my sharing of new insights of the day.

"Annie, what did you see on your walk today?"

"Dogs."

"What were the dogs doing?"

"Running. Catching a…a…a…round thing."

"A frisbee?"

"Yeah. A frisbee."

In addition, my ability with language was regularly being put to the test during meals.

"Please pass the…Please pass the…Please pass the bottle of black stuff with the red cap," being unable to remember the word pepper. And someone would pass me the pepper. Then, 10 minutes later, if I wanted the pepper again, because I had forgotten the word, I had to repeat the process of asking for it in the same way…again!

"Please pass the…Please pass the…Please pass the bottle of the black stuff with the red cap again."

I now know that the term for such a symptom of aphasia, in which the patient can speak, but cannot find the correct word, is termed anomia. Definitely I had…I had…I had…anomia.

Oddly enough, I don't believe I ever felt a surge of helplessness or anguish during this early phase of my recovery, and I rarely (if ever) got angry at myself. For one thing, while my entire re-learning process was no doubt terrifying and difficult for my family, who easily remembered the way I had been before my accident, my early recovery was a reasonably encouraging to me. After all, I barely <u>remembered</u> the old me, and when I compared my actions one day with the new me (the one I knew best) the previous day, I always seemed either to have stayed about the same, or to have gotten better!

Things never got worse.

In fact, everyone kept predicting that I would get better and better. Not much of a prediction, I later came to realize, as I can't imagine what could have caused me to deteriorate. But that continuous improvement was very important to me. Otherwise, I understood so very little of what was going on around me. Yet I honestly don't remember feeling depressed, or even slightly discouraged during those first few months. I suppose my lack of pessimism was due to my extreme ignorance of my condition. I was so very ignorant of what I was going through.

I do remember how surprised I once was, while in Virginia those first few months, by the doctor who questioned me about both crying and sex. He seemed rather surprised, as well as disappointed (?), that I hadn't cried over anything.

"Nothing? Not even the physical pain? Not even when they cut your skin open in the Boston Emergency Room?"

"No, never."

He checked with my family, and sure enough, I apparently didn't remember how to cry...

It wasn't that I had made an effort <u>not</u> to cry, say in self-pity, but rather that I didn't understand what had happened to me, and that I would be going through a process of recovery for quite some time. I simply had no sense that there was anything to cry <u>about</u>.

That situation changed, in a remarkable way, after seeing a TV movie one day, after which I spent most of the rest of the day crying and writing about it.

Thurs. July 18: Crying and crying and crying. Why? Well, I just saw on television a film about a young girl with cerebral palsy. She improves greatly in the film, more than the doctors thought she would. Then in the end, which I just saw, she dies. I have to admit that it was not a great movie, very slow in places, especially. But being as I am these days, I was very interested in the kinds of progress she made, what things they did with her along the way, and what sorts of exercises and activities made her better. Yet here I am, crying and crying, for the first time that I can remember since my accident. I must have cried before, mostly from the pain during Doctor visits and their actions on me, but I don't think that I've cried about myself, and what is my future, especially. Now I am. In other words, I'm not really crying about the movie I just saw, but about my fears for myself...Who would have thought? Not me, that's for sure. I thought that I was very pleased, even happy, about how much I've improved, and how much better I've gotten. Clearly there's more...Certain things don't get better, or do and then get worse again. Is there more wrong with me than I've heard from the doctors? Or that I haven't understood? A soon death is probably unlikely, but are there other possibilities? Things that won't ever get back to normal? Things that will get worse? Given that I haven't heard much in the way of "bad news," I'm beginning to wonder (as I haven't before) if I haven't been included in some conversations.

As opposed to the doctor's concern regarding my apparent inability as yet to cry, I was worried by my complete lack of interest in having sex of any kind. The word sex just didn't mean anything to me, and I didn't miss it. I remembered what sex felt like. It just didn't seem doable anymore. Not that I didn't remember how, or that it didn't seem worth the effort, but the thoughts, feelings and desires just didn't suit each other. I knew what I was supposed to feel and what was supposed to happen, but I felt nothing.

I finally asked the doctor about it. He said not to worry, and not to push it. That my desire for sex would come back, on its own. And boy, did it ever!

As, finally, did my period. Some of my family had wondered if perhaps I had been sexually assaulted, and that I had not been completely checked out by the doctors, since I did not menstruate for over 2 months after the accident. However, as with other matters, the truth was that my body mostly just needed to be left alone, to heal itself, in its own good time.

Dr. James Miller, University of Virginia Neurologist, 7/22/85:

Ms. Mills continues to make splendid recovery from a severe automobile accident in Greece on May 21, which caused her to be amnesiac for two weeks after the injury and to suffer impairment of long and short-term memory, dominant hemisphere deficits with aphasia weakness of the left leg. Additionally, she had some right frontal deficits and a fracture of the right clavicle.

Today she exhibited much better capacity to interpret proverbs, getting them all right and could remember three objects for five minutes and repeat six digits forwards and backwards. She got all of the presidents straight in retrospective succession back to Truman and showed fairly good knowledge of current events.

She could not identify a key case by name, but did recognize a reflex hammer, eyeglasses, and watch. There was no word substitution or no word finding deficit except as noted above. Eye grounds were normal and pupillary responses intact. All cranial, motor, and sensory functions were intact.

Deep tendon reflexes were hyperactive in arms and legs with no ankle clonus [alternative muscular contraction and relaxation in rapid succession] or Babinski response [bending of the big toe toward the ankle joint on stimulating the sole of the foot]. Coordination was satisfactory in upper and lower extremities. Sensation including tests for two point discrimination and visual fields were normal.

Tone was normal throughout the body, but there was still residual weakness of left hip flexion. Other tests of strength were normal.

Impression: Residual right hemisphere deficits consisting of mild nominal [defective use of names of objects] aphasia and left hip weakness with bilateral corticospinal [connection between cortex of brain and spinal cord] tract signs manifested by hyperreflexia [exaggeration of reflexes] only. The patient's voice is quite loud and she gives historical evidence of some decreased inhibition (she announced in a "too loud voice" in a restaurant that her menstrual periods had returned to another member of the family). We discussed her prospective plans to return to teaching at Kenyon College in January and decided to use mid-September as a decision regarding these professional plans. She is on no medication and will undertake all normal activities. She is seeing another physician for management of her clavicle.

Speaking of doctors, I also recall that as my mind slowly began to understand a little of what had happened to me, and what my body (and my family!) was going through, my family inquired about my I.Q. and I asked my doctors about the lack of medications.

"If I'm sick, why am I not taking any medicines?"

"Aren't there any drugs which would fix whatever is wrong with me?"

"Shouldn't I be taking pills, or doing some sort of therapy?"

The doctors would always smile, and then say things such as: "No. No, Harrianne. Your body is doing a fine job of healing itself, of mending your brain, all by itself. You just need to be patient. Relax. Take it slow for about a year. Your recovery will take a while."

A year? A while? What exactly is "a while"? That explanation made no sense to me. Now, many years after my year of recovery, I would consider being in such a predicament unfathomable, not to mention insufferable. Then? "A while" meant nothing. Events never took a while to happen in the world of daytime TV! I had lost all sense of time, as though I were living in another world.

The whole concept of the passage of time came back to me very slowly. While I could tell time quite easily, a sense of the duration of time was a very gradual reacquisition. I suppose my insensitivity to blocks of time was the most similar to that of a young child, to whom "in 5 minutes" means an eternity. I know it sounds odd, but the idea of the passage of time had simply vanished from my injured brain.

The I.Q. of my injured brain? The doctors told my family that I had, indeed, suffered some (probably about 1%) damage, but they were pretty certain that my remaining 99% would suffice, as it had been so high prior to the accident.

Similar to my loss of a sense of the duration of time, when I spoke, I could speak words, but not quite carry on a conversation. And to me, it was not my own voice I heard while answering questions, for example, but just a voice I did not recognize. When I spoke, I thought I sounded a lot like the people on TV. Noise. There was a lot of noise in my world, including voices.

Often I would hear a noise, and after recognizing that it was a new sound, something worth noticing and remarking upon, I would try to figure out how to reply: in what way, in what order, to whom, for what reason, etc., etc., etc. Then, in going through the complex process of analyzing the noise and determining an appropriate response, my memory of the noise would usually disappear! Gone. And the next time I heard that same noise, I would have to go back through the same process, though not remembering that I had been here before.

In much the say way, I sometimes had the sense that what I saw or heard around me were not really there, were not really happening, but were just in my mind, much like the things I saw on TV. I understood that TV was not reality, but just for entertainment. And much of life around me seemed that way as well. Not real. Just things happening for, well, entertainment?

In addition to my watching TV, I visited the University libraries, and looked through (no, not yet read) the books. Since we lived so close to the University, and to its Medical Center in particular, and I was, not surprisingly, very interested in medical matters at that time, I spent a fair amount of time perusing the books in the University of Virginia Medical School library. Their books had more pictures in them and they often referred to one or more of the medical aspects of my life, which was about all my life was in those days.

Not that I really <u>understood</u> the content of the books, any more than the newspaper articles I glanced at each morning. Reading? I wasn't exactly illiterate. I could read. I could recognize words. I just didn't fully understand what I read.

I read and thought I understood each individual word on the page, but they did not fit together. Sentences made no sense. The words seemed to be strung out together with a capital letter at the beginning and a period at the end. Trying to read a sentence from start to finish, my understanding of the sentence would get lost along the way. The ending had no connection with the start.

Many of the books in the Medical School library used the same words as my doctors, and that made the books feel very familiar. Books were also nice to look at, and they felt good to touch. Holding books felt very familiar, and so was very pleasing. I visited the Medical School library, often.

And much like other mental activities during these first few months, I frequently finished reading the words in a newspaper article, listening to NPR, or watching a TV show, without having a clue as to what I had just read, heard or watched. Yet I found those activities, all things considered, relatively enjoyable, or at least as they happened. Once each activity had been completed, my recollection of it seemed little more than a scatter of specific moments. As they had occurred, I was completely consumed by executing the endeavor, moment by moment, since my comprehension of the individual moments never came easy. My ability to perceive those events as a series (not a scatter) of moments, much less my understanding the series of events, was out of the question.

Of course one thing which my doctors would not let me even <u>try</u> to read, was a foreign language.

"Why?" my brother Gene asked. "That's what she does for a living!"

"That's why," they replied. "We don't want her first encounter with foreign languages to result in any negative feelings. No, let's wait for a while, until her English gets back closer to normal, then we'll see how she does with reading and hearing other languages."

Well, I cheated a little on that one, in that I went to the Greek-owned restaurant in town a couple of times, just to try out my Modern Greek. It all sounded very familiar, but I could only remember the most elemental expressions, words such as "Yes" (Nai) and "No" (Ochi). A few others slid easily off my tongue, but it was mostly just a good experience to hear Greek-Americans speaking a very familiar foreign language among themselves — without my trying to make sense of what they were saying.

Unlike the noise of English, the sound of Greek was closer to music — no doubt in large part due to my expectation that I would not be able to understand the conversation, even if I tried. So why bother? Without the stressful goal of trying to comprehend a spoken language, I found listening to the music of other languages to be remarkably entertaining — much like my "reading" books by looking at the pictures.

My memory in my pre-accident life, especially when applied to the acquisition of languages, had always been excellent. I had gradually so far acquired a fundamental knowledge of French, Russian, Greek, and some German, putting into practice the proverb of many foreign language teachers, "Another language, another soul." My ability with languages had always served me well, though sometimes put to excessive use.

I recall a few years earlier, for example, introducing my friend Colette, who spoke only French, to my friend Kostas, who spoke only Greek. Obviously very attracted to each other, they did not speak the others' language at all, and neither one spoke English very well. What was I to do? Standing between them, I enabled their communication for a short while by translating from French to Greek and then Greek to French, each time transitioning through English in my head. It was quite a task, and something I would only have done for close friends. It also provides a good example of something of which I was clearly no longer capable. Was my incapacity for such complex tasks to be temporary, or permanent? That thought was a cause for some concern.

I will say, on the other hand, that my experiences listening to the familiar language of Greek helped me to feel that there was some continuity between my life at that point and my earlier life, about which I remembered very little. But beneath the continuity, I sensed that I had changed considerably and dramatically. I looked different, spoke differently, and acted differently than before the accident. At some level I knew I had changed, but I couldn't for the life of me remember how I used to be. And like my present inabilities, I was totally unsure whether my changes would remain, or change again, or (horrors? hopefully?) would simply keep changing continuously.

My appearance, for example. I would look into the mirror from time to time and, I assure you, that was not me I saw in the mirror, but someone else, who resembled me somewhat, but was not as pretty. I saw photographs taken of me before the accident and they did look like me. I was definitely more beautiful in my mind and in my past than in the mirror.

In addition, my mind was often, well, detached. With no curiosity and no imagination, I even <u>appear</u> detached, in an eerie "voodoo" kind of way, in photos taken of me at the time. I smile a lot, but am not really there. That detachment held true at many levels and in connection with a variety of behaviors. Even food.

Numerous memories of my first few months in Virginia are concerned with meals – an excellent opportunity for social interaction. Unfortunately, food gradually became a bit of a problem. Before the accident, I had always eaten very normally and regularly, in a fairly healthy kind of way, with a resulting weight gain in the winter (to stay warm) and loss in the summer (eating less and exercising more). In the hospital in Athens, I had (I was told) lost a lot of weight. Once I started being fed by my family, however, I gained a lot of weight, and a new health hazard developed. My lifelong weight fluctuations during winter and summer were turning into permanent gain due to my never saying "no" when offered food. One of my doctors mentioned it to me.

"Do you enjoy eating a large meal, and often?"

"Enjoy? Enjoy food? I've never thought about it. No. I don't think so. Not really. But I do eat whatever is set before me." (As when I was a child. I was a good little girl.)

It turned out that my family had gotten in the habit of providing me with more and more food, more and more times a day, thinking that since I was eating it all up, I must have been hungry. But I wasn't hungry. I was just trying to do as I was told, and so to please them.

Thus, by the time I visited Ohio in September, 4 months after the accident, I had gained over 25 pounds. Luckily, my doctor assured me that I was not required to eat 3 full meals a day, if I didn't want to — especially since I hadn't been eating that way before the accident. When I told him that I normally ate one full meal a day, in the evening, he was surprised, but he said it would be OK for me to return to that habit, which I then did, with resulting weight loss.

*   *   *

Ah, the irony of the whole thing. Here I was, the pretty one of the 3 children, the one who had persevered through graduate school in Classics at Stanford, who had lectured, researched and published, feeling quite comfortable in the academic world of ideas. And here I was, lost in a world virtually devoid of ideas, or at least of the means by which either to comprehend or to express them.

My doctors had expressed a similar thought which, at the time, had meant nothing to me. They asked me (and my family) to keep notes, some kind of a record, of my process of recovery.

"You're not just, say, a truck driver," they said. "You're a college Classics professor. Please try to write down your thoughts. It is fairly unusual for this sort of thing to happen to an academic. We would appreciate any reflections you might have. Your thoughts while recovering from your head injury would assist us in understanding the experience."

So I tried. I tried to write, by hand at first, ever so slowly, and then, after being discouraged by that process, I first made some tapes, and then typed on a laptop computer. I did not lack the will power to write. I lacked the means. Writing was incredibly difficult. A few sentences took me hours.

My attempts at doing almost everything, but especially writing, were exhausting. I tired out quickly and simply lost interest. I would then rest, return to the task, tire out quickly and give up again. This book, needless to say, is based on those writings. Rather than summarizing my initial attempt at writing or, even worse, indulging in platitudes about it, let me share my first attempt to write, as my former lucidity began to return.

> *July 1 (Handwritten): This is my first attempt to write since the accident and it isn't at all clear to me where to begin or even how to begin. Though I have been alive since May 21 [date of the accident], much of the time has been anything other than rememberable. Certainly the biggest changes in my ability to do things and to imagine both things and myself and to try to think of the English language for many things, have occurred in the last week or two, since coming to*

Charlottesville on June 16. These changes seem not due to being in Charlottesville, however, or even to living with Mom or seeing Gene often, though all the latter (Mom and Gene) are helpful in the extreme, but the changes seem most due to my recovery.

July 2 (Typed from here): Much easier typing than writing, I must say. Now, if I can even learn to use my fingers for the typing! Anyway, it is now July 2nd, and I continue to try and understand not only who I was, and what has happened to me, but what will be the results of such happenings. Take the recovery which I have already referred to. Certainly my fingers work much better, and my arms, and my right leg. These seem to me to have undergone virtually a complete recovery in the past 2 weeks. I think more often, and sometimes very completely, though often very limited. I speak much better though there are many words (especially nouns) which continue to be difficult to rediscover, or to understand. And of course there are many parts of my body which are much slower to recover. It's hard to know, for example, if my left leg or right shoulder ever will. I assume that I will learn how to speak and how to think, though it's hard to know how long it will take. I know, for example, that I think about much more than when we arrived in Charlottesville 2 weeks ago. I think of names for things (which I sometimes discover) and of changes happening to me. Probably one thing I don't usually think of are the things happening to others or to the world.

Very soon thereafter, I tried my hand at writing my first correspondence — a letter addressed to Timothy — which I seem to have written in order to heal myself, given how incredibly self-absorbed I was at the time.

(July 3): Dear Timothy. Hello. Where to begin? Where to go? There seems so much to write about and so little energy for doing most things, including writing, but I will try. I've been in Charlottesville getting better for over 2 weeks now. Much has increased greatly. Other things remain a bit slower. I assume that Gene has told you about most of it, so I will be brief. I can walk a bit, though it is still very difficult, and the left leg remains full of problems. My arms are much better. They can both move, and the scars are even looking better. They will probably disappear in a few years. My shoulders remain in their brace, and who knows what they will be like. My face looks better and my hair, even though it is now cut short and curly. My behind still hurts, mostly on the right. I do more with each passing day. I can now take a shower by myself (I've done it twice), and only need help washing some places. I've answered the phone once, and talked on it about 3 times. I've learned to wash the dishes, and have even helped

cooking a few times. I've been eating with my right hand instead of my left, for about a week. I go to the bathroom by myself, and brush my teeth, and comb my hair, all of which I've been doing for almost 10 days. I've been doing exercises, suggested by one of the doctors, and can now lift both of my legs. Soon I will surely be able to reach them (i.e. the feet)."

I never sent the letter. Instead, I read what I had written into a microphone, as part of a tape I decided to send him. Most of the tape is about myself, beginning with the state of my body.

(July 7): Dear Timothy. Well, this is Annie, as I told you this morning, July 7, 1985. Um, as I explained to you on the telephone this morning, I've tried to write to you, and it's a little difficult. I thought since I'm getting better at speaking on the telephone, I could make a tape. So that's what I'm going to try and do. (Space)

Maybe I will even get better at recording it as time goes by a little bit. Uh. Anyway, um. Certainly speaking is something that has improved, mostly I would say since I've been in Charlottesville. Actually, most things have been improving the most as far as I can understand it anyway, since I've been in Charlottesville, and I think that's true of my speaking. For example, when I spoke to you, it was I think the third time that

I had spoken on the telephone, um, except, you know, for a little bit say to Gene or to Nancy or something, just saying Hello, I'm fine, you know, I'm getting better, How are you? Or something like that. But maybe the fourth time actually. Um, anyway, at least I feel that this is something that had improved a lot lately, which is obviously one of the reasons that I feel willing to do a tape. I would like to talk about other things about myself, and then talk a little about you. Um. We'll see how long that takes, and if I don't get tired and exhausted and run out of words, I'll even try to, um, put it, oh my god, um, mail, that's it, mail it, tomorrow. (Space)

Let me begin then, by reading from the letter that I wrote to you, um, on July the 3rd, which was a day when I was trying very hard to write. Um. It got a little worse for a couple of days, but I think I will try again today and tomorrow. Anyway, it's dated July 3rd, 1985 and it starts off "Dear Timothy"...(see above)."

Anyway, that's the end of what I wrote on the 3rd of July, and it didn't seem to me anyway, to be enough to send, so I thought I would try this tape instead. In a minute. (Long pause, to take a rest)

Now that I'm done reading the letter that I tried writing to you, let me try talking a little bit more about myself, first going over the things that I talked about in the letter, and then moving on to other things that I didn't talk about in the letter. Um. Let's start with my body I guess. Well, it's now a couple of days later from when I wrote the letter, and my body is basically no better than it was when I wrote it. That is, it improved a lot, pretty much when we got to Charlottesville, which would have been on the, uh, oh, what was it?, the 16th of June. At the beginning things really got better fast. Now I would say everything's either slower or it's just that smaller things are getting better now. So I can tell you about my body, but I'm not sure you'll understand that many things haven't gotten any better in the last, oh, I don't know, maybe the last week or so. But they did for a long time, and my guess is they will again. It's just a little bit slower, and the pieces are much smaller. Like I remember when we first got to Charlottesville, um, because of course they hurt me most of the time when I was in Boston. I remember that but it didn't seem like things were getting any better, because mostly they just kept, they meaning mostly the doctors, taking me to the doctors and touching everything and pulling on things, and hurting me basically. Um. But from the time I got to Charlottesville, although I did see the doctor it was, things were starting to mend themselves. Anyway, um, these days some of the things that I didn't mention in the letter, for example, one of the things is my head. You might remember that there was a big, um, uh, lump, well, a big place that had been bad, that they had, um, what do you call it?, it had been swollen and red and obviously they had put a bandage around it in Greece, and which I understand had been sewn to my head, although I don't remember it at all.

Anyway, um, when I could first feel my head, to remember it, which was in Boston, with my own hands, I could feel that it was very swollen, and they were lots and lots of red things, that would you know, what do you call it, bloody things that would come off all the time. And of course my hair over there wasn't growing at all for a long time. Anyway, now, this is the 7th of July, the hurt place is much smaller than it was before. I mean it's still swollen, but it's much smaller than it was anyway. There's very little bloodiness left, um, when I scratch it with my fingernail, for example, most of the stuff that comes off is white, sort of dead skin I guess you would call it. It doesn't usually anyway, it doesn't hurt as much, and my hair I think is probably, well, it is not quite starting to grow, but it at least covers it a little bit, which is nice.

Other things I should, oh, tell you about, um, well, I suppose one thing is that I'm very bad at moving lots of parts of me, which is a little hard to explain I guess. But, for example, I have a, on my stomach, when my stomach is, um, I was in the shower one day, and Mother came in and asked me if I was holding in my stomach, because it looked so small, and I said no. And then she left, and I tried to hold it in, after she left, and I can't do it. I can't suck it in, or push it out for that matter. Well, I guess I could push it out a little bit, but when I try to suck it in, what's underneath my bosoms sucks in. But my stomach really doesn't. So I've been working on that lately. And there are other things that you would think I can do, like my toes on my feet. The right foot works well. I mean the toes can go forward and backwards towards me, and do all sorts of things. The left, they certainly work a little better than they did, but it's still very hard to move them towards me. It doesn't hurt or anything, but it's just that I guess as Gene explained, the nerve of movement was broken and hasn't really fixed itself.

Um, one thing I should tell you is my fingernails are very nice now because I don't, um, uh, oh, I bit them. That's it. I don't bite them anymore. Didn't I? It seems to me that I used to bite my right hand. Anyway, I don't do that any more. I don't know. It's amazing what a couple of weeks without the use of your hands will do for you. So that the nails on them are looking very nice.

Other things about my body. Well, um, most of the, um, the places where I was hurt. I don't know what you call that, the, uh, aaargh, um. Pause, to take a rest)

Well, I remembered: um, the scars. I remember. I remember very well, when there were scars just about all over my body. As a matter of fact, I remember them on my face even. Anyway, the ones on the rest of my body, aside from my face, um, have gotten much much better. I mean obviously I still have them on both of my hands, arms, and both of my legs, but actually the ones on my legs have really improved a lot. Um. The stuff on my right knee, for example, is almost gone. I think there's maybe one scar left. My left leg is much slower. Um. And of course my arms have scars on them, but they look so much better than they did. Um. It now looks like I was burned or something. I mean it doesn't look like I can't move them, for example. It's mostly just things on them. Oh gosh. Other things about my body. Um. Well, I think I've probably done enough actually. Um.

In terms of me doing things, as I said in the letter, a lot of the things have really gotten better. For example, the taking the shower and talking on the phone a little bit, and I do things a little bit around the apartment here in Charlottesville, like I can wash the dishes. Um. I can take, not only take showers, but oh, sit for example, on all the chairs. Um. Dress myself! There's a good one. I didn't used to be able to dress myself at all, mostly because I couldn't move my right hand. Um. Now I can, although slowly, move my right hand. I have to do it very slowly. A lot slower than the left, which moves at a regular pace, but I am able to dress myself now, which is very nice, and I can take clothes even off. But, well, for example, when we came, I wasn't walking very well, but I certainly couldn't walk up and down stairs. And now I can do that. It's slow, but I can very slowly anyway, walk both up and down stairs, uh, which is very nice. At the beginning, when we were first in Charlottesville, well I guess when I first started walking, um (pause), I could do it if I moved down the stair pretty much with my left leg moving to the new step, and that would mean that my right leg would be the one bending...Now I can do it with both. I can move either my left leg or my right leg to the next stair. So things have definitely been improving there. (Pause, to take a rest)

Well, let me try to talk about other things besides my body. And this is a little harder, in that the examples are strange, and they rehappen a lot, so it's a little difficult to summarize where I am at the moment, because some things get better, some things stay about the same. But things happen every day, which make me more aware than I was the day before. But the next day it might all go away.

I'm not sure I'm making this clear for you. Let me, um, well, try to give an example: speaking, which I have been doing on this tape so far. I know that I spoke, for example, when you were at the hospital, and certainly when Gene was there. And I don't remember anything of those. Um. My memory starts, well, I can remember a few things about the last couple of days in the hospital. But I know that Gene read me things. I mean I've found out that Gene read me things, for example, during those last few days, and I don't remember those at all. So some things are memorable, but I would say my bigger memories, sort of people and places, and what I was doing, for example, doesn't really start until the last day in the hospital. (Pause, to take a rest)

It's hard to know, but I certainly remember going out of the hospital, and going on a plane with Gene, for example, and coming to America, and I remember things in Boston. Well, some things in Boston, anyway. Mostly I remember sleeping a lot. But that's different from my language, because my guess is even at the very beginning I was using a language of some sort anyway. But I certainly don't feel like I had any say over what the language was. In other words, sometimes specific words will be lacking, and sometimes sort of idea of what to talk about are just not there. Um. Or how to talk. It's not so much that the English is gone or missing, as much as the idea is gone. What do you talk about, for example? (There goes a car.) Anyway, um, that certainly has gotten much much better, and I don't think I would time it until probably like, well, I'm trying to think. It was about the 3rd day in Charlottesville that I remember being awake, and sort of lying in bed and looking at the ceiling, and thinking about things. I mean really, I hadn't thought about things for a long time. And I think it was then that thoughts got connected with speaking. That is, I would speak about things because I had thought about them, which hadn't happened for a long time.

Which I suppose brings me to another subject, another idea which I should mention on this tape, and that is how things have changed, or improved, or, I'm afraid to say, stayed about the same with regard to my, um, thinking. Some things have definitely improved. I find myself thinking, not only speaking more, but thinking more, about many things than I remember doing 2 weeks ago or 3 weeks ago. Four weeks ago we won't discuss. I don't remember anything of that. Um. But, um, thinking, well, it's still very strange, as you'll be able to tell from my tapes, because thoughts of some things are very easy, but other things, I just can't imagine thinking about. (Pause, in order to rest)

Um, let me try to think of an example, to make it clear to you that this is not a question of words, as much as a loss, at the moment anyway, of thoughts. Now I have to admit I'm assuming that they will come back. But it's just very hard to think about some things. Like it took me a long time, a long time, to remember what I taught last, this past year, at Kenyon. Now it wasn't that the words weren't there. It's that the idea wasn't there. So far, I've come up with 7 out of the 8 courses that I taught. I still can't come up with the 8th. That happens with me about a lot of things. That is, like I can't remember, obviously I mean I told you this on the phone. I don't remember foods, but, oh, I don't know. I don't remember some of what I used to do, for fun even.

You know, like Mother has asked me something about, oh, I don't know, I was sort of not complaining, but mentioning, all the things that she was trying to get me to do, and that I was doing: going to movies, watching television a few times, although the first time I turned it on, I just turned it off, because I could not understand any of it. But now I have seen a little bit of television, and some of it I understand and some of it I don't. And we went to the bar that my brother plays at one night for example. Anyway, I was telling her of all the things that we've been doing, and I don't want to say I'm not enjoying them at all. They're just so strange to me. Mostly I don't understand what we're doing, and so she asked me what I used to do for fun, in Ohio. And I couldn't think of anything. Well, anyway, there are lots of things like that, that are very strange. Anyway, I feel like I'm going on and one talking about myself. Um, probably getting near the end of this side.

I think I'll talk about you on the other side. Actually, maybe I can talk about things as I remember them, and you won't mind. One thing that I remembered...has to do wit money. Mostly, they won't let me, yet anyway, deal with money. I have mentioned it a couple of times, but I would say for the most part anyway, they keep me out of it.

Well, let's see. Other things on this side of the tape. Gosh, I don't know. It seems like there are so many things I should say to you. Tell you about, but it's, oh, I don't know, maybe I'm just kind of tired from doing the rest of the tape. Hard to tell...A lot of it is that it's hard to remember things. Maybe I should be doing this every day or something, try to get all my ideas down.

Instead, as the exhaustion took over, I decided to continue the tape the very next day, after a re-invigorating night of sleep.

(July 8): Well, hello Timothy again. This is side 2 of the tape. It's now July 8th, in the morning, that is it's now Monday. I'm afraid I got a little tired yesterday, so I quit, but now I'm back, and I think I'd like to try talking with you a little bit about you. (Short pause)

Let me start off with some easy things which I think I mentioned to you a little bit anyway on the telephone. I do remember who you are, a little bit anyway. I know our names, I know that we've been living together, I know that you went to Greece oh, about a month I guess before I did, and I remember some of the things of that month, when you were in Greece and I was still in Ohio. Um, a few things. When I think back to the time before that, again, I remember some things, but there are very strange things that are not there. Um, for example, Mother asks me now and then here, does Tim like, oh, I don't know, hamburgers or something. And I don't know. I don't remember, to put it simply. Which is a little strange.

Um, I certainly know some things about you, and I remember our living together and the problems I would say in living together that we've been having for the last, I don't know, 6 months maybe, a year maybe? It's hard to date it exactly. But I think probably what I need to be sure and tell you on the tape anyway, on this tape, maybe on another one, is that at the moment, and who knows, this may go away, and the old me may come back, but at the moment, it's hard to imagine various things. Like it's hard to imagine at the moment (sigh), loving you I suppose. I mean I like you a lot, and I would like to spend some time with you, and I would like to do things with you, and go places with you, and see you and talk with you. On the other hand, if I try to imagine living with you again, or loving you, or having sex with you, and things like that, it's very hard. I can't imagine it mostly, and I can't remember you well enough to know if I want to do those things. I'm not trying to be mean or to hurt you, so understand that I assume that a lot of this is because of the accident.

And I'm very glad, for example, to get the cassette tapes from you, and I do appreciate, believe me, all the things you did for me the first week after the accident, taking the Kenyon students for what, 3 and 1/2 weeks?! I mean I really do appreciate all of that, and who knows, maybe some day I can even tell you about it in person, and we can talk about what I'd like to do about the things that you did for me. But in addition to those things that I sort of know a little bit about, and really thank you for a lot, there's so much I can't. I'm not sure I can make it clear to you how much there is at the moment that is just gone. Either I don't remember from the past, or I can't imagine from the present. And it doesn't hurt. It's not that it's scary and painful. It's just gone. Now I should tell you that some of the gone things, some of the thing that were gone, say, you know, a week ago, or 10 days ago, do come back from time to time, for a little while anyway. But I think the one thing that is scaring me so far, is that they also go away again. That is, there are things that I don't remember, and then one day, something will come back to me, and I will remember it. It's very exciting. And it may stay for a day, or two, or three. I mean it's very hard to tell. But then it goes away again, and that's very strange. (Pause, to take a rest)

It's been interesting, hearing on your tapes, what you've been going through in Greece, changes and interests, and mostly I guess depression, and things like that. I think I told you on the phone and I'll say it again, I hope that you understand, or you can understand and can put up with the fact that I don't understand a lot of what you say, um, for a number of reasons. But I plan on listening to them again, and hopefully as time goes on I will understand more of them. One thing certainly is that I don't remember names of things. Like you refer to people, and I don't know who you're referring to. Some of them I do. You refer to places, for example, and a lot of times I don't know what you're talking about. But it's OK, because first of all I assume that they will come back, and the other thing is that it's just sort of fun listening to you, and if I don't understand what you're saying it doesn't really seem to make a difference. And as I say, I am planning on listening to it again.

The thing about people is a little strange, in that, well, for example, you talked a little bit about the Kenyon students and I, at that point, when I first got the tape anyway, I couldn't remember any of them. Not just not remember their names. I couldn't remember the people. Now I remember some of the people, anyway, and even a couple of the names of the students, so it's getting a little bit better, but it's still, I would say I listen to the tape, to your tapes, and I haven't been writing down, but I will, how much of it is just gone. I don't know. Like a couple of times you referred to something that I'm supposed to be doing for Kenyon, and I don't know what you're talking about. Who knows? Maybe I can listen to it again tomorrow and I will understand it, but it's very strange. Very odd.

Anyway, I have been enjoying listening to things about you on the tapes, but there are certainly a lot, well, not a lot, a fair amount that hasn't sunk in yet, but I assume that it will. Other things that I could say about you? Well, I don't know. I guess I started talking about this and somehow left it, but you need to understand that I do like you, really I do, and it's not only nice to get the tapes from you and talk to you on the telephone like we did yesterday and things, but to think about seeing you again. I mean all this. I really look forward to, because you're a nice person. Really. Oh, you have sort of strange ways about you, this is true, but you are a nice person, and I do enjoy remembering who you are. At the moment, however, you need to know that there's so much that I don't remember, don't feel like I know about you now, ever knew about you, or ever cared about you, because I can't remember, that, oh, I don't know, at this point anyway, it's my feeling that it is probably not worth trying to start again. That's one of the reasons...Well, who knows? I mean maybe things will get better and it will be [worth it], but at the moment anyway, it's very hard for me to imagine that it would be worth us becoming boyfriend and girlfriend or whatever. Who knows? Maybe that will improve in the next month or something. But without you being here, I doubt it. I doubt it because certainly so far away, the things that have become better known to me have been a result of the work that I've been doing. Either talking to people, or meeting with people, or reading things that people have written. Like I read a little of my brother's Master's Thesis and things like that. Somehow, with you not here, I doubt that I'll be doing an awful lot of that.

Anyway, I hope I've gone on about you enough. I probably will say more things on other tapes, as I go back and listen once again to the 3 tapes I've gotten so far. Certainly one of the problems at the moment is that I have listened to them all, and I remember thinking about certain things as they went by, but I don't remember much of it. So it's a little hard to talk with you about it now. But I will go back and listen to them again, and write down some things. I can write now! Did I tell you that? A little bit anyway. I've tried writing just a time or two I guess. It's still a little hard. My right hand doesn't work very well, but I can write a little bit. Um, in any case, if I listen to them again, I will undoubtedly think of other things about you that I would like to say. (Pause to take a rest)

Well, before the tape comes to an end, let me talk just a little bit about some of the things that I remember at this point you asking on your tapes. You wanted me to talk a little bit about Charlottesville, and America, and the things that I've been doing, some of which may wait for the next tape. About places that I've been going, and fun I've been having, and things I've been doing, and oh, a little bit about what America is like in the summer, because you haven't been here in the summer in a long time. Longer than I haven't, and I haven't been here in a while. So, let me go on about some of that.

Well, I think one of the first things that you need to understand, is that most of my time, my day, my evening, is spent first of all at home, or being taken someplace by somebody, and maybe seeing something, but I wouldn't call it having fun. That is a lot of times I'm doing exercises, or eating, or taking pills, or just doing things which need to be done, to be sure, and they are making me better, but it's hard to call them fun, certainly. In Charlottesville I've certainly spent some time going around the town in a car, sort of seated usually in the front seat, though now, as of yesterday, the day before yesterday, I've learned how to sit in the back seat. The town is very nice. It's very southern in some way, on the other hand I think because of the University of Virginia, it's got a lot of culture to it, I don't know, which you probably wouldn't expect in most southern towns. The houses are quite nice. There seem to be a lot of students, for example, off-campus. There is a fair number of stores, and restaurants, and sort of shopping plazas, and places like that, which seem a lot bigger than the population of Charlottesville. And it turns out that a lot of the rise in population that has happened recently has taken place outside of the city. That is, people living in the suburbs. And they still come into the city to do various things, like eat and buy things and stuff like that, so it's really a "booming town" shall I say?

Um, there are a fair number of blacks, which is nice. I think I asked Gene. I think he said it was 30 or 40% of the city. There are lots of old buildings that have been here since, oh, I guess since the early 1800s, maybe even earlier than that. I've seen some of them and I remember, but I can't remember at the moment. Um. And they've been nicely taken care of, so there are lots of old places with columns, for example, and bricks everywhere. I walk on bricks on the side, uh, sidewalks, and lots of places are built out of bricks. Lots and lots. Um.

There are various things that are a little strange about living in Charlottesville, that I have noticed. One thing is how green it is. Maybe this is true in Ohio during the summer. I don't remember. But you look out and you always see not only green grass, but green trees, absolutely everywhere, and mountains filled with green grass and trees. And things like that, which I don't remember from Ohio anyway. It seemed like it was usually brown, or, I don't know, yellow maybe. So living in Charlottesville in the summer is full of not only bugs and stuff like that, which is certainly true, but also greenery, which has been nice. Um.

Certainly some of the things about living in America that I've been noticing so far is how many kids I've been seeing when we've been going out. For example, we've gone out shopping, a couple of times anyway. We went to a concert. Gene anyway and I went out to a concert in the, uh, what's it called?, amphitheater, amphitheater. Oh, actually I think, who else came? Somebody else came. Anyway, in an amphitheater, and one of the oddest things that I've been noticing anyway, that I don't remember from Ohio, and I don't remember from Greece, is their taking their little kids, lots and lots of people taking their little kids with them everywhere. I mean I remember people taking their, oh, I don't know, 10 year olds or something like than with them, because they're old enough that they can kind of take care of themselves a little bit. But I mean we're talking 1 year olds, or 2 year olds, or maybe 3 year olds, and there are lot and lots and lots of them, absolutely everywhere. I don't remember that happening in Ohio. Maybe it's the part of Ohio that I've been living in, but it's really strange to see, let's say, you know, 100 kids in 10 minutes, or something like that, which has been very strange. (Pause, to take a rest)

And of course you have to understand that when I see them everywhere, they're with their parents. I mean they're not brought out alone, and they're not with babysitters either.

They're with their parents, or one or the other. Sometimes both. Why people would take their kids, little kids, with them everywhere, I haven't really figured out yet. But who knows, give me some time, maybe I will.

I'm getting near the end of this tape. What else should I tell you about? Talk with you about? Spread to Greece? Well, other things I can tell you about America? Um. It's a little hard, as I tried to explain earlier, and I think I stopped in the middle. And that is that most of my time and energy and even thoughts for that matter, are very self-based. For example, there are all that places that still hurt, and mostly I think about how much they hurt, whether they've gotten any better, what I could do to make the hurt go away, and things like that.

I mean you should understand: it's much less than it was. I mean I used to really hurt all over. I mean just everywhere. And now most of them are gone. I would say at this point the only ones that still hurt are my, I'll go from the bottom up, my left leg, my behind, my clavicle, and my head. You know, where my head was hurt. Besides that, you know, like my hands and my right leg, and most of my body for example, you know, the middle of my body, doesn't hurt, which is really nice, I assure you! Not to have it all hurting. But the things that do still hurt, well, obviously I feel them, and it's different at different times. Uh. Well, like, oh, I don't know. It's not worth going on about it.

But when I say that it's hard to describe...K...what's it called? Charlottesville in the summer, or America in the summer, a lot of it is because, to put it very simply, and maybe too strongly, I'm not that interested. I mean I'm interested in myself and getting myself better, and being able to talk, and to think, and to move, and to sleep, and, here's a little example, for example, to have sex. I mean I haven't had sex with anybody for what, 2 months maybe? No, not quite that long. A month and a half? So I have to admit that I probably spend a lot of my day trying to get myself better. I try to read a little bit. I try to talk a little bit. I try to do exercises a lot. I try to figure out about things. Like I think I mentioned to you that I don't understand about food. Um. I don't. Like I go into the food store with my Mother, and I don't recognize most of them, and I don't remember any of them.

Well, anyway, so this is a little bit stronger to me, it's true, than when we go out into the country, or to the bar where Gene plays music, or to a movie. We went and saw a parade a few days ago. Things like that which are fun in a small way. I mean they're interesting, they're different, they're things that I haven't done for a long time, but damn it, it's the wrong time of my life. (Pause, to take a rest)

Well, I can see that I'm coming to the end of this tape, so I probably should start bringing it to a close. It's been nice talking. It's been nice even talking with you, and I hope you can tell from it that it's easier for me to talk than it was. (Long Pause) And of course we can add to that sleeping, and walking, and even cooking, and things like that. But mostly I just want to thank you for sending things to me. THE END

Recording that tape took me 12 days, and as I hope you can discern, I was doing the best I could with what I had been dealt. Certainly I hadn't asked for or want these cards, but I couldn't very well give them back and ask for a better hand. In fact, I would never have expected that an event could be so debilitating without being completely demoralizing.

To the contrary, I experienced an increased awareness of my dependency on such everyday mechanisms and objects as my eyes, my eyeglasses, my right hand and, eventually, computers. Most of all, I quickly came to realize how essential reading and writing are to my life, to my existence, to my self-image. I even thought about it at the time.

(July 16): How to explain what has been going on with me over the past 2 months? It's now July 16. Why bother? Who is interested? Well, briefly put, I write this, and what follows, for myself. In part, to improve my ability to write in English, and in part so that I will remember, by having a memory, what is happening. I have improved enough in the exactly 8 weeks since the accident that I can sit at a typewriter, type a bit, think much more than I've been able to, speak/write better, and perhaps most of all, have become interested in understanding what has happened, is happening, and will happen to me.

That's a lot, I know. Yet, what is the alternative? I am not exactly the same person I was. I cannot think the same, or speak the same, and I certainly don't look or walk the same. Who am I? Who am I becoming? A simple list of the changes my body and mind have been going through is not enough for me, so I shall attempt to provide a more descriptive account. Of course it is dependent, especially for the first 2 weeks, upon information gathered from others, since I do not remember anything of that time. Even here, however, my account cannot be scientific or exact, since though I have heard various things about that time, I don't understand completely. Still, I will try to be as accurate as I am now able to be, with additional hope that the accuracy will improve with the passage of time. The other reasons will come out as I go along.

Those self-assessment thoughts were not infrequent. I may not have cared about others, but I became downright, almost obsessively, introspective.

"After a stroke, anger grows with awareness of what you have lost. The fog of consciousness that held you prisoner from the outside world was, in fact, a blessing in disguise. First you're like a soul with no body, but the soul is drugged. Then the soul awakens into a body you cannot command. You are a prisoner in a private hell. Everybody is just pushing you around. They push your arms and legs, your body. They say things, about things, look at you with expectation, and you don't know what they want. Every minute brings new reminders of the terrible gaps between you and every single thing you have taken for granted all your life. Brushing your teeth, swatting a fly from your face, getting a drink of water, going to the bathroom in the middle of the night." (Patricia Neal <u>As I Am: An Autobiography,</u> NY, 1988, p.261)

Now for some of the specifics of my two months in Virginia, beginning with some high points. I experienced a series of milestones in my newly reclaimed life, in June and July in particular. My first walk (June 19), dance (June 26), write (July 1), swim (July 9), laundry (July 12), cry (July 18), coffee (July 19), driving (July 20), run (July 20) and playing the piano (July 23).

Milestones abounded. I stopped biting my nails after more than 20 years of that bad habit, as a result of having my hands tied down in the Athens hospital. I awoke remembering a dream for the first time (since collapsing onto the floor in Boston) on August 8. I was able to run without my rear end hurting for the first time on Sept.10 — a particularly memorable day.

It was especially encouraging (and fun!) when I first re-learned how to drive a car. The doctor said it would be OK, so Gene let me get behind the wheel in our Mother's automatic car.

"Wheee!" I said. "This is fun!"

It felt new and a little like flying when I first slowly inched the car forward. I wasn't afraid, but it was strange, especially since I knew I used to drive.

The oddity of driving did not last very long. I was much too occupied remembering what all the buttons and switches did, and where all the controls were on this strange automobile. Still, learning to drive my Mom's automatic car was easier than my trying to remember how to drive my stick shift. Having driven mostly cars with clutches and gears, driving her car with automatic transmission was a cinch!

My attempts to reclaim my musical abilities provide a more self-evident illustration of my life at this time — a combination of slight inner confusion and some awareness of my previous life.

I knew I had played the piano, and had loved to dance.

I attempted to dance first, as I couldn't sit down to play a piano until my clavicle brace was removed. Toward the end of June we attended a Jazz concert in the University of Virginia (UVA) amphitheater. Gene first let me watch other people dance and then asked me, "Wanna dance?"

"OK." I stood up and tried to move to the music. That didn't work. I looked like someone pushing at the air on an aerobics dance video. Then I tried copying the steps done by the people dancing around us. That didn't work either. I wanted to imitate their movements, but by the time I figured out how to copy them, the music had changed, and those steps didn't seem to fit the song which followed. Then, I tried copying Gene's motions. That didn't work either. I think men's bodies must move differently.

Finally, Gene leaned over and made a suggestion. "Just try to feel the music."

"OK," without having a clue what he could possibly mean by "feel" the music. I mean Hell, I couldn't even <u>follow</u> the music, since I was certain that the word music meant the tune. And the tune seemed to keep changing, what with the refrains and choruses and instrumental riffs now and then. The only thing I could feel was the beat, so I decided to cheat and to dance to the beat of the music, instead of the melody.

"It works!" I thought. "Nobody's noticing that I can't "feel" the music." I laughed and Gene smiled, thinking I was enjoying myself. And so I was. The only difficulty was that the entire process of re-learning how to dance was exhausting.

Playing the piano was a different matter entirely.

After getting re-acclimated to the fundamentals of life (walking, talking, eating and bathing), my doctors suggested various ways to re-acquaint me with my previous life. Since my memory of that life was rather fuzzy, my family suggested activities, including my interacting with a piano, with remarkable repercussions.

It started off simply enough. Towards the end of July, with my clavicle brace having finally been removed, the doctors approved my trying to play the piano. We found some piano music and Gene showed me a place on campus with an easily accessible piano, in a private room, in the basement a building he often visited, since the Philosophy Department office was on the third floor.

I touched the piano's exterior wood. I touched the keys. I sat down and looked at the black and white keys. I looked up at Gene, standing in the doorway, waiting to leave me alone with the instrument until he knew I could handle it. I played the scale of c-major. He smiled and left.

At that point, the situation became more complicated. The piano music written on the page no longer signified anything to me. The noise of the keys, on the other hand, sounded quite right. And there were definitely…tunes (?) running through my head (?). No, the neither the word tunes nor head quite describes what I was experiencing. The encoding of the melodies seemed to reside not in my head, but in my hands.

I had no interest in reproducing any particular songs on this musical instrument. Rather, my hands just needed to move along the keys in a familiar pattern, and hopefully with predictable results.

It should have worked. Of course, it didn't.

Oh, I could initiate various pieces, Schubert waltzes especially. But very quickly I would falter, and almost immediately upon stumbling, cease playing. As I wrote at the time:

> *(July 23): I can do it some! My guess is that it will all just about come back eventually. Right now, I'm very slow, and don't play very well (i.e. as well as I used to), but the only bad problems are with my energy in the right arm/hand. The right arms gets very tired very easily, and I make mistakes. Still, for the first time since the accident, it could have been a lot worse.*

* * *

All in all, my time spent living with my Mom in a basement apartment near the University of Virginia Medical Center was unlike anything I had ever experienced. It was not like my first time away from home, not like going to summer camp, not like traveling abroad, etc. No, this life was definitely something completely different. Not boring, not exhausting, not exciting. I suppose what comes the closest to describing my memory of that time was that it was a subtle combination of waiting and learning. Waiting for things to get better, and re-learning things I knew I already knew.

Now, years after the accident and my resulting recovery, when I find myself in a situation when I am not doing anything in particular, or when I am with people, but in a non-interactive kind of way (as recently happened when I had laryngitis), I tend to become slightly pensive. The detachment results in my becoming slightly philosophical, thinking about the meaning of life, the philosophy of existence, and so on.

Such was not true during my new life's early recovery. Quite the contrary. Much like...a child? an animal? I am unsure what comparison, what sort of analogy, would best describe the difference, but after the accident, when I wasn't engaging in some activity, and therefore thinking about what I was doing, I wasn't thinking at all.

"Finally, the last reason for my depression was boredom. That can be even more horrible than pain. Perhaps mine was worse than that of some aphasics, because I don't play sports, sew, paint and so forth; my pleasure in life has always come from words – talking, teaching languages, reading and writing." (Dorothea Wender "At the Edge of Silence," <u>Family Circle</u> (March 25, 1986), p.66)

━━━━━━━━━━━━━━━━━━━━━━

I wasn't dumb. I wasn't stupid. I was…well, almost not there at all. I didn't think about much of anything. And not because I was busy with other matters. Just the opposite, which is why I tried using the comparison with children and animals. After something has happened which they want a child to understand, people do not say, "Think about it." What could such an expression possibly mean to a small child? In much the same way, "Think it over" was inconceivable to me.

I did not know how to just sit back and <u>consider</u> things. I probably would have responded with, "Think what? About what?"

I did not understand enough to have asked, "How?"

I could follow directions. I could understand some ideas. I could complete some tasks. But I did not ponder. I did not speculate.

Contemplating now the 2 months I lived in Charlottesville, I am struck by how very detached I recall feeling most of the time. No drive. No goals. No hopes. No dreams.

Much of what was going on around me just seemed so beside the point, as it were. Though I clearly had not a clue as to what the point might have been, nevertheless and oddly enough, I remember tending to feel…well, rather calm, in an out-of-control kind of way.

After all, others (my family, my doctors) were assuming most of the responsibilities in my life. I was required simply to do as I was told, which resulted in a rather tranquil existence.

Perhaps another reason for my relative serenity was my general inability to make distinctions — among people, events, words, etc. A typical list of words which were new to me, for example, included: stapler, shade, brace, brakes, coma, comma, bass, base, and so on.

It was thus often difficult, if not impossible, for me to differentiate between whether I found myself _x_ing (say, moving) or being _x_ed (being moved), and so determine whether an active or passive form of the verb was more appropriate.

I'm sure I did and said many totally idiotic things during those first few months of recovery. My thoughts were cloudy and enigmatic, and it never occurred to me to communicate in a roundabout way (say, by drawing) when I could not express myself with words.

Absolutely everything, including my memories, tended both to run together, and yet not quite fit together.

My writing, for example. In reading letters and postcards I then wrote, they don't seem to have been written by a mixed-up person, but they were.

> *Tues. July 16, 1985: Dear Timothy: Not much worse of course, but a bit. Eight weeks have gone by, as of today, and things have improved greatly. I can walk, I can talk, I can even run in a swimming pool! (Soon, I'll even re-learn how to write so people can read it!) Anyway, in case I forgot to tell you: thank you so very much for your actions – in the hospital, Kenyon In Greece, etc. My modern Greek gets better every day. Ancient languages? We'll have to see in time.... So, ευχαριστώ πολύ και πρέπει να είσαι καλός άνθρωπος γιά το καλοκαίρι. Happy Day, φίλος μου, and more, ... Αριάννα*

The end of the postcard, translated into English, means "I thank you very much, and you should be a happy person for the summer. Happy Day my friend, Arianna."

It took me hours and hours to write comprehensible English.

Greek took me days.

*Αγαπητά Σπίρο και Ελιζάβετ -- Γεία σας! Τί
κάνετε; Εγώ, είμαι καλίτερα, καί κάθε μέρα
γίγνομαι πιό καλά. Σας ευχαριστώ για όλα ποια
κάνατε για μένα, και ελπίζω να σας δώ επόμενο
καλοκαίρι. Μένω τώρα με τη μητέρα μου στη
Βιργίνι, που μένει ο αδελφός μου. Γρήγορα, όταν
οι ιατροί συμφωνούν, θα πάω στη Καλιφόρνια, που
συνηθώς μένει η μητέρα μου. Ακόμη, που μπορω να
γυρίζω στη δουλειά μου (στον Οχαίο), αλλά ίσως
σε λίγο. Γειά σας. Αριάννα*

*Dear Spiro and Elizabeth – Greetings! How are you? I am
better, and every day I become better. I thank you for all that
you did for me, and I hope to see you next summer. I'm living
now with my Mother in Virginia, where my brother lives.
Quickly, when the doctors agree, I will go to California, where
my Mother usually lives. Still, I can't return to work (in Ohio),
but perhaps in a little while. Good-bye, Arianna.*

My struggle in writing English and Greek was not due to my
engaging in an abundance of editing and re-writing.

Phrases came to me in a flash, and I wrote them down immediately,
before they disappeared and became irretrievable. Here's another
postcard, written around the same time:

Wednesday, July 24, 1985: Dear Timothy, Well, it would be nice to talk with you alone, but letters are something anyway...Mom has returned from California, Gene leaves soon for a vacation on an island off the coast of Georgia/South Carolina? Anyway, I look forward to traveling myself some day. What about you? Are you happier? Traveling? I do hope that you manage to make some pleasantness out of the summer. Why? Because you deserve some! I do dream and hope for the best for you – besides work! Take care, have fun, and keep in touch! Annie

Writing such a postcard felt like a magnum opus, after which I would sit quietly for a period of time, either with pen in hand or at the typewriter, waiting for another lucid moment to appear. Turning point moments of competence, of awareness, came without warning, often followed by an abrupt relapse into forgetfulness. And, surprisingly enough, when a thought did come, it often was connected with the previous lucid moment, even though much time had passed in the meantime.

"What were you thinking about during that time?" you might ask. Thank God nobody (including my doctors) ever asked me: "Tell us your thoughts. What are you thinking about?"

The term thought would have been inappropriate to the occasion. For while my mind was busy, and not entirely vacant, nevertheless I would not label it thinking, though I'm sure I must have used just that word at the time.

What did I think about, when alone? Either nothing or something.

Something specific of course. Where are my glasses? When do we leave for the library? What day is today? Who is that on the phone?

Nothing was specific as well. Nothing was emptiness.

In either case, there were no generalities in my world.

I suppose, using my present vocabulary, a more accurate description of my existence during those first few months following the accident would be the word Beingness. Not meditating. Not zoning. Just being. And not thinking about being. Just being. Being and, if anything else, waiting. Not waiting for anything in particular, for I certainly had no idea of what, if anything, I might have been waiting for, but simply waiting…waiting for something.

Chapter 3: Healing My Brain

"To be conscious that we are perceiving or thinking is to be conscious of our own existence."

- Aristotle <u>Nic.Eth.</u> 9.9

"I stood in that room for a long time, watching the sunlight and listening to the sounds on the street outside. I stood there, tasting the room and the sunlight and the sounds, and thinking of the long hospital ward with its wide aisle and its two rows of bed...I turned, finally, and went back through the apartment and through the door that led from my father's bedroom onto our wooden back porch. I sat on the lounge chair in the shade that covered the porch and looked out at the back lawn. Somehow everything had changed. I had spent five days in a hospital and the world around seemed sharpened now and pulsing with life. I lay back and put the palms of my hands under my head. I thought of the baseball game, and I asked myself, Was it only

last Sunday that it happened, only five days ago? I felt I had crossed into another world, that little pieces of my old self had been left behind on the black asphalt floor of the school yard alongside the shattered lens of my glasses."
- Chaim Potok <u>The Chosen</u> p.96

My recovery over the summer in Virginia continued, and I gradually acquired a sense of what I had lost. I began to feel compromised, and experienced an increasing sense of isolation. Not the serene kind of isolation, but one in which I knew I was alone. Utterly alone. With not even myself to guide me.

After all, who knew exactly who me myself was? Certainly not I.

As a result, I was required to reinvent myself. And unlike most contemporary recovery processes (12-step, the child within, etc.), my recovery was not by choice, but by necessity, as I had been (somewhat? completely?) dismantled by a chance occurrence.

In much the say way as the getting acquainted process when meeting someone new, I was getting reacquainted with myself, and thereby, with my previous life.

And I was not just some old wine being poured into a new bottle. Rather, I was given a chance at a new existence, since I now felt so totally solitary, isolated and unattached.

Leaving Hell, Dante said he saw the stars again. By comparison, I regularly saw a mass of puzzling stars, but without much (if any) memory of what Hell had been like, much less any wisdom as to how to make sense of the stars.

I lived in a fragmented world in which everything felt static. I never became fully aware of things, any more than when you turn around to see something you hadn't seen before you turned. That moment isn't really an increase in your awareness, since you knew the object was there before you turned, only you couldn't see it before. And you don't actually <u>think</u> about it when you turn around and see it for the first time. You just see it, head-on. Then you turn back around and see it no longer.

Such was my life at this point.

Now I tend to be a rather patient and tolerant person by disposition, and a month of mostly lying on my back staring at the ceiling, followed by another month of relearning how to talk, walk, read and write, accentuated those characteristics over which I had little control, and which luckily perfectly suited to my recovery. And I did always seem to keep getting better. So while my recuperation proceeded, I attempted to simply exist and wait.

Fortunately, I was unable to remain that inactive, since I was urged, prodded and questioned by my family. Daily.

"So, Annie, what are you going to do today?"

To please them I had to produce a response, which was not that difficult, since they required only the bare minimum of an answer. Rather, our proceeding through the question and answer process was much more important than the activities themselves. Any activity on my part was preferable to my inaction.

Contemplating it now in retrospect, my family often seemed absolutely fascinated by my answer. Perhaps because they were never really sure exactly whom, at that point, they were addressing? Though I appeared the same, my guess is that they were being faced with a rather unknown person most of the time, someone quite distinct from the Annie I had been.

How would she reply? It never occurred to me not to attempt to answer every question. After all, that was how my recovery process had begun, with doctor after doctor asking me question after question.

In time, I'm sure I made a connection between answering questions and feeling less pain.

After a month or so, I settled into a daily routine with a repetitious daily schedule (see below). When asked how I was going to spend the day, I'm certain I came up with virtually the same answer every day.

"I'm going for a walk, and to the medical library."

Each day proceeded much the same as every other day, and yet, without much of a memory, it always seemed new and different to me. My life was terribly simple. I was given and followed a daily schedule, in a very monotonous, almost mechanical kind of way, not knowing under what conditions it might be possible to cut corners.

To give my 3 month stay in Virginia some structure, I followed a very precise daily schedule:

8-9am	Breakfast
9-10am	Rest
10-12	Physical Exercise and Shower
12-1	Rest
1-2	Lunch
2-3	Rest
3-4	Mental Exercise

4-5	Rest
5-6	Recreation
6-7	Dinner
7-11	Socializing, fun, reading, etc.
11pm	Bedtime

The physical and mental exercise portions of my day were spent working on my balance, reading, writing, mathematics, emotional exercises, walking (in front of a mirror), and "setting myself up for success."

The exercises were slightly boring at first — not because of the exercises themselves, but due to my complete lack of cogitation while doing them. I honestly felt I had nothing to think about. That was true even while doing the mental exercises, which were intended to facilitate my re-entry into a thoughtful world. I did the exercises, but I found them quite boring. Not much mental stimulation that I could tell.

Rather, I felt most absorbed with mental activity while on my daily walk, as I responded to external stimuli. Two months after the accident, for example, I began trying to speculate about something I knew better than most: my body. Note the following excerpt from my daily journal.

Sun. July 21: ...Anyway, I spent the rest of the day walking outside, reading, writing, exercises, eating, cooking, etc. One slight problem I continue to have: even when running slowly, my buttock (right) continues to hurt...far more than the left leg, which is also strained at the moment. Hmph. I'll ask Dr. Miller tomorrow. One thing I did for myself: I tried to improve my walking using my left foot, by concentrating on it during a walk. As long as I think about it, I can do it a little. When I'm busy doing other things, my left foot goes back to making noises. Ah well, ...maybe in time.

Gradually, as a result of such ideas germinating in my brain as it healed, when a subject occurred to me which I wanted to think about, I would go for a walk, and eventually, a run.

Visiting libraries, I came to xerox sections of books, even articles, on my many medical problems, especially aphasia.

Aphasia was a new word for me, but one which I came to understand and to use at the library. Aphasia was the reality of my life. I tried to read about it all the time. And slowly, ever so slowly, I came to understand the ailment from which I had to recover.

The injury to the parietal-occipital fissure on the right side of my brain was the cause. Aphasia was the result.

Pouring over the books and articles I found on aphasia (see Appendix A), I very gradually (it took me a while) came to understand that I wasn't stupid, I wasn't illiterate, I wasn't brain-dead. I was an aphasic. I even acquired a deeper understanding of the etymology of the English word dumb, meaning speechless, and therefore stupid.

Without the ability to fully function by means of language, I appeared and so was, for all intents and purposes, stupid. In researching aphasia ("without speech"), the condition of impaired communication skills, I learned the terms for each kind of aphasia.

Of course I could not tell which type, or types, of aphasia I had. And no one ever told me. It might have been simply dysphasia, a term sometimes used for relatively mild aphasia. Then there was dyslexia, a term I knew from teaching college students with impaired reading ability, and dysgraphia, impaired writing ability. I did recognize that I had neither alexia or agraphia, since those classifications of aphasia required the total loss of reading and writing skills.

The most helpful was my discovery of the term anomia, describing a patient who can speak, but cannot find the correct word. This type of aphasia seemed the most applicable to my situation, as when I would say during a meal, "Please pass the...the...oh, you know, the black stuff in the bottle with the red cap." (see above Chapter 2)

The most encouraging discovery from my reading of medical texts was the fact that aphasia was a temporary illness, not a permanent loss, though the volume of aphasic residuals would have to be seen and determined, in due time.

I was especially grateful for the books and articles by Oliver Sacks, a doctor (and now famous author) who had developed aphasia himself, from an accident while hiking in the mountains of Switzerland, and who had undergone much the same kind of recovery I was enduring. I read all his books, especially <u>A Leg to Stand On</u>.

One passage touched me in particular. He was hobbling, and still using a stick to help him walk, after his injured knee had healed, and should have worked just fine.

"The lifeguard unwound himself, slowly, languidly leaned towards me, looked mischievous and suddenly said "Race you!", at the same time taking my stick with his right hand and pushing me in with his left. I was in the water, outraged, before I knew what had happened - and then the impertinence, the provocation, had their effect. I am a good swimmer - a "natural" - and have been since childhood - from infancy, indeed, for my father, a swimming-champ, had thrown us in at six months, when swimming is instinctual and doesn't have to be learnt. I felt challenged by the lifeguard. By God, I'd show him! Provocatively he stayed just a little in front of me, but I kept up a fast crawl for four Olympic lengths, and only stopped then because he yelled "Enough!" I got out of the pool - and found I walked normally. The knee was now working, it had "come back" completely." (Oliver Sacks <u>A Leg to Stand On</u> p.193)

Even writings as similar to my experience as Oliver Sack's could not exactly replicate my direct experience. In much the same way, I fear that this narrative of my memories will not suffice to put others in touch with the ambiguity of my inner thoughtlessness without confusion and my recovery. Hopefully my ramblings can evoke, at the very least, a kind of superficial appreciation of that process.

Some movies have tried. Making abundant use of special effects, films have done remarkably well at putting the audience in close touch with such themes as war, romance, space, etc. But pain? No. Handicaps? No, with the exception perhaps of <u>Children of a Lesser God</u>. Most movies tend to reduce non-physical pain and anguish to discomfort, at least in part because, without physical pain, there is no need for the extremely photogenic use of red blood.

Having been released at approximately the same time as my own recovery, Children of a Lesser God made quite an impression upon me and was, in many ways, my first real exposure to the life of the disabled after the accident. Combined with my personal struggle, the film encouraged me to admire people whom I had previously simply defined as handicapped. I also felt that I had discovered a secret weapon in my recovery, namely my undamaged ears and my ability with learning languages. When I had fully recovered after a year, and returned to work teaching in Ohio, I tried to learn Sign Language. Unfortunately, like ancient Greek, which had been a real challenge to learn, Sign Language is not spoken. Without being able to hear Sign Language, it was not an easy language for me to acquire, and I eventually gave up, after realizing that my facility with learning languages was dependent on hearing the language spoken.

But back to books and movies on aphasia.

In books and movies, aphasia seems little more than a slightly exaggerated form of what we all experience from time to time — forgetfulness. When experienced first hand, however, Aphasia is different because it doesn't go away. You don't usually either finally or a bit later remember the word or behavior you were seeking. Not exactly gone, the memory is just not accessible, which makes you think that it's not there at all. In this case, experience results in a

quintessential apprehension that your memory-skill is completely
gone, and may never return.

"Forgetting dimmed the remembering self: kept it in
hiding. Often he took in experience, half forgetting. He
was not always present in the present; was not always
attentive to what was there to be experienced, kept in
mind, recalled, remembered. Dubin followed his
thoughts where they went, elsewhere. He used to warn
himself to observe and remember…Maud, in any given
experience, saw more details than Dubin saw. He
thought he saw whole forms better than they, but
wasn't sure." (Bernard Malamud Dubin's Lives, NY,
1977l p.332)

I did sometimes wonder if I had simply gone a little crazy, or perhaps
had become slightly mentally retarded, or what is now termed
developmentally disabled. Not because the world around me was so
incomprehensible, but because I kept having the feeling that people
kept looking at me strangely, as if I were a person with some kind of
condition.

Just as many hospital patients feel like an object under scientific investigation, I felt I was under constant observation, by all.

Ah yes, I remember the looks.

First in Boston, then on the train to Charlottesville, around the apartment in Charlottesville, or while visiting Ohio. Wherever I went among friends and acquaintances, I felt I was being watched — and by those I spent the most time with in particular, namely my family, and especially my Mother. The expression on her face was not so bad by the time we reached California, where we lived together for a year. But sometimes even then, and certainly before that, she always looked so hurt. So afraid. Like she had lost her daughter.

I wish I had been able to tell her, "Don't worry Mom. I'll be OK some day."

Fortunately for me at that time, my family's facial expressions, while discernable, were only barely understood, so they were without meaning. Now however, in remembering the way they looked at me, an image burned deep into my memory, I cannot imagine anything more painful to a child who feels so indebted to her family, than to be the cause of such anguish, especially to a parent. Compared to this image, I feel certain that all other pains still to come in my life will be easy.

"The psychology of the seriously ill put barriers between us and those who had the skill and the grace to minister to us.

There was first of all the feeling of helplessness – a serious disease in itself.

There was the subconscious fear of never being able to function normally again – and it produced a wall of separation between us and the world of open movement, open sounds, open expectations.

There was the reluctance to be thought a complainer.

There was the desire not to add to the already great burden of apprehension felt by one's family; this added to the isolation.

There was the conflict between the terror of loneliness and the desire to be left alone.

There was the lack of self-esteem, the subconscious feeling perhaps that our illness was a manifestation of our inadequacy.

There was the fear that decisions were being made behind our backs, that not everything was made known that we wanted to know, yet dreaded knowing.

There was the morbid fear of intrusive technology, fear of being metabolized by a data base, never to / regain our faces again. There was a resentment of strangers who came at us with needles and vials...There was the distress of being wheeled through white corridors to laboratories of all sort of strange encounters with compact machines and blinking lights and whirling discs.

And there was the utter void created by the longing – ineradicable, unremitting, pervasive – for warmth of human contact. A warm smile and an out-stretched hand were valued even above the offerings of modern science, but the latter were far more accessible than the former." (Norman Cousins <u>Anatomy of an Illness as Perceived by the Patient: Reflections on Healing and Regeneration</u>, NY, 1979, pp.153-154)

Friends and acquaintances, more than anything, tended to treat me much like a fragile object, in danger of breaking completely apart.

Perhaps worst of all, I didn't really mind. There was a kind of liberation in my not being responsible for my own actions. ("She's not herself.") I even slightly, well, liked it? I appreciated it, that's for sure, but like is an inappropriate word. I didn't delight in or dislike anything, because I didn't remember how to feel. I never derived pleasure from anything. I had no desires, including to speak, to eat, to go for a walk, or to go swimming. Nothing. I'm guessing feelings were there, mind you, but without a way to encapsulate the emotions in words. Language, after all, is a code, a means of communication, which not only reflects, but shapes, the mind. The two are intimately related. I can now recall previous moments in my life when it was inappropriate to put into words how I felt. Now the cards were turned and without words I had lost not just the words for the feelings, but the feelings themselves. Or so it seemed.

Similarly, it was noted that I would stare ahead most of the time, only rarely glancing from side to side. I didn't notice that, but I know that immediately upon entering a building or room, I always headed strait for the reason I had entered it in the first place. It would never have occurred to me to do anything, or go anywhere, else, for either another or no particular reason.

To go out onto the balcony and look around, for example, or to sit and meditate, simply to relax, was out of the question.

That inability for ideas to evolve was particularly true in terms of conversation. Since I never knew what I would understand the next minute, much less the next day, I tried to reduce those occasions by concentrating hard at the start of each discussion, hoping that the subject matter would not change.

I never did reach the point of being able to stop someone else from explaining something to me I already understood and remembered, by saying, "Don't bother to explain. I remember how this works (or) what this means." I would just let them continue explaining it to me until they were finished.

And when I didn't understand or remember something, I would make a systematic search for it, checking through lists and categories in my brain. Hunting for words that begin with the letter R, or have two syllables, or describe the sky, or rhyme with know, for example, I might finally remember the word rainbow.

What I could <u>not</u> do was what I now tend to do, which is by means of intuitive guess work hazard a theory as to what something is, or what a word means, or how I might already know it, based on my knowledge of similar words, events and objects. I never jumped to related thoughts. I never said "That reminds me of something similar…"

And as difficult as it was for me to respond to many topics of conversation, I almost never initiated a subject for discussion.

I do remember towards the end of my 3 month recovery in Virginia being somewhat close to wondering what good my previously acquired skills (computers, languages, piano) were doing for me. But the closer I came to "Why did I bother to learn them?," it struck me deeply how thankful I was that I had bothered, and that I had managed to live a pretty full life so far.

I had even, at that point, considered the state of existence and the meaning of life from time to time. "Thoughts of death?" you might well ask. No, though I did, having been so close to death, consider my mortality. I even entertained the notion that I might have to remain a 2-dimensional vegetable. But that idea would pass quickly, as I realized I kept improving!

* * *

Before I continue with my ramblings on my recuperation from the accident, I'd like to note one interesting difficulty which I still have, in writing these reminiscences. Recalling the events, I often find myself searching for particular words to describe how I felt when facing various situations. Ah, words, words, words.

Again and again, the word fascination comes to mind, and I reject it. Nothing ever fascinated me at that point in my life. The word fascination suggests thoughtfulness. I was more like a child. It suggests activity. I was passive. It suggests a positive. I was definitely in a state of negatives. Perhaps most of all, the word fascination implies far too many feelings which were inaccessible to me at that time. I was barely feeling at all. More like existing.

Words were necessary not only to express a need or an answer, but words to express those items to request or those questions to try and answer. Still, as a result of my aphasia, words became the trick key, at many levels.

Memory and language were always on my mind, and they came up in practical ways. I would be looking at a picture in a magazine, and immediately see something without a word to describe it, for example.

"What's the word for…?" I would say.

Or, more often, in the course of a conversation with someone, I would utter phrases such as "Here's a…thing." and "This is a…thing." and "There's this…thing." I thought I knew the word, but I couldn't remember it while speaking other words, and I didn't know where to find them. Words were never on the tip of my tongue.

"Unless an aphasic patient is willing to make some mistakes initially, his verbal output will probably not be large enough to produce improvement. It is necessary to get language processes functioning before errors can be reduced, and making errors is part of this process. This is often hard for the educated aphasic to accept emotionally, although the theory makes sense to him. One of the advantages of machine practice for the aphasic patient is that it permits him to make mistakes unobserved." (Hildred Schuell, James J. Jenkins and Edward Jimenez-Pabon Aphasia in Adults: Diagnosis, Prognosis, and Treatment, NY, 1967, p.224)

Having been brought up in a household where almost every topic, but especially contemporary culture and politics, were discussed constantly and coherently, I had, for as long as I could remember, both spoken and written well. Now, however, I seemed to be capable of neither - especially verbal conversation.

For while I did mean what I said, I couldn't ever seem to say what I meant, or wanted to say. When asked a question I did not understand, I didn't even know enough to ask for an explanation, or to respond "I don't understand," much less to enunciate an indirect reply in the refined form "I think...," "I believe...," or "I don't know the answer to that question."

Unlike my difficulty with speaking, I did fairly well at communicating non-verbally with young children and animals. During my wanderings I would stop, and we'd look at each other, roll up our eyes or bare our teeth, shake our shoulders, and the greeting or the anger would be understood. It was comforting to feel so accepted, and somewhat discomforting that I considered them my colleagues.

In trying to converse with adults, on the other hand, I spoke to the extent I was able, made faces and gestured — none of which served any purpose. But I never gave up. And I was so busy paying close attention to the words that I didn't watch for facial expressions or gestures, or listen closely to their voice's inflexion or intonation. I couldn't recognize signs of tension, embarrassment or worry, and I always found it impossible to sit back, wait, and see what subjects people wished to discuss. Once into a conversation, I would often lose my way.

"Wait just a minute," I would say, as I searched for the next correct, or at least acceptable, word.

I would point to the object in need of a noun, or into the air to symbolize an abstraction. I would then pause, frown slightly as if thinking, and if those with whom I was attempting to converse would wait patiently, I would sometimes emit a sound or a gesture or, more likely, I would change the subject ever so slightly, to take advantage of whatever words came to me.

Perhaps more than anything, it seemed to me that the meaning of words in the course of a conversation was defined each time by their context. A change of subject matter in the course of a discussion could prove disastrous, due to my inability to change vocabulary as quickly as the topic.

Even a change in mood, going from a happy to a sad topic of discussion, was out of the question. With no moods of my own (that would require a yearning of some kind), adapting to my interlocutor's change of mood always took me a while.

And though my attempts at conversation may have been abysmal failures, that did not mean they were not valuable. I often experienced, for example, a struggle between my wanting to speak, and my fear that I would make many mistakes. I learned a great deal from my failures.

Sometimes my attempts at conversation were beneficial in odd kinds of ways. I slowly began to "notice" details, for example, which did not come easily, or circumstances which discouraged comfortable feelings. [Please note: I have chosen to express "notice" in quotation marks due to it being a slightly inappropriate word to describe my thought process at the time. I did not notice anything in an "Oh, I see" kind of way. Rather, some incidents and remarks made by others simply felt better to me than other remarks. And of course I preferred feeling good to feeling discomfort or pain.]

Nothing was predictable. Not just other people's words, ideas, or mood changes, but even such trivial articles and devices of daily life, such as doors being on the front of houses, curbs connected with sidewalks, and stop signs at intersections, much less that milk and dairy products are usually kept at the farthest distance from the front doors of food markets. Life's experiences teaches us those sorts of things, and I was devoid of experiential knowledge. Everything was new.

===

"One day Papa felt the time had come for me to face the challenge of going to the grocer's for our supplies. It was not a complex chore...When we got to the store...I felt wretched and was more confused than ever. I stood there staring at all those labels. They were only splinters of color, the writing had no meaning to me at all. I had no idea what to buy. I

began to pull things off the shelf." (Patricia Neal <u>As</u>
<u>I Am: An Autobiography</u>, New York, 1988, p.280)

═══════════════════

Perhaps a catalogue of the negatives during my 3 months stay in Virginia would be a better way to describe my mental state during this time. My life was abounding in negatives.

I couldn't read. I couldn't write. I couldn't work. I couldn't play. Hell, I couldn't even dream.

My existence, more than anything, was filled with an abundance of nothing. Not even anything to miss. Though I was very aimless, I did not miss having a goal, and I was never bored.

There were so many mannerisms which just didn't happen, because they were simply inaccessible, and so out-of-the-question, given my state of mind at the time. Doing or saying something just to prove a point, for example. I couldn't do it. Or wishing for things to happen, such as "Oh, I hope this turns out to be…" or "Oh please, let this be the correct way to respond." I never expressed myself that way.

And I know it sounds crazy, but I have gradually come to realize that much of what I wasn't aware of were items such as puns, jokes, metaphors, which didn't exist as simple objects.

I seemed incapable of comprehending sarcasm, irony, or rhetorical questions, for example. I always answered them – something that continued even after my year of recovery. When asked "How are you?" I developed the horrible habit of replying, not realizing it was a rhetorical question not needing an answer, but just a "Fine. How are you?" Of course given my condition, if my brain had been working, I would have thoughtfully replied "I've been better and I've been worse," or "Compared to what?"

I had virtually no imagination. Certainly not a vivid imagination. Isn't imagination a large part of being alive for a human? You guess. You wonder. You imagine.

I never imagined things. Likewise, I did not recall how to improvise, or to pretend, including how to pretend to be asleep.

═══════════════════════

"Another time, Bill said, "Did you know that aphasics can't lie? If you ask me something, I have to tell you the truth. I have no- no-. (No alternatives?) Yes, that's it. Aphasics have no alternatives." (Hildred Schuell, James J. Jenkins, and Edward Jimenez-Pabon <u>Aphasia in Adults: Diagnosis, Prognosis, and Treatment</u>, NY, 1967, p.214)

═══════════════════════

I never considered subjects unless they were somehow presented to me. Things never just occurred to me.

On the other hand, I was also never combative, irritable, ornery, or restless. And I never worried, was never concerned about anything besides myself – not others, not the world, not the future. I had no illusions, no fantasies, no dreams, not even opinions.

And as difficult it had been for me before the accident, due to my disposition or temperament, I now found myself completely incapable of being devious, manipulative or subtle in any way. Lying was beyond me. Tactful? Circumspect? Not I.

I tried, but nothing ever seemed symbolic. My life, such as it was, was exceedingly, or at least relatively, simple.

I had virtually no dexterity, and I never did things such as whistle or hum or click my tongue or sigh. I never came <u>close</u> to eloquent and I was unable <u>not</u> to say whatever was on the tip of my tongue. I don't remember ever doing anything in the <u>least</u> out of the ordinary, such as shutting my eyes when awake.

Thinking back on it now, I realize that part of the simplicity of my life during this recovery may have been due to the fact that it was not really my life which I was living. Nothing around me was mine – not my room, not my bed, not my town. Having traveled widely, I should have been used to residing in unfamiliar places. But this situation was more than that. It was not my time, not my place, not my world. But it was simple. Simpler than you can imagine.

Unfortunately, in hindsight, my simple life included me having no sense of humor, though I often, almost obsessively, smiled. I even managed to laugh when I heard people laughing around me, or the laugh track on TV. Their laughter assured me that I should laugh, and that made things somewhat funny, insofar as I could appreciate humor. Otherwise I didn't have a clue.

Likewise, I did not know how to tease or be teased, to make fun of anything, especially people, in much the same way (and perhaps for the same reason?) that there was never any randiness, no idiosyncrasy, shenanigans, eccentricities in my behavior. At least not that I could recognize.

And lest you believe that humor is a biological instinct, I don't recall any humorous response, much less humorous remark, just coming to me. I never experienced a flash of recognition or a moment of insight, never developed a sense of perspective, never became aware of anything intuitively. My guess is that somehow my instincts had receded, if not disappeared.

At the same time, perhaps surprisingly, I suffered no profound frustration and no acute depression. Much like someone on antipsychotics, nothing seemed either wonderful or deeply distressing. I was never troubled, never upset by things others around me noticed and considered. With no borders for input to cross, nothing ever nagged me or bothered me. There were no urgent calls, no decisions to be made, no awkward meetings or conferences to attend, no infighting or backbiting to deal with.

If I did have such thoughts verging on depression at some level, those inklings of awareness were easily forgotten, like everything else. I did not feel quite steady, but I didn't sulk, for the simple reason that there was nothing I could perceive to sulk about. I know it sounds odd, but one nice thing about having lost your wits is that you don't know that they have been lost, and you don't understand what people mean, when they tell you that you have lost your wits!

I didn't hope for anything, since I didn't comprehend that there was anything wrong, and therefore something for which I should be hoping.

―――――――――――――――――――――

"And when you came out of your [diabetic] coma, did you come out of it in stages?

Jerry Garcia: I was pretty scrambled. It was as though in my whole library of information, all the books had fallen off the shelves and all the pages had fallen out of the books. I would speak to people and know what I meant to say, but different words would come out. So I had to learn everything over again. I had to learn how to walk, play the guitar, everything.

Did you always have faith that you would accrue your memory again? Did it scare you that you might have lost it forever?

Jerry Garcia: I didn't care. When your memory is gone, you don't care because you don't remember when you had one." (D.J. Brown and R.M. Novick "An Interview with Jerry Garcia," Magical Blend 41 (Jan. 1994), 32-40 & 88-89, p.38)

═══════════════════════════════

Likewise, and perhaps most frightening to me in thinking back to that first year of recovery was my infrequently wanting anything. Not only did I no longer know what I wanted. I never seemed to desire much of anything. The idea of wanting something, anything, seemed to have gotten lost in the shuffle.

I do wonder whether such a reaction may have been a consequence of my newly acquired preference for obtaining what I needed, rather than desiring something (such as a word) and not being able to find, and so attain it.

To this day, I still find it difficult to consider, much less express, what I would like to do, or listen to or watch or eat. I think my mind got out of the habit of making such decisions, when the process of trying to make such a decision was exhausting.

I didn't know how to just go through the motions, so I didn't even try. Oddly enough, I don't recall ever wanting to do something and not being able to accomplish it. And not only because I didn't ever want anything. No, it was as if the desire was difficult enough to fabricate. So much so, that either the desire erupted concomitantly with the pursuit of the goal, or it didn't come out at all. I never did anything against my will, due to the simple fact that I didn't have much of a will.

One thing I noticed quite soon after my year of recovery. Before the accident and my ensuing one-year recuperation, things, especially ideas, would sometimes just hit me out of the blue. You know, when you have no idea where they're even coming from, much less notice that they are approaching? But during my recovery, nothing ever came out of the blue. I had so little to serve as a basic mainframe to use for comparison, and against which something could be compared, there were no preconceptions to surprise or to shock.

In much the same way, I could reject virtually nothing as being not my style, or running against my nature, since I couldn't recollect that I <u>had</u> any personality characteristics, much less what they were...I certainly felt a substantial lack of individuality, which then resulted in a kind of coldness, due to my sense of isolation. Not the serene kind of solitude, but a seclusion, complete with a kind of lonely detachment.

I guess I became a type of generic human, without any real humanity. I recall a complete absence of attitudes such as vigor, vitality, or vivacity, for example, which had been my trademarks. Then, however, I simply had no bounce, and I don't remember actually <u>enjoying</u> myself. For while this state of affairs never really upset me, it also never felt quite right, and it certainly never gave me any pleasure. Along with my not noticing, much less caring, about others, I also never felt ashamed or humiliated.

When I compare the range of feelings I have experienced in the course of writing this book, with the virtual lack of such emotions during my year of recovery, I am astounded. Living in Greece during the summers, for example, I have obtained enormous enjoyment regularly from a drink of cool, clear, water, and a nice cold shower at the end of a long hot day. Similarly, in America, nothing beats a hot fudge sundae with mint chocolate chip ice cream, or excellent Dim Sum in Chinatown. During my year of recovery from aphasia however, I experienced a virtual lack of emotions. But while my complete lack of eloquence was clearly due to the aphasia, where did my lack of assertiveness, of any self-assured aggressive confidence come from? Once I became aware of my emotional deficiency, see Chapter 5 for how I began to remedy the situation.

Finally, I'd like to mention one particularly nice negative before returning to my summer in Virginia. Though I am not entirely certain why not, I was never envious of the ease with which others conduct and maneuver their lives. Psycho-philosophically speaking I suppose it is of some significance that I never asked, <u>Why me</u>? For months at first, I did not realize I was any different. I had too many other things on my mind. Not that I observed anything studiously, but just as I did not notice much (it was all the same to me) so did nothing unnerve me. Why didn't I get agitated? Honestly, I did not care much about other people yet, but was an unbelievably self-centered, like a child. An entire childhood conveniently compressed in my case into 9 months of healing. And I couldn't even enjoy going <u>through</u> the maturing process, because I understood, in some slight way, that I was enduring it.

I never heard things inside my head, never had afterthoughts. I almost never laid awake in bed, and even when I did, I was certainly never lost in thought. In the mornings, for example, I never said "I was thinking last night," since there was no continuity with the previous day's events. I had no more knowledge of, or interest in, last night than I had about tomorrow, having no true awareness of tomorrow. And without expectations, nothing ever struck me as other than predictable. It being virtually impossible for me to gaze into the future, I spent my days looking backwards into my evasive past. Oddly enough, I was never <u>confused</u>. After all, without complexity, nothing obscured anything else. That would require a sense of the future, of connections between events, of life as a process, rather than just a present moment, soon to pass.

* * *

Back to my life in Virginia. Some days during my stay in Virginia included us doing something out-of-the-ordinary, such as going shopping or seeing a movie, which increasingly incited me to speculate about the activities themselves.

Friday July 26: Day of shopping with Mom! We went to stores and looked at clothes for sale in many stores – some cheap and some expensive. Mostly, I was surprised by how ugly most of the stuff looked to me. Maybe it's the new styles, which I do not recognize, but whatever the reason, I could not bring myself to buy any. Then, we joined with Gene and Gayla for an evening of (odd) movies: Man of Flowers (Australian 1984) and The Ploughman's Lunch (British 1984). Both seen at a movie theater, and both very slow, foreign, psychological, etc. I concentrated for the whole time, and understood most of what was going on, but had a hard time being amused or improved by them. Very interesting to me for their ideas on relationships, something I've been giving a lot of thought to. Hard talking about my thoughts so far, but perhaps in time... My walking has gotten much better from all the exercise: I make much less noise, don't get as tired, can walk faster, etc. Maybe I'll be able to get back to "normal," in that regard. Other matters are harder to tell about. They only improve slowly and subtlely, i.e. not completely yet. I got out a book from the public library on "Recovery from Aphasia," so I'll at least be able to learn about what is possible.

I'm afraid I can't explain what I meant (above) by my concentrating and understanding, if I considered myself neither amused or improved by them. I believed that either I would acquire more knowledge and skills, or I would vegetate and never get back to normal. I figured the end result would depend on the items fed into my brain, along with how well I could process them.

I also remember going through a period (some would call it a phase) in Virginia, when I considered that it might help my recovery, lift up my spirits, if I became religious.

In part this new interest resulted from my learning that the church in the village of Ancient Korinth, where I usually lived during the summer, had been praying for me every Sunday. I was not particularly interested in becoming religious, but I did contemplate all kinds of religious possibilities. I even considered the possibility that my accident was perhaps a way to put myself in touch with a former life. I certainly did not feel spiritually impoverished. I just thought that perhaps, with the right frame of mind, I would pick up some signals, from unknown sources, and they would make me feel better. You know: a deity (God?), a planet (the Moon?), a plant (Mother-Nature?). Whatever. I wasn't particular. I even considered numerology, when I realized there were 52 cards in a deck, 52 weeks in a year, and I was born in 1952, as well as there being 7 days in a week and 7 cards across in solitaire. But so what? In the end, I experienced no religious conversion. That kind of religiosity really wouldn't have suited me. It just wasn't my style. I guess I've always felt that embracing a religious belief would have been me giving up.

I recalled a somewhat similar episode of religious deliberation during my childhood. One summer when I was about 12, my parents, out of ignorance, had sent me and Gene to a summer camp in West Virginia, which turned out to be a Christian Church camp. Unbeknownst to them, we spent one week learning Christian hymns and prayers, and memorizing the list of names of the books of the New Testament, in order. When our parents came to visit over the weekend following that first week, they were shocked (to say the least), and decided to take us back home. We convinced them to let us stay, as we were greatly enjoying riding the horses and such, to which they eventually agreed, but only after obtaining a promise from the camp's directors that we would not be harassed by either the counselors or the other kids. That request was easy to promise and impossible to ensure. My brother and I spent most of our second week defending ourselves against the other children at the camp who thought they had never been so close to a Jew, and who prodded and poked us, in an attempt to find our horns and tails, having heard that Jews were the devil incarnate. All in all, my two week childhood experience of being examined by Christian children searching for my obviously satanic paraphernalia, just as my post-accident exploration of religions, confirmed my earlier aversion to religious schools of thought.

In addition to my various escapades in Charlottesville, poking around the various parks, stores, libraries, and offices of the University of Virginia, my family got the idea (from the doctors perhaps?) that it would be good to engage me in an undertaking requiring some conscious planning and involving some responsibilities. They came up with the idea of me and my Mom taking a car-trip to Epcot, in Florida, and I agreed to this trip most heartily.

The trip was great! It felt so good to be on the road, going new places, seeing new things. It was especially helpful that all the newness was being shared by another — in this case my Mom. After all, I had become accustomed to almost everything being new to me, while others always seemed to know what was happening, and what it all meant. That was not true on our car-trip to Epcot, during which there were even some occasions on which I had to help my Mom understand where we were, what we were doing, or where we were going. That felt great.

We stopped often on the drive, both ways, sometimes at funny places along the highway, or just for a meal or rest stop or switching drivers, so neither of us got tired from driving too much.

Epcot? Epcot was wonderful. We saw so much. Did so much. Went many places, and greatly enjoyed not being pressed for time. There was so much to see and do. It felt a bit like I was having a vacation from being sick...

> *Mon. Aug.12: The first day of Mom's and my trip to Florida, to go to the Epcot Center, near Orlando, in Disney World. We left not very early, but got the car, well, serviced at a*

Charlottesville gas station before going, at ca. 8:30am. We took back roads much of the earliest way, going straight south from Charlottesville to Fayetteville, N.C. Then we went on Interstate 95, and spent the night at a Days Inn Motel near Santee, South Carolina, before an early start to Florida. The car did very well, and I did much of the driving, which was nice.

Tues. Aug.13: Spent the early part of the day driving through South Carolina and Georgia on the Interstate. Once we got into Florida, however, we drove more on back roads and stopped for quite a while at various outlet stores. Mom bought some clothes, and then we got to the Embassy Motel (near Epcot) early enough that I got to go for a short swim before dinner at a neighborhood Italian restaurant. The motel was in Kissimee, pronounced Kih-si'-mee.

Wed. Aug.14: Our first day at Epcot, and boy, did we manage to stay a very full day! We had an early breakfast at Waffle House (never again), and got to Epcot by 9:15. We made reservations for dinner (at Morocco) first, and then spent the first half of the day looking around Futureworld, and the second half of the day looking around World Showcase. Wow! And whew! Perhaps rather than indulge myself in various Epcot impressions, I should stick to the specifics of this, our first, day. Well, we started with The Land, which was Gene's favorite building when he and Gayla came for a day about a week earlier. I have to admit, it was wonderful! The ride (on a train sort of track on a cart on water) went through forest, desert, sea, and agriculture, and more!) Very informative, even educational! I learned a lot about recent developments and future possibilities in the world of horticulture. The only other place we went this first day in Futureworld was through Communicore a bit. The lines at the other places were too long. Anyway, we played with computers on possible vacation places, and did some opinion polls on energy, politics, etc. Also spent some time looking at the souvenirs for sale – most of which were souvenirs of Epcot. Had lunch (simple lunch) at Stargate restaurant, in Communicore East, before heading to World Showcase, where we spent most of the afternoon, before having a Moroccan diner, seeing more of World Showcase, and going back to the motel at an early hour (ca.10pm). What to say about the International part of Epcot? Well, it's to increase tourism to the various countries, which is understandable, but to one who has traveled abroad, it could have been better. Oh, it was nice enough, but there was more effort put into the restaurants and stores, than into the attractions or exhibits. Some countries didn't even have exhibits: they just wanted you to spend money. Hmmmm. Most of them taught you a little bit about the country, somehow. But not as well as the buildings in Futureworld taught you about the Future. Anyway, we began with Canada, the United Kingdom, and France (which had a wonderful movie), Japan and Morocco and America. Quite a lot of countries for our first day! But mostly we spent our time looking. America was strange: who would have thought that there would be an America building? The "show," done with movies and audio-animatronics, was quite good. The best part about World Showcase, so far, was the architecture. I wonder if natives built them at all? We saw workers building a new China building, and they were all Americans, but who knows who does the interiors? But the combination of styles is wonderful! Otherwise? Well, enough for now. I'll go on about Epcot, on our 2nd day.

Thurs. Aug.15: Second day at Epcot, and even longer than the last! 9am-11pm: as long as they'll let you stay! Amazing that it continues to be so full of fascinating things. Let's see, Well, the day began with me walking over to World Showcase, in order to make recommendations [reservations] for us for High Tea in the United Kingdom, while Mom saw part of Journey Into Imagination that I thought I'd miss out on. Mistake. She saw the 3-D movies in the Magic Eye Theater, but thought I'd really enjoy it, so she saw it again, with me! And I must say: it was excellent. Not the content (there was almost no plot), but the form, the aesthetics, etc. Amazing! Once, I even reached up with one hand to try and touch the character that seemed right in front of me! Then, after going through a stunning ride which had lot of movie characters, we spent quite a while in The Image World: Mom directed an orchestra, using lights and her hands. I painted art works using a computer, and we both made music by stepping on a lit floor board, and so on. We also went to a wonderful show called "Backstage Magic" at Communicore East, presented by Sperry. It was mostly about computers – including those at work in Epcot! It was so good, that even Mom finally got interested in learning about computers! Who would have thought? The show used a lot of hologram pictorialization, and made the figure appear throughout the Epcot computer center, without a screen. It was excellent, and worth the wait. About the only other

149

*building in Futureworld we went to today was Horizons,
knowing we'd be coming back tomorrow. Horizons: well, I
think it was Mom's favorite. One goes on a long ride/journey
through the future. Homes, fields, businesses, etc., all going on
using animatronics, and the sound track coming into our own
cart. Towards the end, we were supposed to choose our own
New Horizon, but since it didn't work, Mom and I decided to
go through Horizons again! Second time it worked, and we
chose "The Desert" to explore, among the future
environments. Anyway, enough about Future World on our
second day. In World Showcase, we began with lunch in
Germany at the Biergarten, where we got to sit at a table with
5 other Americans. Not the best company. In addition to
Germany, we looked through Italy and China, which had a
great movie, but it was in 360 degrees, which was a bit much!
What we mostly did in World Showcase, early in the day, was
go to our High Tea in the Rose and Crown Pub in the United
Kingdom. Whew! Lots of good eats, including scones,
watercress sandwiches, brandy cakes, etc., and there was an
excellent singer playing the lute very well. I must have
concentrated too much on his playing, for he came over and
sang by me for quite a while, then talked to us and kissed me.
Now one knows how they get their jobs, anyway! He was quite
good on the lute, I must say. So, it was a good high tea! Much
of the rest of our time in World Showcase was spent looking,*

buying, waiting in lines, etc. In the evening, rather than have dinner (we were too full from our high tea) we went to a show at the America gardens, which is a theater in front of the America building. It was a college band, which had been put together from various colleges, and it was their last night at Epcot, so the audience got to listen to a lot of "thank you" speeches. Nice music though, and dancing by the Rockettes, who I guess figured that Florida was better than NY City. After the concert, we decided to stay seated in the theater for the fireworks, which happen every night at 10pm, using laser light, and lots of fireworks. Wow, what a show! I haven't seen anything so well done <u>ever</u> in America, or abroad – not even on the Fourth of July!

After visiting Epcot, we decided to drive back to Virginia via Tarpon Springs, which was a little bit out of the way, but I was certain Mom would like it, and she did! I felt remarkably out-of-place in Tarpon Springs, a very Greek-American city, as I rarely do while living in Greece. A nice enough place to visit, but it seemed terribly touristic. I wouldn't want to live there — a feeling I never have when I'm in Greece.

Come to think of it, our visit to Tarpon Springs provides a good example of my increasing realization of the extraordinary difference between our experiences. My Mother and I were different -- an awareness which would develop more fully while living with her for a year in California (see below, Chapter 4).

One thing I never realized at the time, as I now guess in retrospect, was how many events, how many moments, were…well…organized and orchestrated, virtually fabricated by my family, for my re-education, my re-discovery of life, with one exception — my recovery itself. The accident and the ensuing physical ordeal were apparently considered suitable for discussion, but my recuperation, my journey to selfhood seemed tacitly barred from conversation, as if there was an unspoken fear that I might understand fully what I was going through. I am now positive they thought that would scare me.

In fact, about the only fear I experienced during my early recovery was that my condition would either stay the same and not change at all, or would get much worse. I'm a bit perplexed that I never became intrigued by the recovery process itself, as it was happening. If thoughts about it (the accident, the recovery) ever tried to surface in my cluttered and fully occupied mind, they were quickly and easily pushed aside and ignored. I certainly was not completely unaware of my recovery, but it would not have been possible for me to reflect upon it, given the circumstances of the recovery itself.

Not too long after returning from our Epcot visit, I wrote a fascinating letter to Timothy, which is worth quoting almost in full.

End of August 1985, Dear Timothy: No <u>exact</u> date needs to be put on this, because my guess is that I will add to it from time to time. Let's just say that it's near the end of August, when I am "better." Mostly, I want to try to say something to you which I haven't tried to say to anyone else. Out of my fear, probably, that I'd be thought to have a real mental illness. In any case, I think I owe it to you, my friend.

Put simply, I want to ask you, if you can, to ignore/forget much of what I said when I was worse. I don't remember much of it, but my guess, now, is that it was not the "real" me. How to explain? Well, part of my recuperating has been much slower than my body. In particular, my brain. As time goes on, I think I am becoming more and more "myself," but it's a slow (and hard) process. I have forgotten a lot about my life in recent years, and perhaps more than anything I have been trying to learn how to be "normal." Know what I mean? What to say, what to wear, where to look, what to ask, when to smile – you know, the kinds of things that one does naturally. Well, put simply, they aren't natural for me yet. And if they aren't natural <u>now</u>, when I understand that they're not, they must have been horrible before.

If, by the way, I and my odd brain have caused you any problems, I really am sorry. Maybe, some day, I can get you to tell me what problems I have created for you recently. One thing I have really tried hard to do, is only to say nice things about you to other people. But my guess is that that process has been badly affected by my strange brain. In other words, until recently, I haven't tried to say things to other people which they consider nice, but what I consider nice. Hmmm. We both know that I have been unusual in my beliefs for quite some time, but I think that until recently I knew how to keep them to myself. That hasn't been true lately. What do you think? I really don't want you to be hurt or even angered by my continuing brain-problems, and so I offer to avoid [certain] subjects, if you think that would help. An alternative, I suppose, is for me to say only silly brainless simple things about you, and not make any statements that come from my brain. You know, thoughts could be avoided. Hell, it's what most people talk about most of the time! Anyway, let me know what you think. And please: don't be silly, simplistic or brainless for my benefit. Leave that to me…Yours, Annie

About a week later, Timothy returned to America from Greece, and came to Charlottesville to visit. That was strange, to say the least! By then my memory had returned enough that I remembered who he was, and who he had been to me, but I simply didn't feel anything for him.

I couldn't even remember ever having felt anything...But there he was, visiting me, so we felt awkward with each other for a day and a night, during which he slept on the couch, and I, trying to be friendly, went into the living room and lay down next to him. Nothing felt right. I left and returned to my own bed. He departed the next day.

Others visited as well: I recall a visit from Wesley's parents, Wally and Ann, a Gambier friend Marnie, one of my colleagues, Robert (with his partner Jerry), and an ex-student of mine, Mark. Mostly, I remember them looking at me with a great deal of pity, and apparently feeling sad, though they were all careful to try and keep a grin on their faces most of the time. During the visit there was an almost patronizing put-down, when they noted how well I was doing. Having now caught myself doing exactly the same thing to people recovering from an illness, I realize that such an approach is inevitable, and inescapable, from caring friends.

===

"Many of my visitors left me tired and frustrated. I know that it must have been very difficult for them to figure out if my lagging conversation was caused by speechlessness or simplemindedness. Some guessed speechlessness and talked nonstop the whole time they were there. Others, fearing that the stroke had thrown me back to childhood, spoke in baby talk or pidgin English, which made me furious. It was all right if I called myself an idiot. But I didn't want anyone else to. The frustration seemed to increase in proportion to the number of people in the room. I rarely attempted to speak if there was more than one person with me. Trying to listen to two people was like watching a tennis game, and a roomful of guests was like being on a firing range, words shooting past me like bullets. Once in a while there would be a word I understood, and for a second I knew exactly what was being said. But before I could focus thoughts and trap words of my own, I would forget what I had heard." (Patricia Neal <u>As I Am: An Autobiography</u>, New York, 1988, p.264)

═══════════════════════════════

In addition to visits from friends and acquaintances, I had received an abundance of good wishes for a speedy recovery in various forms, including postcards, letters, and even posters.

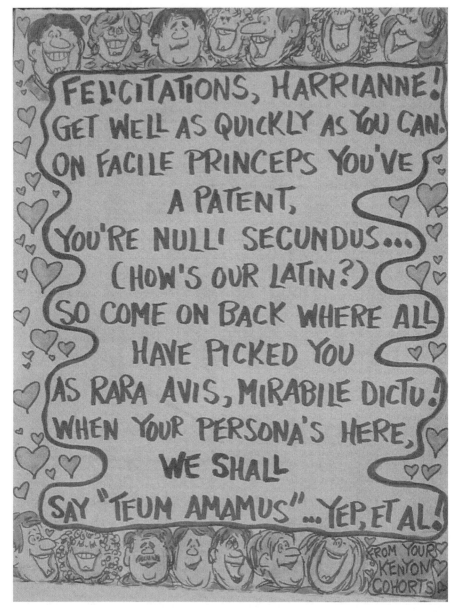

Most of the good wishes had resulted from a press release Kenyon College had released to the community a few weeks following my accident:

NEWS BULLETIN (June 5, 1985)

To the Kenyon Community:

As many of you know, near the end of May Prof. Harrianne Mills of the Classics Department was involved in a motorbike accident in Athens, Greece while leading the "Kenyon in Greece" archaeological project.

Since many rumors are being circulated about her condition, and since so many people are concerned about her welfare, I have decided to use this method of bringing you the latest information. Most of this news comes from a telephone conversation I had this afternoon with Bertha Mills, Harrianne's mother.

Harrianne was in a coma for six to eight hours immediately following the accident. Since then she has had period of "confusion" along with some memory loss. Contrary to rumor, she has not suffered from general amnesia. A CAT scan, done in the Athens hospital where Harrianne is being treated, has revealed no brain damage.

Harrianne has full use of her hands and arms. Her left ankle and foot are unsteady, but she is able to walk a little.

The prognosis seems to be good for complete recovery.

Harrianne and her brother are scheduled to fly from Athens to New York on Friday June 7. After resting for a day in new York, Harrianne will travel home to California with her mother. Her further treatment will take place there.

Cards and letters should be addressed to:
    Harrianne Mills
    c/o Bertha Mills
    410 Sheridan Ave. Apt. 227
    Palo Alto, CA 94306

Timothy Gregory of Ohio State University, co-leader of the trip to Greece, has now joined the Kenyon and OSU students at their archaeological site. A Greek-speaking graduate student from OSU has stayed in the field with the students during the absence of Harrianne and Tim.

Thanks to all of you who have called expressing concern, and especially to those who have helped by tracking down information.

Joan Straumanis
Academic Dean

In an attempt to express my appreciation for all the hopes expressed for my recovery, I wrote a single letter which, again, took me hours to write, to Kenyon College and the town of Gambier friends.

August 24-25, Dear Kenyon and Gambier Friends: The better I get, the more I want to thank you all for your hopes and wishes on my behalf. It has made a real difference in my recovery, and I've been so happy to hear from you! Cards, posters, postcards: they've all been <u>*wonderful*</u>*, and I thank you from the bottom of my heart. To keep you posted, my recovery continues – some of it quickly, some of it slowly. The good news is that I can walk now, and talk, and swim a little, and my reading and running are improving. The bad news, put simply, is that some places still hurt, and the brain recovers more slowly than the body. In any case, everything continues to improve, and I hope to be able to show you and to thank you all in person sometime soon. Best Regards, Harrianne*

One relatively shocking event during my summer in Virginia, was my being told of the death of a Kenyon colleague, Bob, at the young age of 40. He had died in June, I was told in July, but his death did not impact me deeply until I finally read and understood his eulogy, which he had written before his death, during my ensuing 9 months of recovery in California. I mention it here as a good example of something which I knew, but only barely, and certainly not profoundly. Comprehension that deep would have to wait for me to begin developing a new life in a new world, in California. (See Chapter 4)

In my very limited and very private world of those first 3 months in Virginia, on the other hand, I never questioned or reflected upon what I was told, and perhaps more relevantly, I did not exactly encounter difficulty focusing, but I was incapable of changing my mind.

Which mind would I have changed? I barely had one, yet it felt like I had many, and the minds were mostly avoiding each other.

No doubt as a result, I experienced each day as several days, for each time my mind was able to operate more efficiently and critically, it felt like the start of a new day. And while 3 months of recovery in Virginia may be an excellent example of the common expression "the mind goes before the body," my experience then and there suggests that the body returns before the mind.

Dr. James Miller, Univ. of Virginia Neurologist, 9/18/85:

Ms. Mills continues excellent recovery from severe head trauma during a motor vehicle accident on May 21. Currently, she is planning to return to California, where her mother lives and is tentatively planning to return to her role as a Classics professor at Kenyon in January, 1986. She understands that she may not have recovered satisfactory intellectual function by that time to take up academic duties and she also understands that we cannot at this time predict her complete degree of recovery.

Today, she is oriented to place, person, and date and is accurate with regard to current events. She has accurate short-term memory and is able to repeat five numbers forward and backward. Insight is excellent. She still did not interpret a proverb perfectly, reporting that people who live in glass houses should not throw stones because the other persons might throw them back. She first said that a cat, dog and snake were similar because they had ears and tails, and then changed it to eyes. A nickel, dime, penny and quarter were stated first to represent forty five cents, but then she recognized the error and corrected it to forty one cents. There was no evidence of aphasia and no difficulty naming objects or identifying body parts.

There was no difficulty with graphesthesia or stereognosis, and complex tasks were carried out normally. Eye grounds were normal, and both sensory and motor functions were intact throughout.

There was no drift to the outstretched extremities. Tone and strength in all four extremities were normal. Deep tendon reflexes were equally and physiologically hyperactive. Abdominal reflexes were present. She remains weak in left ankle dorsiflexion, but can walk on heels and toes without difficulty.

She could arise from a chair without aid and could stand with feet approximated without difficulty. Cerebellar functions are intact in both upper and lower extremities.

Sensory examination is normal although she reports some subjective hypothesis in the left anterior tibial nerve distribution.

Ms. Mills continues to enjoy excellent recovery, but has recently experienced some depression. She is planning to move to Palo Alto, California, where her ex-husband lives. He is knowledgeable in neurological circles there, and will help her choose an appropriate neurologist, to whom I shall send a copy of my report. No medication is contemplated, and she is encouraged to be patient as she awaits evidence of her final complete degree of recovery.

Before I left Virginia at the end of the summer, and visited Ohio on my way to spending the year in California, I had a few experiences worth sharing. Perhaps the most demonstrative were the events of Tues. Sept. 10, a day which I termed in my diary a crying day. The episode was so suggestive that I decided to write a letter about it, addressed to both ex-husband Wesley and most-recent-boyfriend Timothy:

Tues. Sept. 10, Dear Wesley and Timothy: Hello my dear friends! Here I am, again, crying and crying. Sigh. And yet, I want to try to write about it, so I hope you don't mind my addressing this letter to you both, as a way of stimulating my mind, more than writing in a journal does these days. Now, why am I crying? Well, this is the third time I've cried today, after a week of good humor and no tears. The first time today was while swimming laps at an indoor pool. The second time was while trying (for the first time since the accident) to run without holding on to my painful sciatic nerve in my behind. The third time, just now, was during and after a movie which I saw on TV called Six Weeks*.*

Well, I probably need to explain that I have not been greatly sad during these cries, or at least not sad at the moment of the cry. Quite the contrary. As things get better and better for me, I logically and rationally become increasingly optimistic *about the hopes for my total recovery. No, there must be a way to cry when you're not sad...Well, I guess there is one kind of sadness that I've felt. To myself, who has only recently come to have a full understanding of my condition, I seem worse. Understand that that's because I couldn't understand much when I was <u>really</u> worse. Get it? On the other hand, to people who have known about my problems all along, I seem better, practically all better. So that's part of the sadness I suppose: To myself, I seem bad, part of which is other people's misunderstanding about me and thinking that I'm all better. In other words, it's hard trying to explain why I don't feel all better, especially when I seem so much better to them...*

Hmmm. That last paragraph would be a good think to show them. Is that supposed to be English? Well, anyway, it's an attempt to be English. So, what else is on my mind about all the crying? Well, one thing that Gene and I talked about is the possibility that I'm crying now for past sadnesses, when I hurt too much to want to cry. Or, put another way, when I was much worse, I had too many other things to do and think, so I put off the sad feelings until I was better, which is now. Understand? This is Gene's idea, but it sounds reasonable to me. Does this then mean that it will go away soon? That I will stop crying for past sadness? I wonder. But of course I'm the one feeling in need of tears these days, for whatever reason...so what do I know?

One more thing about my crying before I go. I've noticed that I've also begun to cry a little bit over pain. And yet, the pains have gotten so much better! Odd, if you ask me. When I hurt all over I didn't cry, but now that I only hurt a little bit, I do. Hmph. Perhaps it's from the fear that they won't ever go away? Who knows? But I guess it's possible that I'm starting to worry, which I didn't have the leisure for before. At this point, only my legs and behind have pain, and most of the time bearable pain, with certain exceptions. Until recently I avoided things that caused the pains to increase. Now, I'm encouraging them a bit, in part to make them better, and in part to get used to it. So far, neither is working, but we'll see.

Anyway, sorry to go on and on about myself, but it has helped to try and explain some things to you. I hope to see you both soon. My regards to your lovers. With Deep Friendship, Annie

Much more significant for me, and with much more of an impact on others, was my visit to Ohio — both the city of Columbus and the village of Gambier — in mid-September, for various reasons. This trip was the first time since the accident that I was on my own, without any family around to assist me. Also, for me, this re-entry into the world of Gambier was a test, as I would be confronted by people who had known me before my accident. In so doing, I was repeatedly put in touch with people who felt sorry for me, and who wanted to compare what I was now like, following such an ordeal.

I did find moving around familiar places and people slightly perplexing, in that they were both comfortably familiar and exhausting to process. The college even had a reception in my honor. All my friends, colleagues, and acquaintances were there. Some were sympathetic, some full of pity. Most were just curious.

In addition, I had arrived in Gambier with the hope that my contact with once familiar surroundings would awaken an abundance of dormant memories. As it happened, however, the process was more overwhelming than helpful. I became exhausted viewing so many familiar faces I could not quite recall.

While in Ohio, I stayed first with Libby, Timothy's sister (see Chapter 6) and then with Fred, a close friend of my sister's, for a few weeks in Columbus. They were both wonderful hosts, in that I clearly had their support without them invading my privacy or independence. I also had the use of Timothy's car, which was very nice. And I was very glad I didn't stay at his house.

Mostly, however, I found myself getting emotionally prepared for the process while in California of bringing my recovery to a gradual close. I was decidedly in transition in my recovery. I could tell, though I wasn't exactly sure either where I was coming from, or where I was heading to. I just knew that...well, I guess I knew at some level that I wasn't simply changing zip codes, states, and time zones, but that I was heading into a new version of reality which I could not even imagine.

Chapter 4: Recapturing My Mind

"And dimly she realised one of the great laws of the human soul: that when the emotional soul receives a wounding shock, which does not kill the body, the soul seems to recover as the body recovers. But this is only appearance. It is really only the mechanism of the re-assumed habit. Slowly, slowly the wound to the soul begins to make itself felt, like a bruise, which only slowly deepens its terrible ache, till it fills all the psyche. And when we think we have recovered and forgotten, it is then that the terrible aftereffects have to be encountered at their worst."

- D.H. Lawrence <u>Lady Chatterley's Lover</u>, p.50

"Life isn't about finding yourself. Life is about creating yourself"
- George Bernard Shaw

After my extended solitary visit to Ohio in September, I went to California, to live with my Mom in Palo Alto for 9 months to a year. My new doctors at Stanford Hospital originally thought I might be able to return to teaching by January, for the second semester of 1985-86 at Kenyon, but it rapidly became clear that was not possible. For me, each day was remarkably like every other, with certain exceptions — especially examinations by various doctors, first, at Stanford University Hospital.

Dr. Robert Cutler, Stanford University Hospital, Neurologist, 11/5/85:

The patient is a 33 year old Classics teacher at Kenyon College. She is referred by Dr. James Q. Miller for neurological follow up. The chief complaint is head injury.

The present illness began on May 21, 1985. The evening before she had arrived in Greece for her customary summer work at an archaeological site. She drove to her house in Corinth, unpacked her clothing and went to bed. She recalls nothing further for the next three weeks — her earliest memory after that time is somewhat fragmentary and involved with an evaluation at the Massachusetts General Hospital...

She is aware of having had a right parietal scalp laceration and was told she had a skull fracture. A CAT scan was said to be negative. She was treated with dexamethasone during the acute illness. Her major neurological deficits during the early weeks consisted of a fluent aphasia and weakness of her left lower extremity. At the time she returned to the United States she was unable to walk. She also had complaints of pain in the region of the right sciatic [buttock] notch. At first she had severe difficulty reading with comprehension, recent and remote memory loss, difficulty understanding television programs, and difficulty understanding humorous situations in movies. She was unable to comprehend the "fine points of language." She found herself progressively more facile at covering up for memory loss and difficulty finding words.

Over the summer, she made a very gratifying recovery, both physically and intellectually. Her speech has returned to near normal; she herself notes some residual difficulty finding words occasionally, but says it would not be apparent to others. She continues to read at about 1/2 her normal speed, and often has to reread material several times to appreciate it fully. She believes she has undergone some personality change in that she tends to be more ebullient and outgoing. This affect alternates, however, with bouts of depression and frequent crying spells.

Physically she has recovered to the point where she has only mild difficulty arising on the toes of her left foot. She is not a particularly athletic person, but jogs regularly each day. She also continues to do exercises that were taught to her by a physical therapist. She has no difficulty in the use of her upper extremities.

She returned to Palo Alto one month ago, and is residing with her mother. She spends six to ten hours per day working on her dissertation. This involves managing a computerized data base, reading, and writing.

She is a graduate student in the Stanford Department of Classics...She has recently been invited to give a talk on this subject at the local chapter of the Archaeological Institute of America. She believes she can manage this without difficulty.

Whether she can return to teaching duties during the winter semester remains problematic. She does not feel capable of giving complex courses in Latin or Ancient Greek. She is multilingual, and has noted difficulty in all languages. She believes she could present a passable course in archaeology, but that it would not meet her usual standards. She does not believe that she would have time to prepare for classes because of the slowness of her work at present…

Neurological examination: She was alert, pleasant, and cooperative. There was an apparent mild difficulty in modulating the volume of her voice. She seemed unusually cheerful and smiling.

She gave a comprehensive history and account of her scholarly activities. There was no trace of aphasia except that on two occasions she had difficulty thinking of a word and had to sound out a few alternatives before finding the correct word. She had no difficulty in knowing of current events. She had distinct difficulty with abstract thinking, providing elaborately concrete interpretations. For example, "a rolling stone gathers no moss" was interpreted as follows: moss grows on the north side of a stone and if the stone is rolling all of the time there will be no opportunity to establish a north side. Interestingly, the more obscure the proverb, the more abstract was her interpretation. For example, "the hammer of gold beats down the door of iron" was interpreted in terms of the influence of money and riches over brute power.

The ocular fundi [eye bases] were normal. Examination of the cranial nerves II—XII revealed no abnormalities. Examination

175

of the motor system revealed normal strength and muscle tone throughout save for mild weakness of dorsiflexion and plantar [sole] flexion of the left foot. There was some difficulty in elevation of the right arm secondary to a deformed right clavicle.

The deep tendon reflexes were all quite brisk at 3+, but the plantar [sole of the foot] responses were flexor and there was no clonus [alternate muscular contraction and relaxation in rapid succession]. Tests of coordination were well performed. The sensory examination revealed patchy inconsistent hypalgesia [diminished sensitiveness to pain] over the left arm. Graphesthesia [written figures or numbers] and stereognosis [form and nature of objects by touch] were unimpaired. The gait revealed a mild "favoring" of the left leg.

Impression: Cerebral contusion, remote, recovering.

Disposition: A key issue is whether she can resume her normal professional activities. I would judge that she is an exceptionally intelligent woman who retains some subtle intellectual deficits. I suggested formal neuropsychological evaluation to which she agreed. Following this, I think it would be appropriate to apply for temporary medical leave of absence.

My days in California consisted mostly of an abundance of doctor appointments, giving me an intimate knowledge of medical procedures, and of reading magazines and books on aphasia and classical antiquity at a snail's pace. In addition, I poured over the Stanford Card Catalogue, wrote almost as slowly using my Kaypro computer, and attended an assortment of lectures held in various departments at Stanford – especially Classics, History, Art History and Anthropology.

On each successive day I became further removed from the relatively thoughtless existence I had lived a short time ago.

A kind of anxiety hierarchy characterized my daily activities. I experienced anxiety ranging from very low to extremely high from watching TV, sitting silently, having a serious discussion, interacting with my family (even on mundane topics or about incidental things), engaging in business contacts (dealing with bureaucracies), conversing about any subject with anybody, accepting invitations to a dinner or party, going to a lecture, and attending a seminar where I would be expected to contribute.

Silent passivity was always more comfortable than verbal activity.

There were certain exceptions to my daily pattern of activities. In October, for example, I received by mail a copy of a colleague's eulogy, which he had written himself just before his death. Bob had died in June, and his self-written eulogy had been printed in the October 23, 1985 Kenyon College newspaper. I read it and wept. I read it again and again and again, and I cried each time.

So much of me had died that same summer, and here was someone able to articulate what I could not. I wanted to pass out copies of the eulogy he had written, but when I showed it to a few people, and they read it, I realized that his message, as someone in close proximity to death, did not have anywhere near the same impact on them as it had on me.

Re-reading his eulogy 8 years later, it still drove me to tears. Why is that, I wonder? Well, the section in the eulogy which brought me to tears is towards the end, when he is asking the congregation to celebrate life by acknowledging some people who had been very special to him. He even asks them to stand up for applause — an unusual request in a funerary sermon, to be sure.

Let me quote a few sections:

"You are looking at dear friends; people who put themselves out, who were there when I needed them. Through them I gained a keener awareness of compassion and love and community."

"I have a keen image of him sitting by my hospital bed for hours at a time, simply being there, concerned and loving. With his sensitivity he has taught me how to be sensitive, with his love I have been helped to love."

"[Family and] friends, it hurts to leave you, the pain of separation is intense. But may you also find what I have found, love and peace and joy. Live long and prosper. I love you all very much."

Just typing these excerpts from his eulogy 17 years after my accident, I find myself weeping again. Obviously, I remain deeply touched by the emotions he expressed in his eulogy. He was able, when I was not, to articulate the pain, the suffering, the anguish, the dependence on assistants, the appreciation of others, the need for memories, the hope for meaning, and the desire for continuity and permanence.

Compared with my erratic and gradual recuperation I felt his sense of certainty and finality operated to his advantage. On the other hand, the man was dying when he wrote it — a thing which, in itself, drove me to tears.

By December, I was making note of my linguistic uncertainties.

Tues. Dec.10 Afternoon appointment with Dr. Cutler, followed by a History of Science lecture by Robert Richards (U. of Chicago) on Darwin's Theory of Mortality. Reception after it, with great food. Words in the lecture I couldn't understand: similitude, redolent, dint, amalgamation, eructation, and heritable.

By January, I had retrieved a working mode of existence.

Sun. Jan.19: Stayed up late last night, but, wanting to get out of the habit, I set my alarm for early this morning. Worked at home in the morning, went to the library in the afternoon, and am now back at the computer, it being evening. I'm getting into quite a pattern of action at long last!

I rarely, if ever, noticed such things as the weather or the news, but I frequented Stanford (both Main and Medical) libraries and the Classics Department, and did a fair amount of xeroxing of library books at a local copy center. So often, in fact, that they offered me a job, after noticing how skillful I was at enlarging, reducing, and making double-sided copies.

Oddly enough, the medical examinations I underwent helped to gradually dispel my otherwise docile indifference. Those appointments, ostensibly to evaluate my mental state, made my mental inactivity a nonoption, which I noted at the time with the following comments.

Dr. Ralph Kiernan's neuropsychological examination of me, 27 Nov. 1985, originally written on Dec.4, 1985 and added to and edited over December

Well, a week has gone by since I was examined by Dr. Kiernan (neuropsychologist) at the Stanford Medical Center, but I took some notes at the time, and I really think that it was/is fascinating enough to warrant a full description. First, some comments on the whole process. It was quite long (lasted about 2 1/2 hours), but not very tiring, and it was unlike any other examination I've ever had. And I've had a lot recently. He was nice, and didn't seem to mind when I made some inquiries or made some personal analyses along the way, which I did. Now, let me move on to the tests given me, in no particular order, except for the first and last.

The first one made use of four wooden square blocks. He arranged them in a row, with spaces between each, and then struck them lightly with a pencil eraser in a pattern (at the beginning in a pattern of four) which I was then supposed to repeat with a pencil eraser I had. We did it many times, and after a while he made the patterns longer, increasing to 5 at first, then 6, 7, and 8. I don't think we got bigger than 8, but I got some of the 8-long ones wrong. They were much harder to remember.

Another test asked me to put letters, numbers, and then letters and numbers, into order on a page, by drawing lines between them. They were written inside circles. I didn't make any mistakes, but he said (later) that I was very slow. I remember that I was very slow at the beginning, when I had no idea where on the page to look for the next letter or number. After I figured out that they would be in a direction other than that I just came from, it got easier.

For another one, he asked me to count to 20 backwards and forwards, and then to say the alphabet both backwards and forwards. (hmmm, here's an oddity: why didn't I write forwards and backwards? After all, that's the order in which he asked me, in both cases.) Anyway, I don't think I made any mistakes, but, again, I was very slow.

Another one, which was very difficult for me, was when he told me stories, and then asked me to repeat them to him (one at a time, after each story), as much as I could remember. I remembered the beginning of the first story pretty well. After I had done them, he asked me to repeat whatever I remembered of any of them. I got the total number of stories he told me wrong (I thought he had told me 3 and I couldn't remember one at all. In fact, he had told me 2.) and I couldn't remember much of the first, and almost none of the second. At which point he read them to me again, and we did it again. I got the number of stories right (2) and remembered more of the second one, but forgot more of the first.

For another one, he asked me to tell him as many words as I could think of, in one minute, after he gave me the beginning letter. I think I averaged about 30 words, though this depended a bit on the letters chosen, since we did it more than once. I was surprised that I couldn't think of more for each of them, and that I was so slow at naming all of the ones I did. "A" was the easiest letter he gave me. The others were S, C and L, I think.

In another one, I answered various IQ questions, like what year something happened, or what Marie Curie is known for. My lack of common memory amazed me. Many of them (most of the ones I didn't get) were ones that I know I used to know.

In another one, I was asked for the similarities between 2 named objects. Some of them seemed to have nothing in common at all! Like opposites, for example. I had a hard time trying to explain what they had in common. Also, in general, it was difficult for me, because my vocabulary wasn't good enough to explain what the words meant, much less what they had in common.

For an additional test, I was supposed to put cards with cartoons on them into the order of the "story." He did not tell me the story. I was supposed to figure it out from the cards (4 - 7, depending on the story) which, when given me, were out of order, of course. We did several of these, some of which I couldn't use one of the cards for, because it didn't fit into my story. On at least one set, I told him that there were 2 different possibilities, for 2 different stories.

He also gave me a spelling test, of about 30 words, about 7 of which I missed. This test included verbs, adjectives, and nouns, but all the ones I <u>missed</u> (i.e. mis-spelled) seemed to be nouns. Sounds familiar...

Another one involved my using red and white blocks. They were all the same: red on 2 sides, white on 2 sides, and half red and white on 2 sides. With them, I was supposed to copy designs which he showed me on paper. Needless to say, the paper designs didn't have any lines on them to suggest where the edges of blocks needed to be. And, of course, the designs got more difficult as time went on. I think I did OK on this one.

A long one (apparently the most difficult for me, but it was a very hard test) was when he read over a list of 20 words, and asked me to repeat the ones I remembered. Then, he repeated for me the ones I neglected, but not the ones I had just mentioned, and asked me to say them, again. That is, as many of the list of the original 20 as I could at that point recall. We did this one over and over, probably about 10 times total. Today (Dec. 4), I remember the list included the following: brandy, shark, tennis, clarinet, Norway, Chicago, train, slipper, hand, cup, and desk.

Finally, as a last question, he asked me to repeat anything I remembered about the 2 stories he had told me earlier. I couldn't remember much at all about the first one, and nothing about the second one. Aargh.

After the examination was over, he talked with me about it a little. He said I did some things very well (excellent?). I believe that he referred to my memory of the 20 words in this respect. He also suggested that I not try to read so fast, because it causes the necessity of re-reading. Rather, I should go slower. Read each sentence slowly, and not go on until I understand it. He also gave me his opinion: that I'd be all back to normal by mid-summer, i.e. July 1986! And, he'd like to examine me again then to prove it to me.

Below is Dr. Kiernan's Neuropsychological Report regarding that same examination. The doctor's remarks concerning this same testing session are noteworthy.

NEUROPSYCHOLOGICAL REPORT

MILLS, HARRIANNE   Date of Testing: November 27, 1985

This is a 33-year old woman who sustained a significant head injury on May 21, 1985. She has made a good recovery of functioning since that time, but she continues to complain of minor language and memory problems. In order to closely evaluate these symptoms, she was referred for neuropsychological testing...

At the time of her injury, Ms. Mills was a classics teacher at Kenyon College. She has noticed a loss of vocabulary in both Latin and Greek that is surprising to her. Not only does she fail to recognize many words, but she even fails to remember them after looking them up. She stated that it was "as if I never knew the word." In English, she feels that her reading is still very slow and that her spelling has deteriorated. She stated, "I used to be a really good writer." She is also slow at reading and she feels that her comprehension is less than it usually would be. Her reading is also hampered by problems with memory. She is fairly articulate, although she complains of continuing word-finding difficulty and difficulty with names of people and occasionally of objects. She has no difficulty understanding what is said to her, but she frequently misses the point of idiomatic expressions or jokes.

Ms. Mills also reported a personality change from being a serious scholar and a "workaholic" to a slower paced, more happy, enthusiastic self. During my interview, she appeared almost giddy at times…

Ms. Mills was very cooperative during the testing session, and the results obtained are thought to reflect her best efforts at the present time.

Several subtests of the revised Wechsler Adult Intelligence Scale were administered, including information, digit span, arithmetic, similarities, block design, and picture arrangement. Only the similarities subtest was performed at a below average level, and Ms. Mills had difficulty with this subtest largely because of her continuing word-finding difficulty. She would often be unable to supply the appropriate abstract comparison word and would instead substitute more concrete descriptors.

For example, she stated that a dog and a lion were alike because they have four feet and hair. Her word-finding difficulty was more dramatically apparent when she was asked how an eye and ear were alike and replied, "They are one of your five _____."

She clearly wanted to give the correct answer that they are senses. She was above average in digit repetition, succeeding at eight digits forward and seven backward, and she scored in the bright average range of intelligence on this subtest as well as information and picture arrangement. She struggled somewhat with the block design constructions and obtained only an average score. She was also slower and slightly confused on arithmetic calculations. Again she obtained only an average score. It seems likely from history that this Ms. Mills has functioned in the superior to very superior range of intelligence in the past and that all of these scores represent some decline from her former level of functioning.

She obtained an average score on a direct measure of verbal fluency, but it seems likely that she has had far greater than an average fluency in the past. She demonstrated adequate spelling ability on the spelling subtest of the Wide Range Achievement Test, but it was clear that she struggled with even relatively simply words. For example, she misspelled ruin "ruine." She was above average on a measure of visual attention span, but slower than average in completing two visual motor sequencing tasks. She made no errors on either sequencing task, however. She was near average in repeating two story paragraphs immediately after having them read to her, but she recalled only one of these after a one hour delay interval. Even after repeated prompting with story material, she was unable to recall the first of these stories at all. She was average in reproducing line drawing following a ten second interval. She made steady progress on a demanding twenty word list learning task, and her score on this task was well within the range of normal memory functioning.

In summary, Ms. Mills presumably has functioned in the superior to very superior range of intelligence in the past, but she now obtains IQ scores in the average to bright average range. She appears to be slower and less efficient in general than she presumably has been in the past, and she has mild residual language problems which include decreased word fluency, an increased interference effect with verbal memory, and decreased spelling ability. I believe that her residual problems are relatively mild at the present time, but that her demanding linguistic profession would be particularly difficult for her. She should certainly continue on disability throughout the 1985-1986 academic year, and work on her dissertation would represent an excellent rehabilitation exercise. Ms. Mills has clearly made an excellent recovery of functioning in a very short time, and there is no reason to doubt that she will continue to improve substantially over the next six to twelve months. I would be happy to repeat any of the above tests for comparison purposes at such a time when there has been additional clinical improvement.

Ralph J. Kiernan, Ph.D.

Clinical Neuropsychologist

Thinking back over such medical examinations 8 years later, I was struck by how conscious I recall being at the time, and yet how incoherent I apparently was. Nothing ever seemed incongruous or out of place. Perhaps the best example of how my world always made sense to me comes from the examination just mentioned, when I was shown a carefully chosen collection of cartoon pictures and was asked to put 5 of the cards in "the order of the story."

There I was and there were the cards. But where was the story?

"Obviously," I thought, "I am being asked to make one up. Great! There's no correct or incorrect answer."

Silly me. Of course there was a correct story they expected, and mine wasn't it. Or so I was told, after I had finished. I argued with them. The cards worked quite well for my story, but it was obviously not the story they intended me to create from the cards they handed me.

I recall wondering, "Is that my fault? That's their problem."

Silly me. Looking back over his report, I notice that my score on the picture arrangement subtest was "bright average." Hmmmmm.

Very soon thereafter, I delivered a lecture for the Stanford chapter of the Archaeological Institute of America on "Isthmia: New Discoveries at an Ancient Greek Sanctuary." Having been on the staff of the Isthmia (UCLA/Ohio State) Excavations for several years, I had published (with Timothy) an article on the Roman Arch at that site in <u>Hesperia</u> in 1984, so presenting a talk and slide show on the topic would previously have been a piece of cake. After my accident was another matter.

On My Stanford Lecture, 6 Dec. 1985

Back again. This time, I'd like to write down some things about the lecture I gave for the Stanford AIA (Archaeological Institute of America) Society. Not about the lecture itself, but about my feelings, the audience reactions, my preparations, and so on. In other words, more like a journal entry, though so much time has gone by (1 week) that I wonder how "journalish" it will seem. Still, I think the process of preparing for the talk, and the activity itself, were fascinating, so I don't want to forget about them, and I think Timothy might be interested in hearing more about it than makes sense over the telephone, so, let me give this a try.

Well, I suppose it would make the most sense to start with my preparations. I started working on it about 3 weeks in advance. At that point I didn't have slides, or my Isthmia notes, so much of my time was spent looking through Mom's Greece folders. (She has tons of stuff from the year and 1/2 she lived in Greece.) Also, I went to the public library to use an encyclopedia, and the few archaeological books they had. (I as yet hadn't figured out a way to get into the Stanford library.) I also had to spend most of my time finishing up the Kenyon semester in Greece proposal, so I didn't get much accomplished on the Isthmia lecture, though I did work on it a little every day, some of which time was spent looking through the slides in Prof. Raubitschek's office.

A week in advance, I starting spending most of my time on the lecture. By then, all the slides and my Isthmia folder had arrived from Ohio. By Monday evening, 4 days before the lecture was scheduled, I felt pretty good about my readiness. I had re-learned place names and archaeological terms, and had re-acquainted myself with the terrain around the site by looking at slides and pictures in books. Then came Tuesday morning, and my sense of readiness disappeared.

What happened was simple enough. I was interviewed by a guy from UPI (the director of the California branch). I thought the interview went OK (except that he was pretty dumb) with one major difference from the old Annie appearing: I'll call it my memory. At one point, for example, he asked me a question that I couldn't remember the answer to. I remembered that I used to know it, and had it written down, and had read it many times over the past few days, (even that very morning in preparing for the interview!)...but I couldn't remember the answer when he asked me for it. I excused myself, and went into my bedroom to look at the piece of paper which contained the answer. Then, I returned to the living room, where the reporter was, and <u>by the time I got there</u> (ca.30 seconds), the memory was gone! Aargh. Amazing...I excused myself again, and this time got the piece of paper, and brought it with me into the living room. There, I didn't have to read it or anything. I just had to glance at it, briefly, and the memory returned. Best of all it gave me a chance, before my upcoming lecture, to learn how my mind *had changed, and how to deal with it! Much better than learning such during the lecture!*

I spent the last 3 days writing. Or, at least trying to write, given my speed these days. And I didn't write complete text, by any means. That is, not something I could read aloud to the audience. Mostly, I just wrote notes to myself, but very full ones. Well, let me give one example here, with the beginning of my notes. This one would have been readable, if such had been necessary. It wasn't, and what I said was a little different, but the <u>idea</u> was much the same.

"Good evening. Nice to be back. This evening I'd like to present to you some of the recent discoveries at an ancient Greek sanctuary very familiar to some of you, and completely unknown to others. I hope both groups will be understanding, then, when I seem either completely obvious and simple-minded, or completely incomprehensible. Let's start with geography — an important part of modern archaeology." (First slide)

Most of my notes were far more simplistic. Mostly dates and distances, and stuff like that. Before the evening began, I hid in a back room for a few minutes and looked over my notes, especially the beginning of the talk. Then, I got introduced, the audience clapped, and I began. I was very nervous at the beginning — talking in a strange tone, for example — but as time went on, I got more and more relaxed, and it felt very natural to be back talking to a crowd. I only got mixed up once that I can remember and I did, in addition, quote from my text a few times. But mostly I remember talking like I used to talk, even gesturing like I used to gesture, and looking at the audience a lot. One thing I noticed I didn't do though: I didn't walk around like I used to, because I didn't want to walk away from my notes, except a few times when I pointed at things in the slides. The lecture lasted 55 minutes.

After the talk, various people came up to ask questions, and there was a reception which included wine. Most of the questions were from people (including students) who have been to the site. A few were from Greek-Americans. And a few people (some who knew about the accident) came up just to tell me how much they enjoyed it. As one person said, "it was much better than visiting the site!" Wesley said that either I had improved my speaking style, or he hadn't noticed before, because I was very entertaining.

It's a little of both I think. I think I am a bit more enjoyable (especially to non-classicists) these days. It feels so good to be able to do all these things — like walk, and talk, and point, *and remember <u>anything</u>—...Of course, I do forget more than I used to. For example, I hadn't written down about the handouts I had prepared, so I forgot to mention them, for those interested in picking them up after the lecture. Sigh.*

The UPI interview (Dec. 3) resulted in my also being interviewed by the Paul Harvey radio show "The Rest of the Story." The show's writer, named Meg, interviewed me for about an hour and a half, which amazed me, given that the interview was in preparation for a three minute segment (!). The story would have been on the Roman Arch at Isthmia (an article Timothy and I had written), but I never did hear of it being broadcast on the radio. More significantly, and as I wrote at the time: "I didn't talk about the accident once!"

Come December, I even managed to fill out one of the never-ending supply of bureaucratic forms connected with my disability (compare with my later attempt below, p.208):

Social Security Disability Report (19 Dec.1985)

— Explain how your condition now keeps you from working: *Difficulties with reading and writing, as well as loss of memory, make teaching almost impossible. A good example of my decreased capacities is my filling out of this form: it took* *me an <u>inordinate</u> amount of time writing it, even with the help of my mother...*

- Remarks: *The most painful parts of my disability have gone away by now (December). I started being able to walk a little a month after my accident, and can now walk with only a slight limp. My other muscles are almost back to normal, except for pain in my left foot and right buttock (from sciatic nerve injuries in my fall). Two other injuries are slower to heal, but are no longer painful: My right clavicle has "healed" incorrectly (and will probably need to be re-set someday), and my brain continues to improve. I can speak much better now, but my writing is still very difficult, which makes teaching almost impossible. The doctors think that the damaged nerves in my brain should be sufficiently healed to enable me to return to teaching, part-time, in Sept. 1986.*

By January 1986 I had recovered so much that I felt ready to venture out and explore the outside world. I chose to audition for a part in a play to be performed at Stanford, and I kept notes on the entire endeavor.

Notes on my (Annie's) involvement in
Moliere's <u>School for Women</u>
Jan. - March 1986, at Stanford

197

Introduction: Well, these are notes to add to my file on this part of my life, and to pass on to family and friends, which is much easier for me than writing about it in letters. Hm. Perhaps with a story of how I got into it, and then a bit about the enterprise itself. First, I'll get some basics about the play out of the way. It was written and first performed in 1662, in Paris, in verse. The French title, <u>L'Ecole des Femmes</u>, has normally been translated "School for Wives." Our performance used the first English translation, which dates to about 1750, but the director chose to place it in Yonkers, in 1850, to make it more comfortable for a modern audience to watch, and enjoy. It is a comedy, after all!

My beginning: I saw notices in the <u>Stanford Daily</u> newspaper in December that auditions would be held for three different plays at the beginning of January, and, having never auditioned for anything theatrical before (from fear of rejection I think), I decided to try for a part in the Moliere play. The others didn't sound very interesting. I read the play (in a terrible translation), but didn't really prepare a monologue, though I did look over and try to memorize some of the major lines of the main female character. When I showed up at the first "business" meeting (before any auditions began), I was asked to put down my theatrical *experiences on the form. "None," I answered, in every category (stage, film, music, dance, backstage, etc.), but after thinking about it for a while, I decided to put down "professor." Hell, aren't college classes "audiences" of a sort? My guess is that they are the worst kind of audiences, since they keep coming back for more! Anyway, at the business meeting, I was shocked to find out that the director was planning on cross-casting the Moliere play! In other words, all the male parts (6) were to be played by women, and all the female parts (2) to be played by men! Well, that only intrigued me more, so the next evening, I auditioned for it, and, since I was there, for the pseudo-Shakespeare play <u>Arden of Faversham</u> too.*

Auditions: I didn't enjoy auditioning for <u>Arden of Faversham</u> at all, but I think that was due mostly to the director, who's a very overbearing German. I enjoyed trying out for a part in <u>School for Women</u> a lot, and it took about 10 minutes. I didn't think I did a very good job with the audition. Still, the director was very taken with my name ("Harrianne? That's perfect!") and one of his advisors was very taken with my ability to handle languages. Anyway, boy was I shocked when 2 days later I found out that I was called back for another audition! (About 13 of us were. I don't know exactly how many people auditioned for the play, but about 50 I think. 75? Who knows.)

I went through a fuller second audition process, which lasted an entire evening. Then I waited, for 2 more days, at which point I found out that I had gotten a part! The smallest part in the play, to be sure, but not bad for my first audition ever!

My part: I played Henricus, the rich father of the bride-to-be, Agnes. I have been living in the West Indies for at least 10 years, ever since Agnes was 4 and I turned over her upbringing to a woman servant, since my wife had died when Agnes was born.

Rehearsals: Fascinating, but also time-consuming and sometimes boring. How? Well, having to do the same scene 20 or 30 times, for example. Still, I managed to spend much of the time in which my presence was required doing reading ("What language are you reading today, Henricus?"), until my <u>active</u> presence was needed. I think what amazed me the most about rehearsals is how much <u>work</u> they were! Not only would our bodily movements get changed ("Try moving left, no, right, no, forward, no, back, ...") but our facial expressions ("Try giving us a smile, no, a frown, no, a look of surprise, no, a look of horror.") and our voices ("Emphasize the word <u>emotion</u>, no, <u>soul</u> no, <u>advantageous</u>, no <u>match</u>.") Aargh! Over and over and over again, and then often it would get changed *back to the way we did it the <u>first</u> time! Still, it was fascinating being an active participant in the process.*

My appearance: How about from toe to head? Shiny black tie-up shoes; grey pants (no pockets, side zipper, foot straps) with a cod piece underneath; white suspenders; a white frilly shirt with a stiff cardboard collar; a black and gold striped vest; a black rather short jacket with gold buttons and a monocle in pocket; white gloves; a black foulard tie around neck; a shiny black cape, pushed back to show off its red lining; moustache and goatee for facial hair, with some grey brushed on; bags painted under my eyes; slightly grey hair combed back on the top and pinned up at the bottom; a shiny black top hat; and a wooden cane with curved handle. Whew! No wonder it took me so long to get ready every night! And I wasn't recognizable at all I think. Mom took some pictures.

First performance: (Wed. March 5) My first performance ever! And I was the only one of the cast who had never been on the stage before. Afterwards, Judy congratulated me on losing what she called my "Theatrical Virginity!" The performance itself was not <u>terrible</u>, but not as good as we'd done before, in rehearsals. There was a champagne and cheese reception after the performance, given by the Drama Department.

Performances: Second one (Thurs.) — worst run-through we've ever done, lots of Giancarlo's friends in the audience, lots of laughter, which I'm afraid we all played up to. Third one (Fri.) - much older and more intellectual audience, who didn't laugh at the funny lines as much, but clapped a lot at the end, while both Mitch and Giancarlo were very angry at *them during the performance for what they thought was rejection. Fourth one (Sat.) probably our best one, after which Wiek, Julianna, Giancarlo and I went to a <u>Ram's Head</u> (the Stanford Theatrical Society) dinner/dance.*

Last performance (Sun. matinee): Video-taped by Paul, a friend of mine. Carl Weber (Oliver's advisor) and lots of Jewish senior citizens (students of Wiek's) in the audience, lots of backstage visitors after the performance, followed by us all helping to "strike" (i.e. tear down all the set) and then a dinner over at Oliver's house, to which Wiek, Sophy, Arnold and I went, with friends.

Evaluation Session: (Tues. Mar.10) Done by Drama graduate students, Oliver, and his faculty advisor. They disagreed as much as the audiences had disagreed with each other: what some liked the others hated and vice versa. I just listened to them and learned a lot about the academic world of drama.

My impressions: Well, it was quite an experience, that's for sure! Hard work, time-consuming, and maddening at times, as well as exhilarating, inspiring, and amusing at others! OK, enough with the exclamation marks...Will I ever try to do anything theatrical again? Well, my guess is that I probably will, but only when I see that there's a play coming up that I *really <u>love</u>. And even then, only for a part in it that I really <u>want</u>. Otherwise, just to be there? No, I don't think so. But I did enjoy going through it, and I do hope to do it again sometime! What did I most enjoy? Oh, the learning I suppose: learning about costumes, make-up, lights, music, etc., and improving my vocabulary, with words like "block," "strike," and "up stage." Who would have thought, for example, that you have to stand on stage with your heels together and your toes pointed out, no matter which way you're looking or moving you head! Anyway, it was well worth the time and effort expended, most especially at this point in my life.*

By March, it became clear (to me at least) that my year of recovery from the accident was definitely coming to an end, and would soon be followed by another phase of my life. Nothing was working out for me as well as I had hoped, but that was no doubt in large part because I had finally developed into a real person, and not just an invalid recovering from an illness. Such an awareness had begun about a month or two earlier, and I noted the transformation in my journal.

Thurs. Jan. 16: First day of real work! Wow, what an accomplishment! It was the first day I felt like I was back to "the old me." And, you'll be glad doctors, I didn't push myself, or work non-stop,...I just plodded right along, not getting depressed when my memory didn't work. Yea! And, I *think a few things helped out: being in the library, for one, away from free food, computer & television, and being unconnected to a man, strangely enough. Anyway, I worked on both dissertation and evaluation of an article Marilyn Skinner sent me to comment on for <u>Helios</u>.*

Sun. Jan. 19: Stayed up late last night, but wanting to get out of the habit, I set my alarm for early this morning. Worked at home in the morning, went to the library in the afternoon, and am now back at the computer, it being evening. I'm getting into quite a pattern of action at long last!

Mon. Feb.3: Who would have though that today would turn out to be such a day! Hm. This is hard to explain, because nothing happened to make it an unusual day. And yet, there's no doubt in my mind that it was. Perhaps it was connected with my not so fantastic party two days ago. Or perhaps it was connected with getting (but not yet reading) a letter from Timothy today. Or perhaps it was connected with having visiting relatives. No, I don't think so, for any of the above. Basically, I think what happened is that I got down to work, real work, starting last night, from about midnight to 4am, and then all day today, the afternoon of which I spent in the library. During the morning I worked at home. Still, I'm not making myself clear what was so different about today. Well,

I'm having a hard time saying it because I'm not sure exactly what was so different. I felt different. I didn't feel like I had to be nice all the time, and friendly to everybody. I got angry at myself at one point, and pissed off at another car driver at one point, and I pushed myself a bit, and I was a little late at returning when I said I would, and so on. Is that clearer? In other words, from my point of view. I was more of a real person than I've been of late. Not back to myself, please understand, because who knows who "myself" is? Not I, that's for sure. Still, I think one result of the party is that I no longer feel like I have to be positive all the time. No, it's more important that I learn to be myself, whoever the hell that is...In a way, I think I partly blame all my supporters for how long this process has taken to come. Everybody was so kind and supportive toward me, that I came to think that the same was expected/ required from me. Enough of that. If I fail, or I'm hated, that's the way it goes. I can't spend my time trying to make other people feel happy, especially if they don't show up at my parties! Well, enough for now. I'll be back.

It did me good to get angry, to get sad, to face loneliness, something I had never experienced before, i.e. emotions similar to those felt by most other human beings. I do remember wondering after a while, perhaps subliminally, if feelings and emotional excitement would undermine my recovery. When I became scared, most of all I just wanted and needed someone to remind me of how far I had come, thereby suggesting that the progress would continue. A recovery process with a map, a path to follow, would have been reassuring. I had endured plenty of illnesses, but this one got to me. It had no obvious remedy or antidote for me to pursue. Without a clear path for me to follow, I felt like my essence, my being, hell, perhaps my soul, had been so shaken by the whole experience that it would have been easy for someone to kick it into pieces, to just pull my heart out and throw it away, if they so wished.

Before I could move on, as it were, to a new personal identity, my medical testing and the bureaucracies involved (both governmental offices and insurance companies) had to conclude. In preparation for yet another appointment with yet another doctor, including yet another test no doubt, I kept notes on my language difficulties in the preceding weeks:

Medical Notes, March 1-13
given to Dr. Catherine Poppel on 14 Mar.1986

- *My most common type of mistake involves using the wrong kinds of names for things — referring to Brown Library instead of Green library sorts of things. I do tend to catch this type of error, when I hear it.*

- *I have a major difficulty with the vocabulary of nouns which I have not heard in a long time. They are simply often missing, like not being able to remember the word for the piece of paper in fortune cookies! (Is there one?)*

- *I often forget where I put something, or even forget that I have it, until somebody mentions it, and then I can't remember where I put it...(like a bus pass)*

- *I sometimes experience a reversal of consonants, like writing Rd. instead of Dr. for doctor, and Tre. instead of Rte. for route, when using a typewriter.*

- *Here is a good example of the above: It happened that I made the mistake when using the computer, so I went to jot it down on a piece of paper before I forgot that it happened. But although I had typed Nekyon for Kenyon, I wrote down neknoy on the piece of paper, because I was concentrating so hard on the first 2 consonants (k and n) of the mis-spelled word!*

- *I can't remember the word for a,e,i,o,u (i.e. the opposite of consonant) at the moment.*

- *Less frequently, I erroneously mis-write a reversal of consonants and vowels (I just remembered the word!), as in rebrith for rebirth.*

- *I can't remember the name of the scientist (his name begins with an N) who discovered gravity with apples falling from a tree.*

My response to Dr. Poppel's testing in my journal was brief, simple, and to the point.

> *Mar.14: I took off for Dr. Poppel's at 8:15. Lots of traffic at that hour, that's for sure. Anyway, I got there in time for my 9am appointment, which I thought would take about an hour. 3 1/2 hours later we talked about how long we had been talking! Whew. And the "test" part of it was almost exactly what Dr. Kiernan did about 3 months ago. But it was easier this time! That was nice, even if it means that I won't get any Social Security money...*

Even after my appointment with Dr. Poppel, I continued to keep track, somewhat, of my language difficulties.

> *March 1986:*
> *I can't remember which instrument is a trombone and which is a saxophone.*
> *I wrote arm for leg today, and I didn't notice the error when I read it several times over 2 days.*

> *Thus. March 20:*
> *Happy 10th month re-birthday! I have so much I want to say, but it takes too long! Sigh. I suppose that's part of what I have*

to say. I'm still rather slow, and it does get in the way. But at least now my anger comes from trying to __do__ more (some would say "too much").

By April, I had recuperated to the point of being able to fill out forms and questionnaires from government health agencies and insurance companies — both of which were (not surprisingly) unbelievably slow to pay my medical bills and to provide me with the financial benefits to which I was entitled.

Perhaps most illuminating would be to provide you with my answers to some of their questions, for you to compare with my earlier attempt (see above, p.196).

April 4, 1986, Social Security, California (Fresno):

9. Do you require help with any of the activities mentioned above? [sleeping, dressing, chores, grocery shopping, cooking, driving] (If so, who provides this help?)

I do not usually require help, but I often ask for help to speed up the process, because I'm so slow. In other words, if I need to get somewhere by bus, and I cannot remember ever having taken a bus there before, I will call and ask for assistance, or ask a bus driver, or ask my Mom for help if she's around. I do require help in eating and dressing right. Left to my own devices (i.e. without the assistance of my mother), I make social errors in dressing and nutritional errors in eating.

11. How have your daily activities and the things you normally like to do changed since you became ill?

For me, the biggest change is in mental activities. I used to love to read and write and lecture and compose songs. Now I have to work harder at trying to understand things, because I am so slow. And I often misunderstand things people say. I also have come to deal with my poor memory by keeping a written record of everything as it happens, including phone calls, notes on conversations, activities, and so on. Otherwise, I forget: days, times, places, people's names, etc. Perhaps most of all, writing full sentences is very difficult. Filling out this form, for example, I am writing it on a word processor, so I can come back to it easily, and correct errors and make additions.

12. Are there things you used to do that you are no longer able to do because of your illness? (If so, please list them and describe how your illness prevents you from doing them.)

"No longer able to do" is hard for me to answer. "Worse" would be better in my case, because I prefer to think that they will come back, eventually. I cannot say that my illness <u>prevents</u> me from doing anything, since I have come to understand that I shouldn't expect to be able to do them the same as I used to, since I can't. But "no longer able"? No. So, let me change the question to "not as able to do." The answer to <u>that</u> question is: almost everything. Reading and writing more than anything else, given the things that are important to me. Other things: Well, I do not type as well, dance as well, speak English or foreign languages as well, or cook as well as I used to. And there are more, but they are hard to remember.

13. How do you feel most of the time?

Most of the time I feel tired, depressed, and frustrated, when alone. When I am with others, I feel much the same, but I cover it up and try to appear happy, vibrant, and alive. Also, I often feel embarrassment and shame, because of my bad (almost non-existent) short-term memory.

14. Do you enjoy being around other people? (If not, why?)

I enjoy <u>trying</u> to be around other people, after not being able to talk right for so long, but I am still so bad at it that it gets *me pretty depressed. Even so, I am so much better than I thought I would ever be, that I ordinarily have a smile on my face when with people. I should add that they <u>think</u> that I am enjoying being with them (because of the smile), and, being depressed with them <u>is</u> somewhat better than being depressed alone.*

19. If there is anything else you would like to add concerning your condition and how it affects you, please feel free to do so.

This form really is not very applicable to my case, since it seems so concerned with physical (rather than mental) problems, but I hope my answers have communicated some of my problems in dealing with my condition. I am sorry it has taken me so long to complete it, but such is the way with me these days. Slow, but determined. Perhaps I should say something about the result of my slowed up thought processes on my profession. Well, they hinder me from being able to do the job I used to do (full-time college teacher), and from being able to do the scholarship which I, like most college teachers, used to do during the summers. Still, I have great hopes for the future, especially given how much better I am now (March 1986) than I used to be. Finally, while this has no bearing on my application, I would just like to mention that my brother is taking a loss in his profession, in order to assist me by living nearby starting next school year. Things like that almost make up for the sadness.

At a slightly deeper and more self-conscious level than that requested by bureaucratic offices, I confess that I spent much of my time toward the end of my stay in California trying to escape from the kind of superficial existence which had been my life for the past 10 months. What I had was time. Time to…to what? Ponder and Meditate? No, I couldn't do that. Decide what to do with myself? No, I couldn't do that either. I had lots of time with…well, with nothing to <u>do</u>, really. Of course I could have done pretty much whatever I wanted, but I didn't <u>have</u> to do anything. The proverbial expression about vacations, "Nothing to do and all day to do it" did not exactly apply to my condition, however I felt a great need to figure out who I now was, who had all this time on her hands.

To be more precise, drawing on the twists and turns of my recovery and feeling like a missing person with a vacant smile, I took it into my head to gaze inward. With nothing much to see inside, previously I had only peered out at the world. With some fear of what was being left behind, I began to perceive my circumstances differently and became introspective. Who was to say whether this change in my perspective was more or less real?

My fears had originally been that my condition would either not change at all, or get worse. Now, from underneath it all, emerged the more long-term fear that I would forget what, and how, I had survived — a fear partly responsible for my decision to write this book. The residual fear, which never goes away, is that much like the wound on my head, a scar would first grow, then the skin heal, and eventually I would forget that this experience of a lifetime had ever happened. Only many years later, for example, was I able to express dissatisfaction with, no, criticism of, many aspects of my life during my recovery. Certainly no one else then would have criticized me, with the result that I opened the floodgates once I began to be self-reflective.

Fri. Apr.25: Evening spent being "Greek," first in San Francisco at a lecture on Kazantzakis by Kimon Friar, and then in Berkeley at the Mykonos restaurant, re-learning how to dance Greek, the latter with Stavros and some of his friends. An interesting awareness today for me: I'm very dual. Not schizophrenic or ambivalent, or...is there a word bi-psyche? perhaps the word ambivert? I have two different lots of things: 2 kinds of degrees (History and Classics), 2 professions (classicist and archaeologist), an androgynous name (Harry Ann -> Harrianne), 2 American names (Harrianne and Annie), 2 countries I live in (USA and Greece), 2 places I grew up (Georgia and Virginia), 2 musical instruments I like to play (piano and guitar), 2 physical exercises I like (bicycling and running), 2 meals a day, 2 addresses (Ohio and California), 2 ex-companions (Wesley and Timothy), 2 siblings (Gene and Nancy), and the list goes on and on. In math, it's called antipoints or contrapositives if the two are opposites.

Thus, while the similarity of virtually every day never resulted in boredom, I spent an increasing amount of time wondering who I was and how I was now going to define myself. Was I a classicist? a teacher? a recovering aphasic? I excessively asked questions, which were easier than trying to speak eloquently. Not Socratic questions. Just inquiries based on uncertainty.

Also in my search for identity, I tried out slightly different names (Harrianne, Annie, Arianna), clothing styles (traditional, hippie, professional, casual) and hairstyles (up, down, straightened, curly). And I paid more attention to the personality types I seemed to like, and so tended to repeat, and found myself identifying with the character I had created.

As if to confirm the thoughts rumbling around in my head, I began to perceive people regarding me as not being on exactly the same wavelength, either mentally or physically. The most distressing aspect of feeling myself being observed all the time was the resulting self-criticism of myself, say my appearance. With exotic hair and a dark tan, I felt that I appeared faintly negroid, slightly androgynous and definitely foreign (perhaps aboriginal?). You could hardly blame me if I had become sensitive to the close scrutiny I <u>felt</u> I was under, even though such was undoubtedly not usually the case. I was certain that I stuck out like a sore thumb. My self-imposed predicament was not due to my Jewishness, gender, nationality, Hellenophilism, age, race, size, Liberalism or Secular Humanist religion. My identity difficulties were due to the absence of a me, to be, and not to my membership in any category — not even handicapped, brain injured, or aphasic. Just as I have always considered myself a slightly eccentric conglomeration of many ingredients, so I hoped that my being slightly "out of touch" would be taken as an eccentricity.

And since nothing was evident or instinctive, every so often in California I had the distinct feeling that I had misplaced something. Misplaced what? Well, just as I regularly forgot what I told myself not to forget, and even forgot that I had told myself not to forget something *(!),* so I often misplaced the memory of what it was that I had misplaced.

What I most wanted to happen, of course, was to find the key no doubt hidden away inside the deepest recesses of my mind which would unlock the door and release the secret magical potion or spell for my complete recovery. And if I was carrying that key somewhere, like the Magritte *(?)* painting, all the doors to all the rooms looked alike. And while the key I kept searching for would no doubt open all the doors, inside each door there was a multitude of items I could perceive, but not quite comprehend sufficiently to figure out what to remove and carry away with me. Instead of finding the key to open those doors, I found myself engaged in a considerable array of complicated tasks, and I became absolutely bound to the items and ideas themselves for which I was searching for the word. We became joined together, the word and I, drawn to each other so tightly that I became absorbed by it. The word ceased to exist as something out there somewhere, say in a dictionary, but came to have an internal existence, as the words for the concepts became a part of me. And there were so many, many parts.

I remember as a child how I used to enjoy keeping things I saw or heard to myself now and then, not telling anybody. During the early phase of my recovery, on the other hand, my perceptions did not exist until they were shared, until I told someone. By March, I realized that I had become too much of an open book, and began to explore a private, almost secretive, personal communion with my inmost memories. Previously, for example, I did not keep track of my dreams, in part because I rarely recalled them upon awakening, but also because they did not seem very illuminating about myself. Now, I dreamed about myself constantly, tried to coax some insight from my dreams, and experienced an uncanny sense of myself indulging in compulsive self-reflection — and not just some feigned textbook self-help sort of introspection. I later learned that a partial regression was one prerequisite for a complete recovery. Naive as a child at the time, I engaged in mind-games which I would now consider eccentric, if not abnormal.

As I moved about my Mom's apartment, for example, I remember trying, vicariously, to gain reacquaintance with my past, through her photos and objects. I inspected them. I touched them. Subliminally, I believe I somehow thought that these objects of hers were impregnated with memories which would somehow just rub off on my underdeveloped brain.

I had often been told (in jest) that someday I would have to grow up. Was this it? Had the moment arrived when I would need to learn to accept myself as I was? Had the event that changed my life precipitated my turning into an adult? a grown-up? Noooooo. Not at this point. Rather, I got worse – a necessary reversion to childhood, inflicted upon me by the accident. And the deeper I dug into my personal character, the more I felt I was losing touch with who I, Harrianne, was. I felt shapeless. And I remember thinking at the time: Is this increasing self-awareness that I'm experiencing perhaps necessary for a full recovery?

In much the same way, and perhaps for much the same reason, I had an odd experience both in California and, to a lesser extent, earlier in Virginia, though I didn't recognize it at the time, but only in retrospect. Petty insignificant objects would often elicit an overwhelming emotional response. They would remind me of a happy memory and I would cry. Even watching movies. Tears would flow profusely as I was overwhelmed by general sorrow, or specific empathy with one character. This response was true even if the events were only slightly sad, and the characters only barely empathetic. I remember being almost ashamed by the enormous quantity of tears generated by both my first and second viewings of the movie <u>St. Elmo's Fire</u> back in July and August. For example.

By December, a similar kind of emotional response was still occurring, but with distinct repercussions, as I tried to figure out the meaning of my abundant tears, say in response to a movie. I'm guessing now that crying provided me with a kind of relief, as one needs after having lost something. Hell, just as the journey of recovery transforms the individual, so the memories of the incident itself can be much easier to bear, when devoid of the accompanying pain.

12/26/85 (Thurs.): I saw the movie <u>Maxie</u> on the World Airways flight from SF0 to DC today, sitting between two women, one of whom was watching the movie too. During it, I *laughed in all the right places, and enjoyed it immensely, but at the end, I slowly burst into intense crying. No, I should call it sobbing, to the point of hysteria. Why? Well, the movie was about a woman (named Jan, played by Glenn Close) who was a secretary for a Catholic diocese and her husband (Nick) who was a librarian, and who live together in SF0. In removing wallpaper from their apartment one day, Nick discovers writing/graffiti on the wall under the wallpaper. It says "Maxie Malone, (day) 1927, read it and weep." Later, they find out from an upstairs old woman neighbor, who used to be her partner, that the writing was done by an ex-resident of the apartment, Maxie Malone, who died the day after she wrote it, at a young age, after a very short actress career. One evening, after watching an old film with Maxie in it, Nick meets her ghost, though the body shape is hard for her to keep. She has watched the movie with him, because she never saw it when she was alive. For the rest of the movie, Maxie takes over his wife's (Jan's) body from time to time. Jan doesn't remember anything from when she's Maxie. Jan is very quiet, a hard worker, a jogger, clean cut, with simple tastes. When she becomes Maxie, she becomes outrageous, loud, a plaything, a singer and dancer, a far-out dresser, etc. Nick loves them both, and loses his job as a result of Maxie's outrageous behavior against his female boss who's trying to seduce him. In the course of the film, Maxie gets to have a chance at developing a short acting career, in exchange for leaving Jan's body for good, which she does. And I cried. And not a little bit, either. I cried a lot. And loudly. And I'm afraid I frightened the two women sitting next to me. I tried, while crying, to calm them, by promising to explain. And I did, but I'm not sure I gave them the right explanation. After all, why did I get so upset?*

Well, I think that part of me was happy and part of me was sad. The sad part was for Maxie, who was now really dead, for good. The happy part? Well, that's harder, but I think it had to do with the changes that happen to Jan. Put simply, she becomes both people a little bit. There's a new Jan, in other words, a bit like there's a new Annie, and the new Jan still has bits of the old Jan in her, but she likes the new her even better than before. Hmmmm. I'll have to come back to this and try to do a better job.

I never did "come back to this" – at least not until I began to write this book 8 years later. At the time, the movie and accompanying emotions receded into a blur along with a night's sleep, and were not even recalled the very next day. Nighttime usually made me exaggerate, as my immature emotions came to co-exist with my waking awareness of reality. The lines between the two worlds (my past and my present) grew dimmer at night, and in so doing, they both seemed more familiar, much like a distant, but comforting, friend.

Other than the temporary therapy of crying over movies and reminders of my childhood, my emotional frame of heart was probably the most retarded during my journey of recovery, and one which I do not recall anyone ever warning me about. I received medical attention for my intellectual disposition, but not for my prolonged emotional immaturity, and I was never encouraged to contact other people with aphasia. It would have been very helpful to hook up with people in the same or even a similar situation, for both information and for reassurance.

In much the same way, I can recall few, if any, invigorating moments, or feelings of stress or anxiety. I smiled almost continuously, as I had discovered that it usually made people treat me more nicely, but I never had a <u>desire</u> to laugh. Things and people were just there. Nothing ever startled me. For something to startle you, there must be a solid background against which the event clashes as an oddity. I had no such framework. Likewise, I never stepped gingerly over an sensitive topic, blushed at an embarrassing conversation or felt a sense of relief.

"Relief? What's that? Relief from what?" I would have asked.

I never did anything furiously or enthusiastically. After my eventual re-discovery of enthusiasm I over-reacted and became downright exuberant. In general, however, I found that my emotional life was the most gradual to return.

My behavior itself was often puzzling. It seemed as if an invisible wall separating the real and unreal had collapsed, and with it the structure of my life. When that wall crumbled, I found it impossible to go through the motions of doing what I was expected to do, simply because I had done them for the past 32 years of my life. Without being able to comprehend the extent to which I was acting "normally," I came to depend on others for guidance, however I could never trust my interpretation of their actions. My attempt to define appropriate behavior through my skewed interpretation of other people's actions was much like looking through a kaleidoscope. I'm guessing that my glimpse into their behaviors bore little resemblance to their reality.

Likewise, I once saw myself in the mirror, while trying to converse with someone, and I was absolutely shocked by the look on my face. My intensity of concentration had made my face appear so…severe? I looked almost angry. I wasn't angry, of course. I was concentrating, trying very hard to understand what was being said, and how to respond appropriately. A complex task for me in those days. I blamed such difficulties on my lying in bed for so long, having lost consciousness of normal life; that I had forgotten how things were supposed to work. I spent a fair amount of time trying to come to my senses, to pull myself together, but without knowing which way to turn.

So many memories to be recovered. I had no recent or distant experiences to draw upon, and could not remember those other people told me I had once experienced. Unable to remember my past, it simply didn't exist.

"Don't you remember when…?" I would be asked.

"No, I don't remember." And I would be gently reminded of an event from my past.

Or, when I would recall an event, like a clap of thunder, the memory would all of a sudden exist. And, unlike being reminded of words and names, once the memory was recovered, it would not then disappear again. Once recalled, the memory of an event from my past was there to stay.

I had no involuntary memories or flashes of retrospective lucidity. Rather, memories were usually generated by a memory-jogger of some kind, as was the case with my father. My father Len had died quite young, in his 60s, following a lifetime of smoking cigarettes.

Certainly I remembered him, once my mind woke up after falling down in Boston, but I remembered hardly anything <u>about</u> him for quite some time, which maddened me. Where had all my Dad anecdotes gone? I greatly feared that without him around to stimulate my re-acquisition of memories, he would remain an out-of-focus mirage. As my year of recovery in California progressed, however, I was pleasantly surprised to find him emerging into my consciousness from time to time — sometimes at the oddest moments!

As Chanukah approached, for example, I suddenly remembered how he loved hiding our gifts in crummy brown paper bags, tucked away in the darnedest places, complete with mysterious clues as to where we might find the next brown paper bag. Or when I saw someone on a riding lawnmower while out jogging, I recalled how greatly he had enjoyed sitting out on the lawn with a glass of iced coffee in his hand, just watching me mow our lawn with a riding lawnmower. Or how, when eating horseradish, he would suddenly sit up straight in his chair, enlarge his eyes to bulging, hold his breath, and bounce one hand off the top of his extremely bald head from its hot spiciness.

I'm certain these stories must seem trivial to readers, and insignificant to health care professionals. Such moments of recollection, however, were crucial to me. They gave me a past, and in so doing, created for me an existence, rather than just being alive. Much in the same way as I would never have asked for this accident, with its consequences, but came to appreciate and be thankful for my recovery, so I would obviously never have wanted my father to die, but was ecstatic beyond belief as his memory returned to me during that year. Who knows exactly who the new me would have become if he hadn't? Surely not the Harrianne I now am, for just as he played large part in my childhood and young adulthood the first time, so he re-emerged from the scrapbook and the letters, to accompany me in my recovery.

My Mother's presence during this year was less symbolic and much more essential. Not only did I live with her in her condominium in California, but I gradually came to define myself by comparison with her. Slowly, ever so slowly, I rejected becoming a duplicate of her character, which, though I love her dearly, I had rejected as a child as well. Mom is who she is, and I needed to become me. She loved playing bridge, eating healthy food, listening to opera, knowing of the private lives of entertainers, and reading novels. What about me?

To quote from two entries in my journal:

Sat. Mar.22: [Today] I learned some things, like never again to talk with Mom about my accident. She can't handle it. Funny: I've finally come to handling it almost perfectly, and she was much better when I was sick. Hm. I guess that comes from her nursing days...Anyway, no more.

Mon. Mar.31: Oddly enough, I think it's really good that Mom left me alone. It makes me question and doubt whether the doctor in Virginia knew what he was talking about when he said I ought to live with somebody for a while. Or, maybe the "while" is over? I notice it in everything I do. I had no idea until recently that I was paying so much attention to her ideas! Not that I wanted to become "like her," only that nothing much came naturally, so I figured I could pick things up from her. But she's not me! Some examples: her taste in food, music, clothes, & movies, her attitudes toward dirt, mess, Judaism & money. Not that she's a bad person about any of the above, only that I'm different!

Now while I realize that we don't choose our relatives, I had always deeply admired my parents — not so much for their marriage as for their approach to having a family and raising their children. They shared a sense of purpose in being alive in general, and in raising children in particular — things which no doubt subliminally contributed to my becoming a teacher. In addition, I much appreciated and deeply loved my sister and brother. They each played a part in defining the me who was trying to emerge.

I did wonder what kind of daughter and sister I had previously been. A reasonably decent one I assumed, but after all, who was I to say? And who, when all was said and done, was I now? Not my mother, sister, or brother, all of whom I loved fiercely, and who had been deeply affected by my accident. Without my having much of a mind or memory, my aphasia was much more troublesome for them than me. But for my loving and supportive family, the recovery described here would never have occurred.

Nevertheless, and not to diminish my family's care, I often felt something was lacking, which could not be fabricated for me: I wanted my Daddy. He would make the doctors make me better. He would make all the bad things go away. I missed him greatly.

* * *

In general, my year spent in California was mostly a time not for the complexities, absurdities, and small ironies of daily life, which I was then unable to recognize, but rather for the simplicity of daily mediocrity. There are no real breakthroughs in recovering from aphasia. Just repetitive episodes, which hopefully will occur more frequently. A kind of recovery on the installment plan. As the connections in my brain grew back and developed, my daily life increasingly included some complexity, which I adamantly (if not methodically) embraced, being constantly energized, not-surprisingly, by my improvement.

Lest you are inclined to make light of such commonplace occurrences as mailing a letter or making a long-distance phone call, let me mention one of my philosophies of life developed during this, my year of recovery. Everything you do changes you, has consequences. Not only the peaks and the valleys, the highs and the lows, but the more subtle impressions of regular, daily, average events. Most people, most of the time, do not notice them. During my recovery, however, experiencing mediocre daily events often evoked serious thoughts. I had never previously given much thought to the intimate connection between action and thought, tasks and speculation. I am now fairly certain that our daily lives are composed of a great number of affiliations between these so-called insignificant events. Unfortunately, we spend most of our time simply ignoring them, as if an awareness of the complexity would make us slightly neurotic.

In those days I lived in a strange illusionary world. I am reminded of the Vladimir Nabokov story "Signs and Symbols," in which one of the main characters suffered from "Referential mania."

> "In these very rare cases the patient imagines that everything happening around him is a veiled reference to his personality and existence…Everything is a cipher and of everything he is the theme." (Nabokov's Dozen p.69)

Not that I considered myself the center of the universe, however I did become obsessed with details, to the exclusion of the big picture, which I could not see.

In most situations, I was incapable of focusing on particulars (which I perceived as disjointed details), in order to grasp a complex situation. My senses were simply missing something, which appeared as disinterest. I could recognize individual items, but not compounds with multiple dimensions. Exclusively mental encounters? Those seldom occurred.

> *Thurs. May 1: ...Actually, now that I think about it being the beginning of my last month of "Rebirth," I should really try & write more about my mental rebirth, which I have no good name for yet, but which I'll call my re-education. Hard to explain all the reasons for it, but my guess is that the accident & recovery is only part of the reason. Other reasons? Being in California, growing middle aged, becoming single for the first time in my life, just to name a few...Some examples to come back to: learning about CDs (compact disks), VCRs, Mtn. Bikes, Computer graphics, etc.*

Unlike my months in Virginia I attempted to sometimes just think about things during my year in California. The result was most often incomprehensible. Not quite confusing; just puzzling. And when something I perceived as insignificant would happen, I wouldn't bother to try and figure it out. Then later, when I realized that it <u>did</u> matter, I often <u>still</u> wouldn't attempt to work it out. How much to tip at a restaurant, for example. It took too much brain power, so I left such matters to others.

Earlier, in Virginia, I never considered such matters, either at the time they first occurred to me or later. By California however, I think I was able to think about such matters, but chose <u>not</u> to, and I have no idea why. I cannot now understand how I could have simultaneously realized that a matter was important, and so should be comprehended, and at the same time rejected giving it any more thought than absolutely necessary. I suppose it was a question of conserving my energy and/or resources. To put it crudely, I became enormously selfish, and was oblivious to how something could possibly matter if it didn't directly affect me. I was innocent and egotistic, like many a young child.

At the same time while in California, similarities, connections and comparisons between entities began to fascinate me. There were so many relationships to discern — between everything! People, places, events, colors, music. You name it. Not only did nouns (such as thermometer, oyster and eucalyptus) stand for a object, which was difficult enough to comprehend, but some things (such as icons or logos) stood for other things, and words (such as acronyms) stood for other words. The most incomprehensible for me, as I recall, was when equations (such as E=mc^2) symbolized ideas. As if just understanding the idea all by itself wasn't difficult enough! Trying to understand, and then to describe, the complexity of those relationships became a sort of game for me.

I have heard that random ideas can mess you up. Virtually all ideas were random to me, but my confusion was not <u>due</u> to the random thoughts. Rather, my random thoughts <u>resulted</u> from my confusion. Similar to the ancient riddle leading to the paradox, "which came first, the chicken or the egg?," but in my case the damage to my brain was definitely creating the chaos.

I had never considered myself one to be lacking in imagination, however the haphazard connections made by my damaged brain astounded me. Just when I needed some order among the abundance of confusion, my increased consciousness brought with it an increase in disorder. Why? Because my pieces of knowledge were just that — pieces that didn't fit.

It is a basic premise of scholarship that our understanding of an issue or event is only as valid as the available evidence. But I could not apply the same methods to dealing with aphasia. The pieces of evidence didn't fit. And this new puzzle had no picture on the cover. Prior to my accident I usually avoided puzzles, and so was disinclined to even attempt them. Now my entire life had evolved into one large puzzle, apparently impossible to solve, with no box-top image to imitate. Oddly enough for me, the most valuable approach was not for me to attempt to discover the correct solution to the puzzle (i.e. the scene on the non-existent cover), but to try and attach pieces randomly, and see if any of them fit.

Mulling over my year in California living with my Mom, I probably could have just run around all day in a cool nightgown. After all, brain damage would have been a legitimate reason for enjoying myself and relaxing. But I discovered many traps, crossed wires and hazards in inactivity, so I ventured to adapt to this new life of mine, full of uncertainties. I had no need for certainty at first. Only improvement. Then I began questioning, doubting and suspecting that things might be other than they first appeared. And just when I thought I understood something, the rules of the game would change! It was so easy for me to fall and so difficult to rise back up. Yet once down I never considered not trying to climb back up. I wonder why not? Ignorance perhaps of how far I had to go? My dealing with bureaucracies such as Ohio Workers Compensation is only one example of such agony.

Wed. Apr.23: Aargh! What a morning! Grrr...Dealing with Ohio Workers Compensation is starting to drive me crazy. It's been bad all along, but never to the point of making me want to kill them, but I think this morning finally did it. The hardest to take was about why they didn't fully pay the Massachusetts General Hospital bill: They didn't pay for x-rays of my right wrist and knees because "they weren't injured." Yes they were! Well, they replied, you didn't say so on the form you filled out. That's because they weren't broken! Not good enough. Now they want me to fill out another form, asking for reconsideration of the claim, to be backed up by a physician! But the accident was 11 months ago! Can't they be satisfied with photos of the scars? "No, we can't be sure that they aren't from wounds acquired yesterday." Aargh!

Engaging in discussions with governmental officials, I gradually noticed that I never paused in the course of a conversation — neither in order to concentrate while listening, or when speaking. And while I never felt defeated when attempting to discuss something, I also could never figure out a way to force my mind to remain alert. I did develop the habit of scanning my environment, looking for clues as to which of my internal dictionaries would be most helpful to bring to the surface. Words concerning food? music? work? children? political events? For while conversation always <u>seemed</u> possible, I was definitely lacking the full vocabulary of many subjects.

During a conversation, I would often have to ask my interlocutor to repeat what they had just said — hoping the repetition would suffice to allow the meaning of the message to sink in. It rarely worked, but I improved greatly at pretending that it did, and that became the most frequently employed of my multitude of pretenses.

By requesting a repeat performance I doubled my chances of understanding the sentence I had missed. And a doubling of events was familiar, as I often experienced things twice myself — not through different senses, but as if I perceived the world in double, much like a split screen or stereo. When that happened, I had no way of determining which experience was true. Both simply played a part in my world.

In conversations, I often wasn't certain exactly what I was supposed to say, but could tell by the expressions on people's faces whether what I spoke had made any sense. Also, sometimes, when I was communicating fairly well, I would start to feel as though there were disaster in the air. I could tell that I was losing it, and that I could do nothing to stop it from disappearing. Now I have it; Now I don't. My ability to converse would simply melt away, and my confidence along with it, which would remind me of my general disorientation, and how the boundaries of my universe had once again changed.

My thought threads had become so tangled that I wondered such counter-productive things as: What was the point of someone telling me, "It's raining today."? Or why would someone want to know,

"How are you?"? Not thinking clearly, I vaguely expected that I would someday find out that there was a hidden truth behind all these questions. Were they referring to my insensitivity to the weather by remarking on it raining? to my not being very well, by inquiring as to how I was? I was clueless. And yet I didn't know how to make use of verbal defenses, by asking, "What do you mean?," or saying "I don't understand," much less "Huh?"

At the same time, the notion that there might have been some sort of underlying truth to matters other than how they appeared on the surface was unfathomable. The unspoken merely did not exist. Without the words, I could not comprehend that I had been deprived of certain experiences. Among my deficiencies, a lack of appreciation of opposites (heat/cold, day/night, life/death, here/there, tears/laughter, up/down, us/them, and left/right), and grappling with contradictions - including those made by myself!

I was not able to be both pensive and engaged in an activity (including speaking) at the same time. In the course of a conversation, for example, I was incapable of both listening or talking, and at the same time thinking such things as: I'm bored. (or) She's just trying to be nice. (or) I'd like to leave, but I can't. (or) I wonder if he's going to ask me for my phone number? etc. Thoughts such as these could not co-exist with either conversation or activity. They could not compete with my need to concentrate on following the conversation. They now

<u>do</u> coincide, which is why I remember their absence. All I could do then was to express my thoughts, or to postpone thinking until later, when I was alone, and did not have to grapple with human interaction.

Perhaps I can make my situation more comprehensible by using the metaphor of sound. People conversing sounded not exactly like cacophony, but more like a meandering tune, going nowhere. My life was proceeding as if I had been playing in a different key and with different strings, yet with the same fingers, and on the same bow. Could I still play the same sort of music? The music was slow, randomly lilting, with no sign of a tune, but a multitude of echoes, as if to confirm that it was music…

Chapter 5: The Socio-Sexual Recovery in Particular

"More or less, they educated one another concerning their natures."
- Bernard Malamud <u>Dubin's Lives</u> (NY, 1977) p.107

"To write is to put the seeming insignificance of human existence into a different perspective. It is the need, the wish, and, please God, the ability, to reorder our physical fate by mental means, a leap of the imagination, an act of faith."
- Alfred Kazin "The Self as History: Reflections on Autobiography" in <u>Telling Lives: The Biographer's Art</u> (ed. Marc Pachter, NY, 1979, 75-89), p.88

My unexpected accident had, among other things, succeeded in almost completely desocializing me. I had not become completely antisocial, but my experiences had transformed me into a social nonentity, living a limited, mostly isolated, life. In my effort to cease my seclusion, I decided to concentrate, with deliberate focus, upon my social detachment, in a way many would consider slightly odd, if not suspicious. I began to explore being a single woman, complete with dating, personal ads, and bars, and with no preconceived expectations of what I would find. After all, that was one reason I was doing it: to learn about such matters! I needed to feel <u>at home</u> interacting with other people, and especially that other species called men.

I wrote about my encounters, so my socio-sexual rebirth can be gleaned from the following letters and journal entries, which I have interspersed with some after the fact reflections. I wrote this excerpt, for example, about 8 months after the accident, in January 1986.

> *How to begin? Well, historian that I am, how about with some simple factual background? In this case, on my sexuality before the accident. Simply put, until the accident, I had never been single before. Not that I was always monogamous, whether married or not, but I never took meeting men very seriously, because of my intense/serious involvement with men: first Wesley, then Timothy. Now (post-accident) I find that I am single, for the first time in my life really!*

Needing to broaden my social matrix from the limitations of family members and friends, I met and became acquainted with an immense assortment of single men, each of whom contributed to my social renewal. Not having known me prior to the accident, these men could easily ignore the momentary lapses in my English or my memory, due to their need to concentrate on assessing so many other aspects of my personality. Unlike my family and friends, they were not on the lookout for my errors.

First, some basics I remembered from my previous socio-sexual life. I had been married for the approximately proverbial 7 years to Wesley who, about 5 years earlier, had left me for another (older, married) woman. As my year of recuperation in California progressed, I remembered more and more about our marriage. And since Wesley lived and worked quite close to where I lived with my Mom, we visited frequently. In fact, while we had not parted on the friendliest terms (divorces never are), our interaction these many years later was remarkably comfortable. And since we had first met in high school, he reminded me of my adolescence in Virginia, and of some very pleasant memories of my 20s in the 1970s. There were even some humorous escapades (such as our taking separate honeymoons) which came to mind from time to time.

It was tremendously difficult for me to connect with my emotional life prior to the accident, and I wondered: Had I previously suppressed my emotions? Was that why I was having such difficulty rekindling them? I first explored my emotional life in writing, and then finally in person, during Timothy's (my boyfriend at the time of the accident) visit near the end of August. I wrote him 3 letters prior to his visit, in which I explained that I hadn't yet recovered any romantic feelings toward any man, and that I had observed plenty of couples (on the street, on TV, in movies) but hadn't understood their staying in a relationship filled with hatred and anger.

My attempt to re-connect with the emotional relationship portion of my life through writing letters was an utter failure. I was trying to pull a rabbit out of a hat. Not a magician's hat — appearing to be empty but containing magical tricks. This hat was full of misunderstandings, competing ideas and random thoughts, fighting tooth and nail — not to get <u>out</u> of the hat, but to reign supreme. It never happened that summer.

Before Timothy's visit? No sex of any kind. I couldn't even recall what sex felt like. I wasn't attracted to any men, and I wasn't drawn toward looking at or reading pornography. It was as if that part of my body was dead.

During Timothy's visit? Again, no sex. Oh sure, we slept together once, which was pretty yucky, and we tried to kiss, but it didn't feel right, to either of us.

After Timothy's visit and my leaving Virginia to live with my Mom in California for a year? I didn't involve Timothy in my search to understand men and relationships. He became my ex, and as such was no longer included in my future. I did not stop thinking about him, or writing to him now and then, but the rules of the game had changed, and he became a friend from my increasingly distant past life.

About 2 months after Timothy's visit, and almost exactly 5 months after the accident which changed my life, I met a man.

* * * DEREK JOURNAL * * *

Thursday, 24 Oct.1985: There have been so many new beginnings for me since the accident, that I hardly know how to explain what I am about to start trying to do. Simply put, I guess one would call it a special kind of journal. But the type of specialty is more difficult to describe. How's this: A journal about the history of a relationship, begun at its beginning, without any assumptions about where it will go. Hmm, not too bad. It's very different from anything else I've ever written about my relationships with men, because they've only been started either after the relationship is very serious, or after the relationship is over. This one is neither of those. I just met him. And who knows if anything will develop at all? Maybe

I'll never see him again. Maybe we'll end up getting married years from now. Maybe, maybe, maybe. Perhaps that's one of the reasons that I am inclined to try and write about it: because I want to have some record of it no matter where it ends up going. Also, I have the time, since I am presently on disablement [disability] insurance and can't yet work all day on my as yet unfinished dissertation. We'll see how this works, both at improving my slow linguistic recovery, and at keeping track (at the very least for memory purposes) of my emotional life.

Monday 28 Oct. 1985: Whew! Most of all, we talked and talked and talked: about all sorts of things, but mostly about relationships between women and men, ourselves included. What a wonderful experience for me! I had a great time, was very relaxed, re-learned a lot about feelings, and above all, enjoyed myself without any expectations about the future. Who knows? In a way, who cares? I certainly got more than I expected from a brief romantic interlude! Perhaps most of all, I had a chance to think about and talk about the old me, the uncertain new me, etc, etc, with a very friendly and very helpful (not to mention very sexy) man! Ah, it was perfect. Of course, he's not perfect, thank god. That would have been too much for me to deal with I think. But I wasn't really in the mood to "fall in love." I just wanted to get back into a more

normal lifestyle than I've had for the past 5 months. And I did!
And it felt wonderful! To be able to touch a man, be touched,
talk with a man, play with a man, and so on, felt very easy
compared with my fears of how complex I thought it would be.

Sat.2 Nov.1985: ...As for our close and involved
conversations: well, they're hard to encapsulate. We're very
different persons, in many ways, but we both seem to enjoy
finding out about each other...some. We're also both avoiding
getting very involved, on the other hand. He talked more about
his work, about old girlfriends, and about likes and dislikes. I
talked some about my work, showed him some recent (past 5
years) photos, answered some questions about my marriage,
and my lack of belief in monogamy.

Thursday 7 Nov. 1985: Whew! These forays with Derek are
getting more and more difficult to summarize, but I don't want
to stop the process of trying...What do we talk about so much?
Oh, mostly ordinary things (music, jokes, politics, movies)
plus each other. Who knows why we both seem to enjoy
talking about each other? I suppose it may be due to both of us
wanting to avoid getting "trapped," so we spend a fair
amount of time telling each other two kinds of things: 1) what
we each like about the other, and 2) what we aren't interested
in becoming for the other. Hm, is that clear? Given that

neither of us is the other's "type," and yet we seem to enjoy each other's company (for various reasons), I think we are both careful to make it clear that neither of us should expect it (the relationship) to become any more than it now is. Is that clearer? I doubt it.

Friday 8 Nov. 1985: Hmmm. It's funny, but things between me and Derek keep getting harder and harder to summarize. I suppose that's because interpersonal relations inevitably become more confused as time goes by? No, that's too simplistic...Certainly from my point of view, the highest point of our night together occurred at ca.3am, when I awoke and had to go to the bathroom. Simply put, I was very moved: Derek was sound asleep, and holding on to me very closely. Sigh. Who knows why it struck me so hard? Truly, my eyes filled with tears. And yet, I don't feel at all "in love" with him, and I assume that he doesn't feel that way about me. So, why was I so moved? Am I more of a romantic than I'm willing to admit? Am I changing in this regard? Honestly speaking, I really am not interested in becoming heavily involved with him. Oh, sure, I like him enough to want to spend some time with him now and then, but not lots, by any means. As an example, it turns out that he'll be going to Sacramento during the coming week. I haven't yet told him, but I won't be going, for the simple reason that I'm not interested enough. How to explain to him? Well, given how much I have used him, and how much I have learned from him, and how little I have asked from him, perhaps the most concrete way to put it is: What more can I get out of him?

He was very important to me when I needed to feel desired, and accepted,...but what about now? Oh sure, I still like feeling desired and being accepted for who I am, but it's not so much a need anymore, so it has become more important to me, than it was before, how I feel about him. How do I feel about him? See below. How does he seem to feel about me? Well, he has never seemed to open up very much to me, or to think very much about me when I wasn't around him, or to do very much for me when we saw each other, and that continues to be true. In other words, from my point of view, he's good fun, sometimes, but he makes for a fairly boring and superficial "boyfriend," because he's not much interested in developing a relationship. And I don't mean a commitment, or even monogamy. I just mean companionship, tender affection, interest in me as a person (including my mind), and not just as a sex object, which only includes sexuality. So, why bother? He would probably say: for good sex. Well, that has never been enough for me. Good sex has always been relatively easy to find, or to do without...No, there are other things that have been more important to me, and apparently still are. I doubt that I can explain them, but I could try, and perhaps someday shall, to somebody.

Thursday 14 Nov. 1985: One more thing I should mention about these past 2 days with Derek. I have become more and more aware of things about him that, while I don't dislike him for them, I'd rather not be around them (and therefore him) so much: he asks me almost no questions, he's a definite sexist, he's interested in physical violence more than I like, he's rather cheap (always counts his change), a collector of objects, a non-traveler, non-intellectual (no books, no newspapers), no men friends, a slight liar (to women, to business associates), he would like to have a woman to care for him (especially cook, clean, and sex), says he has a "woman's bike" (no top bar), and so on. One result of my increasing awareness of our differences, is that I think I should end our relationship before either of us gets hurt or feels exploited or taken advantage of.

Despite his attractiveness, Derek felt inappropriate to my partially in-hiding personality. He was thoughtful enough to give me positive, at times eloquent, feedback on my attempts at social interaction, so I even wrote him letters now and then.

A Mind of My Own
memoir of recovery from Aphasia

Friday 15 Nov.1985: Dear Derek, Greetings from your overlinguistic friend! Words, words, words. You must be getting tired of them by now. For me, I am in part re-learning some of my old loves: talking, reading, and writing. In this case, you get to try your hand at dealing with the last. Let me know if I'm incomprehensible

In particular, I thought I would try my mind and hands at attempting to communicate with you about 2 things which came up during out most recent visit: 1) the way I've been "using" you, and 2) what I like better (and need more?) than either talking or sex. (I believe you thought talking won with me...)

On the first. Well, "use" is such a terrible word, but I can't think of a better one those days. Put another way, there are various things that I have been learning from you, trying out with you, and so on. Oddly enough, I think these may be the same sorts of things which attracted me to you. Put simply (and I'd be glad to try to describe to you the more complicated version some time), you are the first completely "not my type" man that I've ever tried to be with, to please, and to enjoy. Not merely to see if I could do it (that would fit the standard meaning of "use"), but to help me figure out who I am/have become these days. In other words, who am I becoming?

I know that I'm sounding a bit like a child, or at least an adolescent, but I guess such is the way during the process of rebirth. Oh, I know who I used to be, and, without the accident, I would almost certainly be the same person — one, I'm afraid, who would have had nothing personal/intimate to do with you. But now? Who knows? I would have liked you just fine, maybe even been intrigued by you. But I doubt that I would have let myself (or wanted) to get close to you. No, I know that I wouldn't have. Anyway, enough of this. I doubt that I've made myself completely clear, but perhaps clearer than before...In Friendship, Annie

Mostly, however, I wrote to myself, in the form of my journal of rediscovery, in the hope of keeping track of my rebirth.

Tuesday 19 Nov. 1985: Well, I must be addicted to this process, because here I am again...I continue to be intrigued by the whole process of self-rediscovery.

Wednesday 20 Nov. 1985: Just a short batch of reminders... Derek. Well, we didn't have much of a chance to talk much, but during our short conversation there was one part well worth mentioning. Towards the end of our time together, Derek made a comment about Mom seeming to like him by

how friendly she is toward him. I said it was more than that.
He asked what, and I just said that she was glad he wasn't a
runner-up for son-in-law. Put simply, he was flabbergasted,
and asked why. Given his response, I chose not to go into
great detail from Mom's point of view, but to simplify and give
him one thing about him that both Mom and I have noticed. In
other words, from both our points of view. And, instead of
using the term Mom and I have used (egocentric), which I
wasn't sure he would understand, I called it his self-
centeredness. He asked if that was the same as selfish, and I
said no. Because it isn't. And he isn't selfish.

Needless to say, my involvement with Derek didn't last very long. I
tried to bring our relationship to a friendly end with a letter I wrote in
December.

Thursday 12 Dec.1985: Dear Derek, Well, here's another
small opus from your over-linguistic friend! I've finally gotten
to the point where I don't need to talk or listen all the time, but
we haven't had a chance for either for a while, and I doubt
that we will this evening, so I thought I would write something
to you which you could read while I'm gone, if you wish. If
you're still up when I return, I'd be glad to talk with you about
it, but my guess is that it will have to wait until your next visit
to Palo Alto. Feel free just to leave this text here, if taking it

home would be a problem, or throw it away and ignore it, if you prefer.

What's up? Oh, not that much, really. I just thought that you might like to hear a little about my feelings toward you these days, especially since I am in no mood to have sex with you. I know this is an important subject for you, so let me explain.

Well, first of all, you need to know, and understand, that my feelings are not in any way connected with our sexuality together. Much the opposite! I really enjoy having sex with you, ...but I'd rather not today. In other words, my aversion to such has nothing to do with the pleasures (or non-existent displeasures) of our sex life.

And it has very little to do with my feelings toward you! Oddly enough, I still like you, Derek, in much the same ways that I used to! No, the difference has more to do with me. Or, put another way, I'm not exactly the same person I was a month ago. From my point of view, I'm not a better person, or a worse person, but perhaps a more self-confident person than I was.

Here's an example: I have tried to imagine, from your point of view, why you want to visit down here. Because you enjoy *being with me? I doubt it, though I think you do enjoy being with me! But,...I doubt that that's the <u>reason</u>. Understand? Hmm, I guess it is a little complex. Perhaps this will help: Here are what I think your reasons may be — a free place to sleep close to San Jose (and thus cut down on driving); a free place to do laundry; a place full of free food (dinner, breakfast, lunch); and a place with good (sometimes even great!) sex. I can't think of any others.*

Please, understand that I don't think badly of you, or dislike you, or anything like that. I just need more from my sex life.

Understand? I hope so, my friend. And, who knows? Maybe some day we'll be more to each other than a good lay!

Anyway, I've gone on about this long enough. Again, I'd be glad to talk with you about the above if you'd wish, but please, don't feel that you <u>need</u> to, for my sake. I've had my say,... here. So Derek, many thanks for listening, and I hope to be seeing, smelling, and hearing you again soon. In Friendship, Annie

Not surprisingly, such thoughts and feelings on my part ushered in the end of our relationship, if I dare use such a term for the first intimate coupling of my new life. I had tried pretending otherwise, but our attraction could not be characterized as anything but doomed, and any effort on my part to overcome the impending doom was too great to be worth much effort.

Friday 13 Dec.1985: Hello there, Derek journal! Long time no see! Needless to say, that's because I haven't seen Derek in a long time, for various reasons. We were supposed to get together day before yesterday, but there seems to have been a mix-up. Where to begin? Well, perhaps I should start by referring you to the letter which I wrote to Derek yesterday (and today), since I gave it to him very soon after he arrived today, and it had a big impact upon our time together, and, my guess is, our time together from now on...

Put simply, he was furious. We talked a bit about it, and it became clear to me that he doesn't read very well, because he missed some of the basic things I was saying. He got all the things he considered criticism of him though...We talked some about my lecture which he missed, according to him because he thought he'd be bored. He made some phone calls, including to his roommate, Sophie. He wanted to come with me to the party I was going to, and I said no, telling him I didn't think he'd enjoy a party filled with classicists, but feeling that I'd rather be more available to other men.

Monday 16 Dec. 1985: Let me stick to facts. Derek and I went to see Rocky IV. He arrived, ate a bit (juice, bread, an apple), used the bathroom, and we left for the movie. The timing was just perfect for a non-sex time together, because there was no time for him to get bored.

We didn't talk at all in the car. He paid my way in. I bought us popcorn and coke. When the movie was over, we had to leave in a hurry, so he'd make it to pick up his roommate Sophie at the right time. He asked me while getting into the car if that (watching the movie) was more fun than having sex. I couldn't answer. I asked him what his favorite parts of the movie were, and he said the beginning (with Apollo Creed) and the flashbacks to earlier Rocky movies. He said that it was a really inspiring movie, and that he was very in need of that these days. "There's always one more round" he quoted to me from the movie. I said he must have enjoyed Rocky's statement to his wife (Adrian), while on the stairs of their home, that he was striving for more than a big house, nice cars, lots of money, etc. Derek said No, those were what he (Derek) was striving for, and then he changed it to "freedom," presumably meaning freedom from poverty.

Finally, while dropping me off at the condo, he said he thought there was a lot more to him than I had described in

255

my letter to him (like his kindness), and he complained that I didn't correct Julia in her assumption that he was a good fuck and no more. Then, before I got out, he asked me if we could get together for sex on Wednesday. I said no, I was busy, and he said he'd call me next week. The end.

11:30pm: Aargh. I was just going to read the newspaper review of Rocky IV which was in yesterday's paper, and it's gone! Alas, I know where it is. Derek has it. I showed it to him before we went to the movie, and mentioned that I didn't like to read reviews until after I had seen the movie. He read it while drinking juice in the kitchen, and apparently took it (4 pages) home with him, without asking. Definitely the end.

One week later, I decided to take the bull by the horns and face my social situation directly, in a head-on kind of way, by taking advantage of the California singles scene. Before moving on to exploring/discovering other men, however, I had to put Derek to rest.

Tuesday 24 Dec. 1985: Well Derek journal, this is my last entry. And it will be short. Derek stopped by for a short visit today, around noon, bringing with him an exact replica of the bottle of champagne I gave to him as a house-warming gift, as a Xmas present for me. We talked a little bit, but mostly it was a very awkward time together, lasting about 30 minutes. He was very uncomfortable, and I doubt that I'll ever hear from him again. And, if I do, I'll encourage him not to bother. It's not worth it. So, diary of sorts, I guess this is good-bye. It's been nice knowing you, and I've really enjoyed our time together. And who knows? Maybe I'll do this again...

Whew! My involvement with Derek was over. And since it was not possible for me to feel love without someone <u>to</u> love, I decided to write a personal classified in order to meet men. What ensued was Annie's Rediscovery of Men, an undertaking which I was determined to explore widely. I had learned not to bother entrusting my undeveloped emotions to just one man.

22 Dec.1985: Today was quite a day! And one not appropriate for some short notes to myself, which have been serving as a kind of diary of sorts over the past 5 months. But they have been aided by other writing I've been doing, like letters, my Derek file, and so on. No more. Well, at least for a while. I'd like to get into writing into a diary of men more regularly, and today seems like a good time to start. Hell, if I didn't write about them, in a fuller framework, I'd never understand my notes to myself a few days from now, much less the distant future!

I had met one man a few months earlier, after deciding to respond to an intriguing personal ad in the newspaper with a letter — a letter which, as always, took me quite a long time to write.

Dear Possible Friend,

Where to begin? Well, as a recent returnee to California, I've been reading things I used to avoid, and your personal classified struck my attention. If you've found your perfect woman friend, feel free to ignore my letter, but if you're still interested, feel free to read on and perhaps make contact with me. But please, don't feel any obligation. Let me tell you a little about myself, since I know a bit about you.

I'm a SWF, fairly tall (5'6"), slightly athletic, finishing a PhD at Stanford (I'm writing the dissertation), very presentable (some would say beautiful), a young-looking 33 yr. old (people guess much younger), quite well traveled (though I've been returning to much the same places for summers for the past 5 years), gregarious to the point of having too many friends, lover of the outdoors (especially hiking and camping in out-of-the-way forests and sunning at uncrowded beaches), strong sense of humor, very honest and cheerful, non-smoker, not very "grown-up" (and probably never will be), lover of dancing, no children yet (but looking forward to probably having one some day), and so far a

successful professional (though still early in my career).
Whew!

As a recent returnee to California (2 months ago), I don't
know many men around here (Palo Alto), and am looking
forward to meeting some, but am not interested in trying the
bar scene. I seek romance (of either the brief or long-term
kind), adventure, and excitement, with a self-satisfied single
man who knows that he's not entirely perfect but thinks he
comes pretty close, and wants to share it with someone. Sound
interesting? If so, here's my phone number: 415-321-2045,
and ask for Annie.

Hope to hear from you, nameless, and meet you. Again,
I've really enjoyed reading your ad. If nothing else, I've
gotten great pleasure out of that, as well as writing this letter.
It sure beats writing a dissertation!

Stay Well and Take Care.

Your possible friend, Annie

During my year in California, I repeatedly used that letter, slightly re-
written, and received a reasonable number of responses. Dating men
began in earnest in December, when I slightly re-wrote my personal
ad response letter and began to send it out to whatever personal ads
impressed me, with a variety of results. I pursued a life I could not yet
live, and a love I could not yet feel. Instead of describing the
intricacies of each affiliation, I wrote rather brief summaries, not to

keep track of the relationship, but as memory-joggers, to assist me in case of repeated contact.

I had to keep records of absolutely everything. Not just their names and phone numbers, but how they appeared, <u>exactly</u> where and when we met, what they liked and disliked, etc. Otherwise? I would never have remembered. Below are 4 examples.

1) <u>Karl</u>: Met Mar. 14 when I went to Stanford Hillel for the first time ever. Hm. Not great, and I'm not sure if I'll ever go again, given how little I know about Judaism, but it was interesting to see how little I do know, and how dedicated other people are. And I did meet a few guys. In fact, I ended up spending the rest of the evening with Karl at Bechtel, drinking Cafe Mocha and listening to a great guitarist, who looked very familiar, but I can't remember where I've met him before. Karl? Well, he's very Jewish, very taken with me, a lawyer, and very research oriented, but not with law as much as with what he was involved with for years before practicing law: "risk," meaning health-related chemicals. He stopped by the dept. a couple of times to try and see me. First date: movie Hannah and her Sisters. Very Jewish, loves talking on the phone. Called Apr.4 and he talked for > 1 1/2 hours. Called again June 10 and talked to me for a long time again. Hopefully for the last time.

2) <u>Gary</u>: *Called Apr.11, A 4th generation Californian. Works as a contractor, on own house and others. Bicyclist. Wanted to become an Egyptologist. Has 2 small children of whom he has partial custody by his ex-wife, who left him. We met Apr.14, at coffee shop next to St. Michael's Alley. Has brown curly hair, glasses, rugged looking, according to him not very handsome. Went out to dinner at the Good Earth. Health food lover. Is a yacht hand sometimes. Has at least 2 other women in his life: one teaches jazzercise and one works as GTE engineer. Leftist politics (anti-Reagan). Went to Vietnam in the Navy intelligence. Active in the Beyond War anti-war group. Drives a baby blue pick-up truck. Is afraid of computers.*

Tues. Apr.15: Wow! (Almost no sleep last night with Gary, but it was worth it...) Actually, I spent much of the day thinking more about last night with Gary. Incredible, to feel so much for a man. And it makes me think less of Horoscopes, since it had nothing to say about such a possibility. First time in a long time I've felt that way; long before the accident, to be sure...He called Apr.25 and came over for ca.2 hrs, but no go.

3) <u>Jake</u>: *Called the number early in morning on May 2, he called me long-distance from NY for our first talk May 4. He buys and sells money around the country, has 7 yr. old*

daughter, considers himself an ex-chubby Capitalist Republican, loves bicycling long distances, spoke last week at Berkeley grad. business school, keeps on Cal. time while traveling around the country, coming to California this weekend and wants to meet me. We never met.

4) Joe: He's British, 27, slightly bald, a marathon runner, PhD in physics (took him 3 years in England). Works with semi-conductors. Earns about 3x as much as he would in England. Considers himself right-wing, loves to travel, argue about politics, have dinner parties. Met at a party in his apt. Apr.20, had a date Apr.24, went to dinner at the British Bankers Club. Spent day and evening Apr.27 together, including a beautiful drive. He has no short-term problem with the age difference, but does for any long-term relationship. Left a note at door Thursday morning (May 1) asking me out for a date Sat. Called him in the evening to tell him I already had one, then went over to his apartment for a short chat. Strange to me that we have such good rapport, given how different we are. Missed me while I was in the east, so he called me in Ohio and Boston. Keeps calling me from time to time in Ohio.

I met plenty of men that year — about 3 dozen, of considerably varying ages, religions, backgrounds, habits, and so on. I had sex with a few, which ranged from empty to wonderful. No true conversation would occur with some, and at other times I was aware of a significant improvement in both my linguistic and social skills. No one could have suspected that I was as ignorant at understanding the intricacies, the subtle permutations of social interaction, as I was. I did not even recognize the most basic social rules and cues. I had no appreciation of propriety, and thus of impropriety. It never occurred to me to believe some things said, and to completely dismiss others as fabrications. Often an important aspect of a social situation eluded me, with the result that I was faced with (and then had to deal with) unforeseen outcomes to situations. My Mother, in particular, tried to impress upon me the need for me to re-learn how to imagine circumstances with which I might need to reckon. I eventually became accustomed to visualizing future possibilities in general, but it took me even longer to envision social behaviors in particular. That skill did not come back easily. There were too many gaps and the gaps were too large. I did try to comprehend my emotional chasm and even began to interpret my venture into the world of a single woman dating, speculating about my socio-sexual recovery.

Sun. Jan.12: Day full of thoughts about meeting men: I've always fallen in love with men, and gone on with my life from there. And recently, I've been dating for much the same reason: to find a man to fall in love with. But now it occurs to me, that I'm really enjoying meeting and interacting with

different men, and I'm enjoying not falling in love with them!
Hmm. In other words, I wonder if I'm not becoming more my
own person...Not that I'm opposed to falling in love. It just
doesn't seem as necessary as it used to. Men can be more fun
in small doses than in large doses I think.

My enjoyment of the process of just meeting men, rather than looking for a man to fall in love with, got a bit out of hand for a few months. In the process, I became increasingly aware of my personal emptiness. Not scary or terrifying, that emptiness became, however, another problem to solve. Forging a bond with any of these men would have required me to have a fully-developed psyche, a soul as it were, with which to experience deep feelings. It just wasn't there.

My social canyon was similar to an observation I have often made when watching American-made movies, especially comedies, in foreign countries. I find myself laughing long before most of the audience finishes reading the subtitles. In much the same way, I often awoke the morning after a date realizing a social cue I had missed, as well as an appropriate response, had I recognized the signal at the time. I kept trying to catch moments of social significance, but with little success. I even tried applying the "I think I can" line from my favorite childhood book, The Little Engine That Could, but to no avail. It didn't seem to work at socializing, in spite of the overwhelming quantity of hills (i.e. men) I tried to get my social train's engine to climb.

I had eased myself out of the frying pan of being newly single (Oct. 24 - Jan. 12), only to be thrown into the fire of the singles dating scene (Feb. 6 - May 4), and things got <u>out of hand.</u> I had received numerous responses to my social overtures, and yet did not feel, as a result, that I had socially developed substantially at all. I recall a (book? movie?) review I once read in which a character was criticized for their inability to convey more than one emotion at a time. That was me, if even that! Which is odd, since I also recall how social situations during my recovery could simultaneously feel both scary and insignificant, at exactly the same moment. What I could not do was to feel anything very deeply or in any complicated way.

In that regard, it's worth noting how I answered two social life questions on a Social Security questionnaire (April 1986).

> 10. What things do you do with your time during the day? h) Do you participate in any evening social activities (parties, going out to dinner, movies, going to bars, etc.)?
>
> *I do go out to dinner sometimes with men I've met through singles activities. I have not been to any real parties since the accident (except parties for me) and I*

have only been taken to a bar for dancing, since I do not drink much alcohol anymore.

i) Do you visit with friends or relatives or have them visit you? (If so, how often?)

Not very often now. Early in my recovery, they used to invite me over to visit them, but then seemed to get uncomfortable, and since I did not want to impose upon them, I have pretty much stopped inviting them over to visit me. Now, I am trying to make new friends, who do not know about the accident.

I was apparently remarkably lacking in some basic social skills, which may have been due to the lesion having occurred in my right hemisphere. I was perceived by others as being emotionally somewhat flat, and I often misinterpreted facial expressions, gestures and body language in general. While not exactly language skills, these behaviors are necessary prerequisites for successful social interaction such as, well, love.

―――――――――――

"The language of socialization, courtship, and love is often unspoken, hinted at, and embellished by gestures, facial expressions, and body language that may neither be expressed nor perceived by the individual with these deficits. Language may be misinterpreted. For example, "I feel like retiring," said with a come-hither smile might be answered, "Well, goodnight," thus missing the gentle cue for lovemaking." (Griffith and Lemberg, p.46)

═══════════════════

Engaging in both teamwork and relationships is quite difficult if one is misinterpreting the facial expressions and gestures which comprise so much of communication and social interaction. (For more information on the significance of right hemisphere brain injury on social behavior, see Appendix 1.)

My conclusions regarding the California phase of my new life? I tried to sum up my socio-sexual rebirth in May 1986, a year following the accident, when I felt it was almost complete.

> *Hm. Well, this part of the file is not really about sex. It's about men, which I suppose is at least partly about sex...Actually, though, it's an attempt on my part, now that the year is almost over, to summarize my re-entry into the singles dating scene. First, some general observations:*
>
> *1. Most of the men have something they're hiding, usually something "wrong" (from their point of view) with them:*

alcoholic, mentally retarded or blind, for example, but it goes farther than that. Some, for example, are not willing to tell you the positive things at first either, like wealth, education, etc., for fear that you will be attracted to them for the wrong reasons.

2. *The ones most attracted to me I was not attracted to, and vice versa. Odd.*

3. *Age has very little to do with numerical age. Joe is old for his age. Greg is young for his. My turning out to be older than I look did seem to put off 2, though not as friends, and some of the younger men seemed to really like it.*

4. *Many sexual firsts for me: First time single, my first virgin, first uncircumcised, first Jew, first non-driver.*

All in all, based on my reading on victims of aphasia, I'd say that my social healing, though somewhat odd in form, was remarkably typical in content. It began with my awareness of the difference from my pre-accident existence, and developed to recognizing my need for some behavior modification, to be considered normal. Perhaps most similar to many aphasia survivors from traumatic head injuries was my enormous egocentricity. The most excessive aspect was my emotionalism, especially my fits of severe depression, with uncontrollable and prolonged tears.

Finally, neither as obvious nor as easy to describe their ramifications on my personality, I experienced real difficulty with concepts and decisions. I could deal with simple facts, events and questions as concretely as they appeared to me, by listing them, memorizing them, describing them, etc. Not perceiving abstract ideas, however, I encountered true obstacles when faced with intricate thoughts, complicated feelings, or subtle situations. My engaging in critical thinking or value judgments was out of the question, which certainly hampered my social recovery.

* * *

In many ways, my year while recovering from the accident in California should not be considered as my being single, as I was not yet entirely me, but a creature still in a state of formation. The next year, back to work in Ohio and living alone for the first time in my life, was my true new self being single, and yet a very abnormal time for me. I had originally considered my year in California as a transitional phase, before I was able to go home — to Ohio, to Kenyon, to my job, my friends, my life. It didn't turn out that way.

Socially speaking, for example, that first year back at work in Ohio was often very lonely and very sad — a combination resulting from my being very busy, getting re-acquainted with working and teaching for a living, and my crying over what I will call my socio-emotional depression. That depression was in large part due to the difference in men in Ohio from those I had met while in California. Also, I apparently continued to appear either completely lacking, or overflowing, with feelings, as I attempted to leap the emotional chasm which seemed to lay between us.

Early in my return to Ohio I continued to be plagued by social questions:

Sun. June 22: Listened to a "Sex Call-In Show" on the radio, toward the end [of the show], which brought the following question to my mind: When, if ever, does my dating game turn into my mating game?

Mon. June 30: ...Ah, the airport: why are there so many couples of older men and younger women, given the mortality ages (men first) and the age of a male not ever a problem for fathering a child? Do women perhaps need fathers more than men need mothers?

What I found, that first year back at work in Ohio, was that I achieved a certain amount of satisfaction in concealing considerable internal intellectual and emotional disorientation with a calm and casual exterior manner. Such a personality was quite a change from my pre-accident days, when I had been known as a very outgoing person. Now, I became slightly shy. Such was not my nature, but it pervaded my whole life. So much so that I was not 100% outgoing even with my family.

I always felt I had to be careful not to give myself away, not to let others recognize how frequently I was confused — especially regarding appropriate social behavior. I suppose my socio-sexual recovery would not have been so troublesome once back to work in Ohio had I been surrounded by some family. But as it was, and I assured people that I wanted to make it on my own, I had to admit that I mostly felt very alone, and very depressed, for quite some time…

Chapter 6: Starting a New Life

"Know Thyself"

- γνῶϑι σ'αυτόν, Gnothi se auton, Socrates' motto, the admonition he ascribed to the god Apollo at Delphi (by others to Thales and Pythagoras), inscribed on the Temple of Apollo at Delphi. See Plato <u>Alcibiades</u> 129a and <u>Charmides</u> 164d-165b; Xenophon <u>Mem.</u> 4, 2, 24

"Non sum qualis eram!" (I'm not what I used to be)
- Horace <u>Odes</u> IV,1,3

In the end, though my doctors had said my complete recovery would take a year and ½, it took 9 months in California, after my first 3 months in Virginia, i.e. 12 months in all, for my doctors to approve my return to work. I returned to Kenyon, where my previous teaching position no longer existed, to find a job, as no reconnection with academia, no matter how tenuous, would have been unbearable.

Sat. May 31: ...Got two job offers! Assistant Director of Admissions, by phone at Robert's ca. 1pm & teaching for IPHS at the Ransom Hall reception for the new chaplain at ca.4:30pm by Reed Browning (new Provost).

Luckily, I was able to choose between the full-time staff position in Admissions, and the two-year part-time teaching position in an Interdisciplinary Program in Humane Studies (IPHS, a type of Great Books Program), which I accepted. It made sense that my illness was finally coming to an end.

Sat. July 19: ...a fascinating day: from my point of view, my first day of the next part of my life...People in town don't treat me so special any more, which is nice in a way, but a little bit boring too...

After all, prior to this accident, I had never lived a particularly turbulent life. The late 60s had been for High School, the early 70s for college, the late 70s for graduate school and the early 80s for launching my career, learning how to teach, taking life for granted, and engaging in very ordinary, healthy, authentic activities. I knew nothing else. Such was life. Or so I supposed, having always assumed that my life would proceed along fairly satisfactory and evenhanded stages of life, with the variety of joys and crises, wins and losses.

And I know this might sound strange, but though most people considered my accident my misfortune, I had so far refused to approach it as a life-altering transformation. Beginning in September of 1986 I came to realize that it was. After all, I had been abruptly disconnected from life as I knew it — a life for which I had been promised a happy ending, like movies in the good 'ole days.

So I buckled down to the start of my new life, the way it now was. I had to get used to it and deal with it. I was determined (some would say obstinate) not to remain a poor helpless invalid leading a life of private desperation, but it quickly became apparent to me that my return to work was only on probation. After all, I had not suffered a disease, from which I had finally recovered, but rather I had a condition, and conditions do not just go away.

Life has a way of surprising you, when you least expect it. When I felt I was finally returning to being considered normal, I realized I had not completely recovered, was not all better, or that I necessarily would ever be. My life had definitely changed, and rather dramatically.

Mon. Sept. 1: Wow! First day teaching again! It was hard, and I wasn't quite as <u>good</u> as I used to be, but not too *bad...Mostly, I think it wasn't as well organized as it should have been. Better next time! It's strange not having done it for over a year...*

Wed. Sept. 3: Not such a great lecture of mine today. I need to spend more time preparing.

Fri. Sept. 5: Much better lecture! And it should have been, given how long it took me to put together! I was up preparing it for most of the night.

Come to think of it, my readjustment to my new life was similar to the loss of my Georgia accent when my family moved from Augusta Georgia to Northern Virginia when I was 9. I opened my mouth on the first day of school and everyone laughed. I shut my mouth and wouldn't open it for about a month, which I spent listening to the radio, trying to speak English without an accent. I didn't ever have to go through that again. More than a linguistic tone shift had occurred. I gradually ceased to be a Georgia peach and people no longer stared at me, or laughed at me when I spoke, but considered me normal, as if I belonged in Northern Virginia. In much the same way, my re-entry into the workforce consisted of more than me becoming reemployed.

About a week after returning to work, I took aside a close colleague, looked him straight in the face, and asked him:

"So, have I changed very much?"

With a huge grin on his face, he chuckled slightly and replied,

"You're the same, only worse."

"The same? Worse?"

"Harrianne," he explained, "you've always been fairly cheerful, friendly, and easy-to-get-along-with. Now? You're worse."

It's true that when interacting with people, I never did stop smiling.

I guess that's what happens when you almost die.

═══════════════════════════════════════

"It has been said that aphasics act as they did before their CVA [cerebrovascular accident; stroke], only more so. It seems as if personality characteristics of the person are often exaggerated." (Libby Kumin, Aphasia, p.16)

═══════════════════════════════════════

In re-encountering work, and the daily interaction with people, I discovered that the process of meeting or even just greeting someone was remarkably similar from encounter to encounter. Running into people already known, for example, invariably resulted in their asking me, "How are you?" which I proceeded to answer.

"Oh, not too bad, though I've been having a difficult time lately with my…"

I always tried to completely answer their questions as best I could, not realizing that their rhetorical question required no reply, but was merely a social convention. They expected an exchange of formalized greetings, and nothing more. I never did become accustomed to decorative conversations, and I never developed an automatic response. In fact, it took me years not to answer "How are you?" fully, but to adopt the veneer and automatically reply with, "I'm fine. How about you?"

Social formalities are about the slowest to recover.

In an attempt to ameliorate, if not overcome, my inability to socialize by engaging in small talk, I tried to develop a series of automatic responses which could be applied in various situations. Of course I had to remember to use them. I tried not to converse about my accident and recovery following the typical "How are you?". My best developed response, due to its frequent use, concerned my name.

"Harrianne?" people would often ask upon first meeting. "What an unusual name!"

"Very," I would reply at that time, "since I'm the only one! Honest. I'm in the Guinness Book of Names."

> *Wed. May 7: ...Fascinating letter from the Guinness Book of Names: it seems they can't find any other Harriannes!*

Sometimes, the conversation would continue.

"Where did you get it? How did your parents think up such a name?"

At first, my favorite reply was "I came out the wrong sex." As time passed, I explained that I had been called Harry for 9 months before being born, and had just barely avoided becoming a Harriet due to the fortuitous birth of a cousin a few months earlier. I became rather comfortable with this conversation, to the point that I would encourage it, by pronouncing my name as clearly and succinctly as possible, knowing that people would tend to assume they had mis-heard the name Marianne. If I clearly pronounced Harrianne, the chances increased significantly that a rather familiar conversation would ensue — and one therefore not as exhausting as being asked yet another new question for which I was not prepared, like "Some weather we've been having, eh?"

I never did manage to chat easily about the weather.

More often than not, conversations upon meeting someone for the first time tended to fall into predictable patterns, such as: Where are you from? What do you do? Do you like it here? and so on. Over time I developed quite an array of explanations of what I did for a living.

"I teach Classics" was rarely appropriate to the audience, for whom the word Classic meant everything from Shakespeare to a type of Coca Cola, but rarely having anything to do with Ancient Greece and Rome.

Instead, my default reply was most often "Ancient Stuff, like Caesar and Socrates."

Then, if their response went beyond the "Oh, how interesting." as far as "Really?" I would continue with "You know, Ancient Greek, Latin, Ancient Greek and Roman History, Archaeology. Stuff like that."

Such a prolonged interchange rarely occurred, due no doubt to people's inclination to avoid sounding dumb on subjects of which they are ignorant. I do recall being amazed by how infrequently anyone ever asked me a probing question, such as "How did you choose that subject?"

I was only rarely asked that question, and my answer was, as usual, much too long-winded. It was so nice to be asked, to be able to reply, and even to remember my distant past!

"Well," I would say, "There I was, a first-year student in college, determined to major in history, when I asked the professor after the first class how it happened that the historical situation got that way – how it came to the point at which the course began." After being told it was a good question, I was encouraged to take an earlier History class, which I did. That same question and reply occurred on the first day's class on the Renaissance, and then on the Middle Ages. So I took Ancient Greek History, where I felt I ran into a wall from which I could proceed forward through the centuries again. No such luck of course. I got trapped, becoming more and more intrigued by the amazing world of Ancient Greece. That attraction developed into an obsession when I even began to study Ancient Greek, having always excelled at learning modern languages.

"Give me two weeks and I'll learn a new language," I used to say.

Languages had been remarkably easy for me to acquire, even those with a different alphabet, such as Russian. By my final year of college I was almost fluent in French and Russian, having studied them (instead of study-hall) in High School and continued them both in College, so having spoken them for 8 and 6 years, respectively. And given my intention to attend graduate school in Ancient History and my facility with languages, I convinced a Philosophy professor at my college (it no longer exists) to tutor me in Ancient Greek, as Windham College did not offer Ancient Greek.

Boy oh boy, was <u>that</u> a surprise!

I had never realized, or been told, that my ease with modern languages was due to my having a good ear – something no doubt also responsible for my ability to play the piano at a young age. My attempt to learn the Ancient Greek language solely from a book was an utter disaster, even though, being my third language, I had acquired a reasonable sophisticated understanding of grammar and syntax. Nevertheless, I positively drowned, and did not really learn the language, though I did manage to pass the course. As a result, my first year of graduate school was quite an adventure — not only due to my attempt to survive intermediate Ancient Greek, but as a result of all 3 languages (Ancient Greek, Latin and German) I was required to take that year, as well as History classes.

Let me explain.

My first 2 years of graduate school were spent in the Cornell University History Department, where I had been accepted while the residing Ancient Historian was on sabbatical. He was clearly not pleased with my acceptance, and his disapproval became abundantly clear when I asked him, as my faculty advisor, what courses I should take.

"How's your Greek?"

"Not very good."

"Take Greek. How's your Latin?"

"Non-existent."

"Take Latin. How's your German?"

"Non-existent."

"Take German. Now, what courses shall we have you take?"

"What courses? You've just told me to register for three!"

"Ah, yes, but those don't count. You should have learned those languages before attempting to do graduate work in Ancient History. It's not my fault you aren't sufficiently prepared. They should never have accepted you. You don't need the credit in those languages for a graduate degree in Ancient History, just the skill, and those 3 classes don't count toward an eventual degree."

I almost died. I took 2 History courses in addition to the 3 languages and slept very little. I learned a great deal and survived my trial by fire, no doubt to his surprise.

Such was my first year of graduate school — an excellent example of my character prior to the accident — a strong, self-assured academic, an assertive hard worker and researcher, very comfortable with languages and various forms of communication, but especially reading, writing, and public speaking.

The contrast with this, my condition at the close of my year of recuperation from aphasia exactly 12 years later, was extraordinary.

I could still communicate by means of the spoken word fairly well, though I often had to engage in short-cuts in order to find (i.e. remember) a word. I became amazingly adept at engaging in an expeditious internal dialogue, in which I used opposites as a short-cut to recall words in the enormous grey area between the two opposites. I would engage in free-association using opposites.

Easy, difficult, light, heavy, adept, inept, awkward, graceful, competent, incompetent — cumbersome! (the word I was searching).

Or, finding myself unable one day to recall the term for a dental procedure, and being nowhere near a thesaurus, I first tried searching for words beginning with the letter f, thinking that was the consonant with which the word began. False teeth? Fillings? (I thought to myself) No, that didn't work. Then I fabricated an internal conversation with both positive and negative (again, opposites), between a parent and a teenager.

"We'll have to get you..."

"Do I really have to get...?"

That technique didn't work this time either. I quickly gave up trying to recall the word I was seeking, and resorted instead to a description of the dental work, instead of the missing word. My first thought when I woke up the next morning was: braces!

This search method allowed me to overcome (bypass really) the linguistic roadblocks of my aphasia. I even developed a fantasy in which I compressed the impediment so thin that I could pass through the almost transparent obstruction to instantaneously find the desired word among the morass of alternatives.

My writing had not reached that point. By the start of my first year back at work, I remained incapable of expressing myself easily or very well in writing, though it became gradually less painful, and certainly no longer disabling. One large difference worthy of note: hearing the vocabulary of a topic under discussion by others would often awaken more words which would prompt memories of other words, and so on. Eventually I could try to join in the conversation, hopefully still in progress, and not having moved on to another topic.

That gradual and progressive sequence never happened that year in my writing. Just as I could not stimulate a thought to then utter all by myself, so putting a pen in hand would not generate even a phrase, much less a sentence. Still, my increasing facility with my restrictions confirmed my suspicion that I had mostly returned to my regular mode of existence. I wondered from time to time if there were nuances which might still improve over time, but I knew not to <u>expect</u> them.

There were also some drawbacks to my return to being normal. With the beneficial loss of total confusion, I was also deprived of the vague free-associations of my dreamy state of mind. My private world of mental imaginings was no longer out of sync with my experiential world.

Emotionally? Well, at the start of my first year of once again working I would sometimes wake up crying in the middle of the night, feeling as if the good things in my life had faded away and gotten lost. It interrupted my sleep. Almost nothing intensified or altered my mood when awake. Nothing seemed very good or bad and I was neither very happy nor very sad. Likewise, most of the time I couldn't comprehend, and so be traumatized by, the horrors of life, even when watching the news.

When tears while being awake did finally come, with them arose a kind of demonic excitement, for which no resolution seemed possible, since it wasn't the result of anything in particular. When that violent anger erupted, I could suppress nothing, not weeping quietly, but sobbing fully, and at the slightest provocation. I was just angry and sad, at the same time, with an abundance of tears. And I recall feeling very helpless.

The intensity of my feelings took me by surprise. Something seemed to be working its way upward, starting in my guts and ending up in my tear ducts. Those feelings were heavy, scary and almost disgusting. Perhaps due to the newness of such high-powered feelings, I was inclined to be dead serious about everything, both work and play.

And none of these feelings assisted me in my continuing discomfort when socializing. For while I had never in my life been particularly popular, I had also never been completely unaccepted, or out of it. And though I had sometimes been known not to notice life's details, I had become much worse. I frequently missed jokes, slang, puns, references to movies, and other commonsense asides.

One thing surprised me, as I completed my year of recovery and started returning to ordinary life: I barely sought, or pushed myself, to be accepted as an ordinary, normal person. Not at all really. I still don't, come to think of it. Not that I just sit back and wait for acceptance as "one of us," but pretty close. What seems most important to me? Avoidance of turbulence I guess. Otherwise? I gave myself a great deal of latitude and found I could construct a fairly comfortable reality around myself.

Also, the means by which I constructed words, even sentences, began to approximate my innovativeness with food. I had always combined ingredients other people would never have considered mixing together, and I discovered I could do much the same with my vocabulary. If I couldn't think of the appropriate word, I would create a new one! Usually, such words were simply combinations of English words already in existence, perhaps with a Greek or Latin prefix or suffix.

Some examples: burple (blue and purple), linner (a meal between lunch and dinner), antidominant (opposed to power), exrelatives (ex-husband's family), biethnic (restaurants) and monospirituality (believe in only one religion).

Finally, rather than my attempting to summarize all the ups and downs, pluses and minuses, of my first year back being a part of the workaday world, below are a few extracts from my journal. I have selectively chosen diary entries which should illuminate my recuperation from aphasia during that year, academic year 1986-87.

Sat. Sept. 6: Another "accident" occurrence: I had planned all day on going to see "Out of Africa" before "Jaws," instead of going to the "Evening of the Bizarre" music concert. I went to Rosse, picked up a program, which surprised me, but didn't look at it, choosing instead to have a short conversation with Nadine George who was sitting next to me. Then the lights went down, and it turned out that I had made a mistake, and was at the "Evening of the Bizarre" concert! Aargh. What to do? Well, I sat there & thought about it for a little while, then walked out, looked at my calendar & saw I had the wrong day for "Africa:" it was yesterday & will play again tomorrow. So, here I am, back in my office, "working."

Sun. Sept.7: Evening: went to see "Out of Africa" movie, and was amazed at how much I cried. Why I wonder? Well, I cried at: 1) not being in love, 2) question of name(s), 3) health problems, 4) relations between women and men, 5) watching the landscape of Africa, which is very much like Greece in parts, and 6) free spirited (live for today) versus traditional (commitment) ways of living.

Mon. Sept. 8: Interesting how many mistakes by others I notice now, always thinking that it's my brain at fault. A good example: the pamphlets for my new car (which as yet doesn't have a name). I was told by the salesman that he would put them in the car. They weren't there, so I called him & told him so. He said he'd mail them to me. I waited a week & they didn't come. I called back & he said he couldn't find them. He called me back to say the original owner still had them, and he would get them, and mail them to me. We'll see. I'll believe him when I see them.

Tues. Sept.9
Amazing how many things I do all day! They clearly don't pay me enough...

Wed. Sept.10: Whew! Probably the most fascinating event of the day was my finding the Senate meeting. I was early getting to Lower Dempsey, where the letter said the meeting would be, so I went to the library slide collection. Then I headed over to the meeting, and there was nobody there! Hm. My first thought, as always, was that my brain wasn't working/remembering. Or, maybe I was just early, so I checked again. Then I recalled that over the phone, Bill Klein had told me Weaver, & since I knew the letter had been wrong about the date (it had said "Wednesday Sept.11"), I assumed it was going to be in Weaver. But I found nobody there either! By now I was very late, so I called the English Dept. secretary, and she told me that Senate was meeting in Pierce Lounge! Aargh! Nobody called to let me know...

Sun. Sept. 14: Long full day...Things I learned: I am more Greek than many Greek-Americans; I am more Greek than Jewish; I was born in Japan and reborn in Greece; I am prettier in appearance than I used to be; I was told I should write an autobiography.

Mon. Sept.15: ...Then, in the evening, I became a DJ again! After all these years, it was amazing how quickly it came back to me. Who would have thought? Anyway, it was fun, and it went so fast!

Tues. Sept.16: ...A striking instance of "post-accident" Harrianne in the late afternoon: I wanted to get the card for Gene in the mail today, and had forgotten that his address was only at home, so I stopped off at the post office before 4 (when they close), in order to get the postage right. Then home, got Gene's address, but couldn't remember anything else I needed from home. Heading back into town, I remembered that I also wanted Ben's phone # (also at home), but decided it could wait. Then, when I parked by Timberlake, I also remembered that I had forgotten to mail the card (mail goes out at 4:30)! I drove back home for the phone #, and planned to mail the card on the way back. But I forgot to do it again, until I was past the post office! So, I drove around the block, and mailed it. Aargh! What an experience!

Thurs. Sept.18: Another interesting "post-accident" experience this morning: dealing with Ohio Workers' Comp. over the phone. I received a letter which told me, if I had questions, to call Mansfield. I thought I knew better, so I called OWC in Columbus. They said they didn't handle questions about payments to OWC, and that I should call Mansfield. I did. They had no knowledge of the new status of my claim, and told me to call the Attorney General in Cols. I did. They told me they had no file for me yet (since I didn't not pay up yet) and that I should call OWC in Columbus! That was where I had started! But this time, I knew the right words to use, and I had success!

Wed. Sept. 24: Some general comments about this phase of my recovery: it's harder than I thought it would be...Bad memory is the worst, but things also take me a long time.

Mon. Sept. 29: Unusual morning, both because of the way I feel, and because of the way people seem to be treating me. Until now, they have tended to say, in passing, "hello," and pass by. This morning, everybody seemed to say, "How are you?" Odd...Got a wonderful letter from Spiros and Elizavet Marinos, which moved me to tears.

Tues. Oct. 7: Whew! A busy but a very yucky day, oddly enough. Why so yucky? Well, I think part of it was my brain not working as fast as Lenny Gordon talks. Also, he is talking about things (the Hebrew Bible) I know nothing about. Most of the rest of the day I just felt overworked and alone. Oh, I know lots of people, but, as I realized in trying to come up with somebody to change cars with next weekend (for Mom, Nancy & Jessie's visit), I'm not very close friends with any of them.

When I mention my need, many offer, but I don't feel inclined toward them...In other words, I don't have a good friend I feel right about depending on, or leaning on. And not just about the car. I wish there was somebody I could just talk to when I'm feeling low, feeling blue, feeling unneeded, etc. Robert (Bennett) comes about the closest. But who can I talk to about job and career decisions? Only you, computer...Hm. I guess this is a sign of me having my period.

Fri. Oct.11: The biggest event of the day came during my drive to the Bergamo Center in Dayton for the GLCA Women's Studies Conference. During the drive, I was amazed and astounded by my self-doubt and others' incompetence. Put simply: I tried to follow the directions which had been xeroxed for me. Not only are they slightly wrong and out of date, but they are impossible to follow after dark. Also, I have to learn to stop trusting things in print, and even what people say. I did fine to Dayton, and then, trusting Martin's directions about a new "quick" way, I took a just finished interstate, got off & turned right where he told me, but I should have turned left. Robert went the same way, but turned off when he saw a sign for the next street mentioned in the directions. I saw the same sign, but thought the directions were right. I drove a while and still didn't find the first road, so I asked somebody at a gas station. They turned me around, I found that road, but I couldn't find the next one, because the street signs aren't lit at night. I asked again & found it – "it" being the right block, but I couldn't find it (the center)! No signs and, since I didn't know what kind of structure I was looking for (tall? small? spread out?), I gave up and decided to call the phone number on the map. But, given the hour (ca. midnight by then), I got a recording! By then I was ready to kill, but instead I asked again (this time at a fast food place) and was told that the street names had been changed! It turned out that I was looking on the wrong street. Aaargh. By the time I found the center with the conference, I had missed the Halloween Party...

Thurs. Dec.18: ...The most fascinating part of the conversation, from my point of view, was my answer to a question about how I got into the study of ancient history. In going through the story, I made the connection between my love of the archaic period (the historical period of the birth of the mind) and teaching college (the human period of the birth of the mind). I didn't mention, but I thought of the connection with the accident too: the rebirth of my mind. Interesting, to say the least.

Fri. Mar. 13: Interesting thought today: After the accident, I felt so dependent on others that I promised myself that I'd never feel that way again. Result? I have become more independent than ever.

Sun. June 21: Saw the movie "Breakfast at Tiffany's," during which I shocked myself by crying twice: first when she said she wasn't her old name anymore, and again when she said she wasn't either her old name (Harrianne?) or hew new name (Annie?)...

Mon. June 22: ...I think I'm a bit eccentric in that I'm more devoted to comfort than elegance. Also, not teaching Classics, I feel like a missionary without a crusade.

THE PRESENT

All of which brings me to the present. It had been a long, slow, at times problematic, nine months in California, even by Midwest standards. A year since the accident when I went back to work. Eight years before I wrote most of this book. Eighteen years before I finally edited it for publication.

I still cannot recall names, which bothers me, though I am still excellent at recalling numbers.

I couldn't walk or talk with as much ease and facility, and stumbled frequently, until about 7 years after the accident, when I found myself alone in Greece, and decided to consciously work on my balance. I concentrated, regularly, on how and where I was walking. Instead of engaging in other activities (reading signs, looking at people, making decisions on what to do next, etc.), I actually focused just on walking, for two months. The results were remarkable, and I rarely bump into things any more.

My difficulty with language at present is easily apparent, at least to me. Right now, for example, in writing this book. Without the vocabulary readily at hand, the ideas can't germinate or flow. It's as if my mind is asleep, by default, unless I wake it up, which I often do, by reading.

I understand the words when I read them. I may even use one or two if I write or converse soon after reading. But if I want to employ the 'new' (i.e. newly-reminded) word much later that same day, or the next day? Not only is the <u>word</u> not there, but the concept connected with the word is virtually impossible to arouse. So I learned to write them down, and keep files: file of words, of phrases, of expressions, that I...might want to use? No, of phrases I want to have available for use, since the ideas aren't there without the words to express them. The ideas are there, but they're...well, asleep, dormant, waiting for a transfusion.

I used to be able to sit down and write whatever thoughts were running through my mind. Now? My thoughts seem to require stimulation, some incitement, before they can turn themselves into words. Reading puts me into the writing frame of mind. My thoughts in some sense are always there, but they cannot seem to find their way out. They don't know how to be generated all by themselves, and the way they are, is quite strange.

For example: I wanted to refer to how frequently I needed to check both spellings and definitions in a dictionary, and then one day, while reading a novel, I came upon the phrase "event glamour," which prompted for me the word dictionary-dependent.

I also now find that I tend to think in sentences — not words, not phrases, not paragraphs, but just sentences. Not all of which, like this one, contain a verb. But they do have a capital letter at the beginning, and a period at the end, which makes them seem correct.

APHASIA LEFT-OVERS

Up until about 10 years ago, I was often asked, "Are you OK now?"

Even now, when the subject of my accident and healing comes up, people sometimes say, "Everything certainly seems back to normal!"

I never know quite how to respond.

For a long time, I preferred not be reminded either of my accident or the resulting loose ends of my life. Now I don't mind at all. I sometimes even enjoy entertaining folks with the story. But I have tended to avoid mentioning the clearly (to me at least) aphasic residuals, which seems like a losing proposition. The few times I have tried to explain them, I've noticed people changing their opinion of me.

Residuals? Let me relate a few examples of my leftovers from having aphasia, beginning with a listing of residuals not requiring an explanation.

I sometimes still bump into things. I do not dance as well. My handwriting is less legible. I make more typos. Oddly enough, I now probably write better than I speak. After meeting people with extensive fantasy lives, I realize that I once imagined things, which now I rarely do. And I believe that because I re-learned to speak before I re-learned to listen, I tend to talk more than listen.

In teaching, I came to rely on notes to teach a class — something which I never did in my pre-accident years of teaching, depending instead on my having reviewed the material the day before. I also came to habitually consult dictionaries and the thesaurus. And I do mean routinely! They lived on my dining room table for years, for spellings, meanings and synonyms. So much so that I am still addicted to consulting a thesaurus.

A few years ago, I found myself in a work situation in which a group of employees was engineering something like a…coup, in order to get someone fired. I kept repeating the word coup to myself because I remembered that the word began with a c, but otherwise, nothing. And for the <u>life</u> of me, I seemed incapable of retrieving the word conspiracy. Revolution? Overthrow? Takeover? Engaging in self-talk, there was no sign of the missing word conspiracy, and I was nowhere near a thesaurus. Finally, after about the 20th attempt to retrieve the word conspiracy, I revised my memory jogger to "It starts with 'con' (rather than just the first letter C)." Still, though I have recalled it accurately 10-15 times, I still need the memory-jogger "con" in order to retrieve the word "conspiracy."

Or, regarding the same incident, in conversations with interested parties, I would search for a word which I <u>knew</u> began with the letter B, but in searching my brain, I kept coming up with the incorrect word bribe, instead of blackmail, the correct term for the allegation. In that case, I must have been searching for the wrong second letter, so I even created some self-directed humor about how my replacement of the sound r for the letter l must have been due to my having been born in Japan...

More recently, I was talking with a friend on the phone, during which we agreed to meet for coffee, and I mentioned that I wanted first to do some xeroxing, so it made sense for us to do coffee near Kepler's.

"Why Kepler's?" he asked.

"Because I need to make copies."

"But why at Kepler's?"

"I told you." I said. "I need to do some xeroxing."

"At Kepler's?"

"Yea, sure!" (Note: Having re-heard the word 3 times, I still did not realize my mistake.)

"Oh," he said. "You must mean Kinko's."

"Oops. Yea. Sorry."

I have noticed that when I make such errors in speaking, I normally catch them. But not when the first letter is either exactly the same consonant or sounds the same, such as ph and f. In that case, I never do…

One of the strangest realizations I have experienced while writing this book, is how much better I wrote during my aphasia! When I was incapable of speaking a coherent sentence, I wrote fairly well. When my spoken English returned, my ability to write decent first drafts declined, as if the editing process used to occur in my head, instead of on paper. If so, that may explain why it took me so long to write, and how I now always edit my writing, so no one has ever seen a first draft since the accident. I won't say that I now write quickly, but certainly much faster by comparison!

A few other aphasia residuals are worth noting.

While I had previously been loquacious, sometimes to the point of eloquence, I now speak more simply, clearly, and to the point, always in fear of making a verbal mistake.

While my personality is no longer as passive as immediately following the accident, it took me years to become reasonably active, and I still have not returned to my level of activity prior to the accident. Of course that may be due in part to my acquisition of a television during my recovery – something I very consciously did not previously own, lest I become a couch potato.

SOCIAL SKILLS IN PARTICULAR

Though subtle, changes in my social abilities are among the most meaningful and intimate leftovers of my aphasia.

Having had doubts about many things throughout my life, my looks, intellect, work, creativity, etc., I had <u>never</u> doubted my ability to get along with just about anybody and everybody. This changed, and for a while after the accident I was incapable of holding my own in social situations — no doubt to some extent due to my obsession with myself and disinterest in others. While living in California for 9 months, I would run, hot tub, hang out in the Stanford library, in bookstores, especially used bookstores (my favorite), and I even tried my hand at the singles dating scene, both via bars with dancing and through one personal classified. (see Ch.5) However, my continued efforts as an observer of social interaction notwithstanding, my re-acquisition of social skills was unbelievably slow. It was much like trying to pull a white rabbit out of a hat, because I constantly had to make a conscious effort to improve my ability to socialize, frequently at the most basic level, since I was challenged by the most trivial daily situations. I do not recall such predicaments as a child. And I couldn't say:

"Excuse me. I'm recovering from a head injury and have not yet developed my confidence in interacting with people."

Some examples of my social ineptitude: I never understood why people glared at me for taking so much time to write a personal check in line at a cash register or at the bank. When I encountered someone walking towards me on the sidewalk, I could not figure out which way to move, so as not to bump into each other. I was reasonably compliant and willing to learn the rules of this game, but for a long time everything seemed all wrong, as if I had fallen into a time warp. My attempts at learning how to interact in social situations were not unlike trying teach a small child to lace their shoes or a person with limited sight to thread a needle. Doing it correctly once does not suffice.

Again, perhaps a sequence of negatives would help. I had no sense of propriety, of discretion, and virtually no social graces. I seemed to have lost my awareness of what would surprise, shock, perhaps ever terrify, people. Lacking in the most basic rules of society, I was forced to study people, and not just by reading about them or watching TV.

I had always been a great reader, consuming books as my peers had consumed marijuana. Now, being determined to understand the social proprieties, I wondered if I had read too much during the last 6 months of my healing, when I should have been stockpiling a rudimentary knowledge of ordinary social behaviors. Perhaps I didn't have a sufficiently full storehouse of social skills from which to draw? Presumably that reservoir would have included defense mechanisms, with which to ward off the invectives. At the outset, of course, I had no need of such resources, either because I couldn't recognize disparagement when it appeared, or because there simply <u>was</u> none, which I doubt. After all, I would guess that not everyone likes me.

Scrutinizing my notes and diaries kept during my recovery, I am struck by how very formal and isolated they are. I noted my re-birthdays (21st of each month), with whom I spoke, movies I watched, my period, talks by speakers, cleaning the apartment, and so on. I kept track of events and my activities, but in a very abstract way, and with a great detachment, much as I imagine soldiers speak of the enemy in their journals, keeping some distance from any personal involvement in killing.

Listening to what people were talking about around me, I always felt very formal. Comparing my thoughts to their conversations, I didn't tend to think about daily life kinds of things — neither silly ones like wishing I hadn't bought that expensive purse or hoping it wouldn't rain, nor more substantial ones like wondering about the next election or deciding where to be buried. I kept hoping that my irregularity would simply go away, and that I would be just like them, presumably like I used to be. But there seemed to be no vestiges of my pre-accident personality which were <u>trying</u> to come out. Were they never there, and I just hadn't noticed?

This feeling of abnormality was no doubt responsible for the sensation I frequently experienced that people were smiling at me, in a condescending, smirking kind of way, as if thinking "Poor thing." My Mom, in particular, became locked in to the habit of beginning almost every conversation with "Do you remember...?" Of course being treated like an invalid, I must confess, did excuse my erratic behavior. In general, however, I found that I was more comfortable in the company of recent acquaintances who knew nothing of my condition, rather than family and close long-time friends who, remarkably often, reminded me of my head injury.

"I wonder if you remember..." they would say.

"How are you feeling?" they would ask.

"Wasn't X wonderful to you after your accident?" they would remind me.

Now I can scarcely blame my family for continuing to treat me a bit like an invalid at first. After all, my friends have known me either before or since my head injury. But my family, and especially my Mom, living far from Ohio and whom I visited as an adult only once or twice a year, became most acquainted with me as an adult during my year of recuperation. Such a re-acquaintance is inevitably influenced by the context, and I doubt that I could do anything to change their memory of me during that year. Only time will tell.

As for now? Well, I am able, once again, to hold my own in most social situations. I rarely drown, but I do often flounder, and I have grown to appreciate the company of those more sociable than myself, children and animals.

In moving around the world, I used to feel as though my whole history was discernable.

"Don't they all see how different from them I am?"

Of course they (i.e. ordinary people) don't see any difference, because my sense of abnormality was all inside me, a concealed inner dialogue. And while I am certainly not the only person to have ever experienced such a recovery, I don't personally know anyone else, so I feel very unique. Other people? Oh, people are nice enough. We get along just fine. They just haven't <u>been</u> there.

I can use an expression about myself, for example, but am no longer capable of saying about others, "Have you lost your mind?"

I did lose my mind. Luckily, I found most of it again.

*   *   *

You know the feeling of having lost or forgotten something, but you can't quite remember exactly what it was? Well, while I was mending, I definitely felt as if I had lost some crucial element, and nothing seemed able to take its place, whatever the Hell it was that I had lost.

Looking back over the experience, I have tried (with little, if any, success) to convince people that though I would never have asked for the accident, and certainly would not wish it on anybody, the experience has had some very pleasant, one could say even desirable, repercussions.

"Yea, right." I can hear you say. "Maybe I should consider getting almost killed for a nice summer vacation."

No, but the experience, once it has been forced upon you, can be remarkably...well...liberating. I had been given a challenging new beginning, a chance at giving rebirth to myself. Put in close contact with death and mindlessness opened me up to a wide range of opportunities, in an almost metaphysical way. Like military combat, one acquires a broader perspective when facing death, including the mental death of aphasia. I felt as if I was being handed a road not yet taken both to discover and to explore.

Now on most journeys, the particular route you choose to take is of relatively little importance, as you can reach your destination in many ways. In this case, however, since the route I took would <u>determine</u> the conclusion of my healing, I felt I could not waste or squander any time or efforts along the way.

Previously, as mentioned at the start of this chapter, I had been certain of a vigorous life — one full of its ups and downs, to be sure, but perhaps most of all, I was secure in my conviction that little could endanger this bumpy life of mine, and that if someone or something tried to, that I could meet it head on, and with success. That was no longer the case. As a result, and with no medications or physical therapy, my wrestling with the unknown was remarkably liberating, in that I couldn't be held responsible for having done something <u>wrong</u>, which might have impeded my recovery. Thus, I felt remarkably free about expressing my opinions and preferences. Not only was I protected from responsibilities and obligations, but I also had no real sense of the disconnection. Oddly enough, it is possible to relax completely and live in the moment (though without the normally accompanying pleasure) when you have no sense of what the next moment will be. My character seemed to have changed, and I often felt very weak or very fragile, but not usually very unhappy.

To explain: in looking back over the whole process, I consider it to have been a remarkably liberating experience, in that at the time, and to a certain extent for several years, I didn't have to account for my behavior. After all, I wasn't (literally) myself, and frequently was often not (figuratively) myself.

Put another way: Before the accident, though I had expected to go through many gradual minor changes in my life, I basically thought that I had already turned out a certain way, and that whatever was going to happen to me had, for the most part, already happened. Times would change, people would change, but there was a <u>me</u> inside me who would endure, who would continue to exist, no matter what.

Not that I was averse to change. In fact, I have always tended to seek out alternatives to the norm. But that was before the accident. Now? Well, as my healing process sped up towards the end of that first year, I gradually found myself waking up just about every day to find that I had changed, fairly significantly, since the day before. And I did not appear to be capable of looking ahead, to consider or imagine who and what I was going to become. In thinking back over the ordeal, I do wonder why I never considered myself engaged in an experiment, being tested to see how well I would do? For I was definitely being given the chance for a new existence. Isn't one's personal identity intimately and intricately bound up with...dare I say it?...Fate?

Now, as is common among many (most?) humans, I have always held very inconsistent views of fate and free will. I did <u>not</u> believe I could fashion events according to my wishes (free will) or that the accidence was a happenstance of fate (it was preordained that I would be at the wrong place at the wrong time). But I also believed that I was responsible for fashioning my recovery from said event of fate. I had, for example, chosen to survive and to become well again.

At the same time, unlike my lack of control over the fateful event, there did not seem to be many, if any, barriers or obstacles to my recuperation, with the exception, perhaps, of the evil spirit I called "normality." I often had the sense, in other words, that I was, more than anything, trying to be normal, trying to <u>force</u> myself to be normal, or at least to <u>appear</u> to be normal, out of fear that any time I did not <u>seem</u> normal would be attributed (by them? by me myself?) to the accident, i.e. to my slightly demented brain.

In much the same way, I kept waiting to feel better. I never gave a thought to the possible long-term consequences. Reading over my diary and letters written at the time, I am struck by how, being out of touch with the concept of recognizing one's limitations, I was sure that any day now I would return to normal, that it would all just go away, that I would lose this ambiguous sense that everything was at once both wrong for me and yet comfortable. When that duplicitous feeling occurred, I tried to pretend it wasn't there, but I never got very good at it. I'm not very good at pretending. It doesn't suit my character. At that time, however, things were different. I didn't even <u>try</u> to cover up the pretense. That would have been much too difficult, on top of everything else.

At first I was clearly accomplishing activities for others, for my family basically, who wanted me to improve. Only in time did I do such things for myself, as I became increasingly self-centered that is, after I acquired a sense of who myself was. It's difficult to say exactly when that happened, but after it happened, I continued to sometimes engage in activities as much for them as for myself because I liked it. Only gradually during my ordeal did I begin to feel compromised, as I got a sense of what I had lost.

Much of life for most people consists of taking actions which, though necessary, cost them something. Sometimes the activity costs them emotionally, sometimes physically, and only rarely financially. It now occurs to me that during my recovery this sense of my being in distress and having to sacrifice something in order to get well, never developed — I think because there was nothing (at least nothing apparent to me) with which to engage in "give and take." On the other hand, I always kept getting better, so I was not frequently, but only occasionally, depressed. I had not anticipated that an event could be so debilitating, yet at the same time without really being totally demoralizing. I had always thought that the two coincided, but not in my case.

Another thing. It had been considered (and even suggested to me) that I no doubt would have determined never to return to Greece, or at least to the place where the accident had happened, or to the hospital to which I had been taken. People regularly asked me, "Isn't it difficult to see places which remind you? Places like where it happened? Or the hospitals you were in?" I answer them truthfully, though I know it surprises them: "No." How to explain?

Well, it was inevitable that I should come back again in Greece to the place near the bridge, the scene of the accident. But again and again and again and again? Almost daily one summer. And each time, I was reminded not of the accident itself of course, which I do not remember, but of my whole journey of recuperation. As such, I found myself oblivious to reminders of the unexpected event, but I regularly renewed my acquaintance with my gradual "recovery of function" (as medical terminology calls it). In retrospect, I chose to devote my attention to regaining my autonomy, and not to my traumatic experience which required it.

Likewise, my physical ailments (broken bone and infected wounds) were not the problem, but the mental consequences, the aftermath of the illness. My recuperative life, full of its intricacies and uncertainties, became the center of my attention, even though I knew that the prognosis was pretty good. I felt my personality was in a race against the accident and neither one was winning, but rather my improvement from aphasia.

For a long time, I felt as if others (other people, other places, other times) governed and directed my life, in that I never invested my own memories (lack of memories really) with any strong significance. Much in the same way as people can look at or listen to things with indifference so I found that it was possible to <u>know</u> things with indifference, so that my natural good humor had been transformed into nothing ever coming to assume enormous importance. That changed with Libby's death. Libby had originally simply been Timothy's sister to me — a nice enough person, who lived an interesting and active life, dedicating herself to political activism and community organizing, when she wasn't running her businesses of the King Avenue Coffee House and her imports/bead store. Then, in 1986, when I was supposed to be working on returning to being ordinary, she suddenly died in an airplane crash.

In a flash, upon hearing of the catastrophe, I finally experienced a true crisis. Previously, I had tried feeling deep emotions such as guilt, but

Libby's death resulted in a deep correspondence between reality (not movies, in other words) and emotions. I've never completely spoken of it until now, but I recall very clearly how my initial state of disquiet gradually evolved into a combination of severe depression and a sense of loss. I not only missed her greatly, but I was struck by an intimate consciousness of human mortality such as I never had – not even when my father died. I found myself reacting — not simply to her absence, or with any preconceived notions of grief, but with an incredulous overindulgence with her passing. I virtually deified her deathbed. I obsessed for a short time, and this worried me. Here was a concrete manifestation of how my agitation was increasing, rather than lessening, with the passage of time.

A large part of my life had been dedicated to "moderation in all things," (Medio tutissimus ibis) as Terence (160 B.C.) said. But my natural good humor and pleasant disposition, one of balance, harmony, symmetry, and equilibrium, like a good Libra, had been transformed into an irascible monster, subject to fits of penetrating irritability. When that happened, my mind would regress to the time when, as a child, I had been bruised — either when falling down the marble stairs in the art museum at the age of 5, or being thrown off a horse into the huge bramble bush at the age of about 11. Now, as in both cases, I wanted somebody other than my family to make everything all right, and to bring everything back to normal, back to a sunny, happy reality.

The tears still reappear every now and then in my new life in my new world, though never in predictable ways, and I no longer have need for diversions when they appear. After all, the tears are no longer touching aspects of my mental fatigue, but an expression of either a dilemma, a disaster, or a crisis. Only rarely are they due to reminders of my aphasia. One relatively recent summer, for example, while attending a wonderful Cultural Kaleidoscope festival in East Palo Alto, I found myself suddenly carried away with sobs, for no apparent reason.

I stopped, frozen by my inexplicable tears, and noted where I stood when they erupted. I felt nothing special. No sadness. No grief. All in all, my tears seemed inconsistent with an otherwise enjoyable afternoon community festival. Only much later, upon reflection at a considerable distance could I reconstruct the mental model resulting in those tears which the festival no doubt subconsciously created. Of course once created, the tears were easily perpetuated by their infrequency. It felt so <u>good</u> to cry! Why?

Well, I think one of the most important results of my year of recovery was my increased awareness of, and empathy with, those considered "other." I never felt like I fit in during that year, and there was no turning point after which I felt like I <u>did</u> fit in. There was another reason. I was never conscious of myself while going through the process of recuperation, but I was always, increasingly, conscious of others. And they always seemed better than me. At everything. I felt that I had created the smallest minority group possible, consisting of only one person, namely me. Not that I was embarrassed to be me. I just wasn't as good as all the other people in the world because I wasn't completely normal, and probably never would be. It was, as they say, a bad scene. I felt inferior to the rest of the world of humanity. Others, observing my behavior, would never have guessed I harbored such thoughts. I didn't even admit it to myself, or think about it too often, as it was far too depressing. But the concept was always there. And there was nothing I could do about it. So I used to cry about it sometimes…

Deep down? The entire experience? I don't know why I remember some things and not others, and I don't know which is harder, trying to change yourself or trying to change other people, but I've thought and thought over and over again about this phase of my life. At one level, I felt I was living an illusion, and I was not who I claimed to be. At another level, it forced humility upon me. But perhaps most of all, there was an enormous difference between the way I no doubt appeared to the world during the process and the way that I felt, down deep inside, where I felt there was nothing. There was nothing there, deep inside of me. Or at least nothing I could find…My life lacked quality. There was quantity, with lots and lots of things to try and process; only they were in bits and pieces. My mental re-development came in anything but a quiet and commonplace way. It came in fits and starts, bits and pieces, and in a most circuitous way. After all, my thoughts getting lost in their attempt to find their way over damaged nerves was what made them lacking in quality. With no Random Access Memory (RAM), just Read Only Memory (ROM), the circuitry of my memory (both Small-Term-Memory and Long-Term-Memory) could have been compared to Theseus' trailing a string through the labyrinth. I once read such a comparison of memory to the Minotaur's labyrinth, in which the cortex is a labyrinth and the string of memory is a trace — a chain of nerve cells linked by synapses, where nerve impulses jump from one cell to another. Nerves I had. Memory traces I had. Mostly, however, they were just jumping around all around my injured brain.

Allow me to engage in an analogy, for which you need to understand that most of this book has been written during my summers, either in Greece or California, and not while in Ohio, where I used to live and where there are no mountains. The presence of mountains in California had an enormous affect upon me during my year of healing. Seeing them convinced me that the absence of mountains, which I experienced living in Ohio, is not just the presence of plains. No, it is definitely an <u>absence,</u> a lack, a deficiency, and not simply of mountains. Much like my aphasia.

There are other similarities besides mountains between California and Greece, like the anomaly of foliage and grassland. Unlike Ohio, where the weather grows cold in the autumn, so the deciduous trees lose their leaves and the grass turns from green to brown, and where the leaves and the grass return with the spring rains and the rise in temperatures, both Greece and California have quite different seasons. In both, it rains only in the winter and, even then, it never gets really cold, but just a bit cool, so the grass turns green only during the winter. Yet the deciduous trees still lose their leaves in the fall.

It may have just been a coincidence, but I recognized a correspondence between such Mediterranean seasons and my recovery from aphasia in California and, later, in Greece.

Like the climate changes in both California and Greece, my brain returned at the surface level, like grass, with the equivalent of rain, in the winter. But it took until the spring, when I considered returning to work and began to grasp the ramifications of my unfortunate accident and recovery that, like tree roots, I began to re-sprout my leaves.

Until then, everything I encountered conspired to give me a pleasant illusion of normality, so I often felt as though I was living an illusion, in that I was no longer who I claimed to be. I would (i.e. could) never have put it that way at the time. Only now, in retrospect, does such an insight appear to me.

At the time it all seemed so unalterable, yet at the same time, so unreal, like a wild but now caged animal, re-born into a kind of captivity, allowed not even a glimpse of real life outside the cage, until eventually liberated, by a combination of love and work, I would like to say. I have a strange feeling that I have been most freed by writing this book. That's not why I wrote it, but in completing it I find that I have experienced a kind of reconciliation with the accident, and consider myself to have been fortunate for surviving such an arduous journey. I haven't thought about my accident half as much as I have while writing about it, but I know I will remember it, and my process of recuperation, always. That was the time during which I finally and irrevocably discovered that I had a mind of my own.

My life now, 18 years after the accident, is much the same as it was prior to the accident, but I am not the same person. The process of recovery changed me, and while I would never have wished for it to happen, I do like myself better.

I enjoy noticing things, such as the alphabet song having the same tune as Twinkle, Twinkle, Little Star.

More importantly, I'm kinder, gentler, more patient, more content, more thankful to be alive, and more appreciative of the all the assistance I received while recovering that mind of my own.

I began writing the book to understand.

I completed it in celebration.

"I hope nothing. I fear nothing. I am free.

Δεν ελπίζω τίποτα. Δεν φοβούμαι τίποτα. Είμαι ελεύθερος.

Kazantakis' Epigram

THE END

Epilogue

I have postponed writing these reminiscences of my recovery from aphasia in an attempt to know and understand it all. These memoirs began in the form of a short essay for my family and friends, turned into an article for the likes of <u>Reader's Digest</u>, and gradually evolved into this book. Not only could I originally not have written it, but even when I could have, I opted to wait a bit because I do not believe that you can simultaneously live your life and write your life. One needs some distance, some perspective.

I do not present myself as other than I am. And I am not a writer, have never been a writer, anyway. A scholar at times, publishing articles, but not an author. A slight bookworm, yes, but as a <u>reader</u>, not a writer. By profession a teacher and researcher, I have delved into the depths of my memories, my notes, my doctors' examination notes, and my family's memos and recollections. For while a few books have been written on aphasia, I feel that my case is also deserving of attention, both due to the distinctive form which it took in my case, and because of my non-professional point of view. I am not a doctor, nurse, or medical technician. In fact, until recently (2002) I was not connected with the medical profession in any way. I was a Classics professor at a small liberal arts college and am now an administrator at a private graduate school.

Perhaps I can offer people, both sufferers and healers alike, some insight into, and an understanding of, recovery from extensive brain damage.

I consider myself a recorder, a commemorator, and somewhat of an analyst, or at least an interpreter, of my aphasia. This work is clearly not meant to be a comprehensive study, or case history. Nor do I claim to be able to assess or evaluate my recovery. I do not believe that to be possible in this type of self-study.

Yet just as some of the best insights into old age and approaching death come not from scientists or doctors, but from poets, so I am convinced that these memoirs of my aphasia have much to contribute to the dialogue, hopefully with both some pathos and some glory, to wax a bit poetic myself.

And while there is no secret agenda, my memory of the recover process is both subjectively accurate and no doubt slightly fictionalized (some names have been changed) — especially in that while I was present the entire time, and tried to keep notes, through letters, tapes, or journal entries, some recollections (especially thoughts) had to wait until I had the verbal means by which to express them. I also thought at the time that I would, perhaps more than anything, want to forget about the whole business, if it were ever 'over.' That turned out not to be true.

Not that I am attempting to raise the general level of discourse on recovery of function from brain injury by my reminiscing. Rather, I am perceptive enough that these ramblings qualify as an aphasic's narrative, and perhaps even personal history, based on the fact that they are as true as I can remember them. And since they are true, the reader should not expect them either to have an encoded message or to exemplify a moral position. On the other hand, they do not necessarily lack either or both. In that regard, this being a 'story' about a temporarily disabled, invalid, handicapped person (I do not like any of those words!), I really should have tried to spice up my narrative with a combination of hope and misery. Unfortunately, those don't work in this case, for the simple reason that I profoundly remember: I experienced neither hope nor misery while in recovery.

Finally, the reader may wonder how, after having been in such a state of existence, I can now remember what happened. In addition to the need for you to understand the explanations offered throughout, I'm hoping you can also give me the benefit of a slight cessation of doubt, and extend the boundaries of autobiographical narrative. Rest assured that you can completely believe some things. And I use "some" advisedly, for I have always believed that the genre of autobiography is rather dubious in terms of truth, to say the least. Thus, I know that I embarked upon a perilous journey in presenting these writings. As for all the rest? Well, I also believe that there is a certain insight to be gained from a recovered person's remembrance of that recovery, perhaps at a level even more truthful than superficial reality.

If you've let your mind float free, an understanding of the process of my recovering "a mind of my own" should have followed.

Appendix I on Aphasia

I have neglected to provide you with any due consideration of the multifaceted aspects of aphasia, and would like to summarize some of the literature I have read and studied connected with head injuries in general, and aphasia in particular. Because I have wanted, over the years, to gain some educated insight into the workings of the human brain (having lost mine for a while), I feel I must touch briefly on my understanding of: 1) some of the basics regarding brain structure, 2) mental function involving aphasia, in particular, and 3) a few representative varieties of aphasia. In addition, I would like to take the opportunity to discuss some of my theoretical suggestions 4) for the relationship between language and thought, as well as 5) for a relationship between my living through this traumatic disorder and some analogous experiences in my earlier life (LSD).

I apologize for the abundance of quotations, however this portion of my writings on aphasia is both unfamiliar territory and a true struggle for my convalescent language.

1) My knowledge of the structure and workings of the human brain is based on my study of a variety of scholars: biologists, physiologists, neurobiologists, psychologists, psycholinguists, neuropsychologists, neurolinguists, anatomists, etc. These scientists and others deal, in other words, with both the hardware (structure) and the software (function) of the brain in general, and of memory in particular, as understanding brain damage from head injury requires a knowledge of both the anatomy and psychology of the brain. Now any description of the structure of the brain, the hardware of memory, involves at least 2 levels, for the brain has both an anatomy of parts, and a circuitry, providing the connections (by means of neurons) between the different anatomical parts of the brain. Those neurons, through their synapses, receive, process, and then transmit information along their axons to other neurons, which engage in the identical process in turn. In much the same way, in other words, that the various segments, the lobes, of the brain, are connected by means of neurons, so too are the cell bodies of the neurons themselves connected to each other by means of axons. The circuitry, the interconnections, that is to say, is much like a spider web, or a quilt, of information, whether that information is of fact, of feelings, of languages, of images, of procedures (how to <u>do</u> things) — whatever.

In my case, the connections inherent in my working brain were where the (my?) problem, which came to be termed "aphasia," occurred. Brain damage, after all, tends to be a very selective type of injury, for while some abilities may be completely lost, others will re-emerge completely unscathed. At the same time, those abilities virtually unaffected by the injury, may lose the connections necessary to exercise those facilities. In the case of memory, for example, whether short-term memory (STM) or long-term memory (LTM), a brain may still have the memories residing somewhere, however one may have forgotten exactly how to "reach" them, as the memories have been filed away, catalogued, and cross indexed by many subject headings. Indeed, can one say that the memories have been retained, should the person completely loose the map by which to find them?

Brain injury/healing research has experienced a fairly intense revolution in the past 20—30 years, however some of the basics regarding the brain damage I experienced can be summarized rather briefly. Understand, however, that much of our knowledge regarding the anatomical sites of such things as memories and language is not so much due to injury to particular areas where those memories and languages are stored, as to damage done to the pathways by which the language and memory areas are connected. In fact, because of the immense increase in our knowledge of linguistic mental processes in recent years, the linguistic symptoms are now often used to predict the location of the injury, when such is otherwise unknown.

Due to the lesion caused by the helmet when it broke, my doctors knew that my explicit brain injury occurred on the right side of my brain, between the occipital and parietal lobes. This area, termed the parieto-occipital sulcus, is mainly located on the surface of the brain, and the parietal lobe in particular is thought to be:

> "where we assemble our world. It is probably here that letters come together as words, and words get put together in thoughts." (Ornstein, Robt. & Thompson, Richard F. The Amazing Brain, Boston, 1984, p.36)

In addition, however, my brain undoubtedly also experienced an implicit contrecoup — namely a force exerted on the area at the opposite side of the brain, where the blow is therefore also experienced. In fact,

> "the force of the blow is relatively more important than its location. It can cause what has been termed the coup, or trauma due to cortical contact with bone directly under the blow,…" (Arnadottir p.83)

Thus, between the two, if not more, regions of my brain affected by my broken helmet, I developed aphasia, the fundamental loss of human's "most characteristic attribute, language." (Norman Geschwind p.83) Typically aphasia results from damage inflicted on the left temporal lobe — the kind of harm often caused by a stroke, for example, or from force exerted against the left temporal lobe. My injury, however, was heavily localized (in its explicit aspect anyway) on the right side of my brain, with a variety of (mostly very positive) results.

Before I tell you more about my aphasia, indulge me for a moment while I broaden your horizons regarding head injuries in general.

The human brain is a part of the central nervous system (CNS), which controls the body's activities, including speech, language and body movement. The nervous system controls these activities by means of a complicated array of chemical and electrical networks, connected by fibers. In order to reduce the injury from blows to the head, these nerves are also protected by the bones (the skull), a membrane and a cushion of fluid. The human brain itself consists of 3 sections: the cerebrum, the cerebellum (the bottom of the back of the head), and the brainstem, which runs down along the spinal cord. The cerebellum is the largest part of the brain and is composed of 2 hemispheres — left (verbal) and right (spatial) – which are connected by the corpus callosum, to allow communication between the 2 halves. Each hemisphere also has 4 lobes, each specializing in certain functions, as well as an outer layer, known as the cerebral cortex, with depressions (known as fissures) which mark the divisions between various portions of the cerebrum. Of the 4 lobes – frontal, temporal, parietal and occipital – the frontal lobe appears to be the most important for rational thinking, including language in the left hemisphere. The temporal lobe is connected with hearing, and thus the ability to understand spoken language. The parietal lobe specializes in sensory messages, such as touch and temperature, and the occipital lobe in vision, so that blindness can result from damage to the occipital lobe.

Aphasia, language impairment resulting from brain damage, can occur due to an injury on any of the various parts of the brain – either hemisphere, any of the 4 lobes, not to mention on a particular region of any of the lobes, many of which have been named for the aphasia researcher who discovered them (Broca, Wernicke, etc.) – so much so that aphasia has been termed a "constellation of neurological impairments." (L. Kumin p.14)

In addition, several language disorders are considered related to aphasia, in that they tend to accompany aphasia due to the damage to the nervous system (agnosia, hemiplegia, dysarthria, etc.). Given the intimate connection between these disorders and aphasia, I will consider them together. In general, it needs to be understood that aphasia is "an acquired impairment of language processes underlying receptive and expressive modalities and caused by damage to areas of the brain which are primarily responsible for the language function." (G. A. Davis <u>A Survey of Adult Aphasia</u> p.1)

In the early phase of my recovery, I experienced some motor dysfunction, fairly typical of brain injury victims. The problems most in evidence to me were physical (hemiplegia, hemiparesis) and sensory (agnosia, especially prosopagnosia). Hemiplegia (paralysis) or hemiparesis (muscle weakness), though usually temporary, is a common problem to head injury victims, as are severe headaches. Muscular dysfunction mostly affects the side of the body opposite the brain damage, and is often recoverable through exercise. Having suffered right brain injury, the left side of my body, especially my left leg, was affected, both with difficulty of balance and motor control, so using my left leg was exhausting.

Agnosias are sensory disorders. Similar to aphasia, an impairment in which a person may be able to recognize and "understand" a language, however has difficulty obtaining any deep or subtle meaning from that language, people inflicted with agnosia have the ability to hear, see or touch, but cannot make <u>sense</u> out of what they so perceive. Three-dimensional spatial disorientation, in particular, is common with damage to the right hemisphere parietal lobe. I bumped into things.

I also recall being told that I experienced prosopagnosia (common to right hemisphere occipital lobe damage), the inability to recognize previously known people, including both very familiar people and those just met – in my case even my family. I am certain there were other non-aphasic disorders, however I most recall the ones just mentioned.

Until fairly recently, there was relatively limited access to information regarding brain injuries due to the fact that people involved in serious accidents (say in automobiles) tended either to die or to become "brain dead." More recently, however, due to both safety devices (such as seat belts) and improved medical facilities, people sustaining brain injuries are more likely to survive, and even to "recover." "Indeed, it has been suggested that brain injuries may represent a 'silent epidemic' of Western civilizations…" (Kolb p. 176), given that 0.25% of the population sustains a closed head injury each year, with the result that the chance of suffering a head injury during one's lifetime is about 1/20.

Prior to what came to be termed the "Decade of the Brain" (1960s-70s), brain damage was thought to be permanent and virtually irrevocable, given that brain tissue, once destroyed, is "forever beyond repair." (Gardner "Brain Damage" p.29) Thus, treatment of brain injury patients was "left to psychiatrists and rehabilitation workers who 'might' be able to help patients copy more effectively with their permanent disabilities." (Stein & Glasier p.4) When activities connected with the areas destroyed (so-called "recovery of function") did occur, it was simply thought that "other brain areas 'took over' the functions of the injured tissue." (Stein & Glasier p.5)

But with continuing, and more sensitive research techniques in neuroanatomy, noting that fairly extensive cortical reorganization after brain injury was observed in both primates and children, "the view that the adult central nervous pathways were fixed and immutable began to change." (Stein & Glasier p.6) Gradually, it became evident that "a brain injury itself is not a monolithic event" (Stein & Glasier p.8), and that, due to the "plasticity" of adult neurons, partially damaged nerve fibers were capable of producing new terminal branches. In addition to creating new branches to replace those destroyed by the injury, it was also discovered that those intact nerve fibers in close vicinity to the injured area would also produce new terminal branches — in order to better communicate with the damaged area.

There were other milestones. Pharmacologists, for example, found that the injured human brain developed a whole "pharmacology of recovery" — a set of chemical mechanisms that facilitate brain injury repair, complete both with agents to block the negative processes and with proteins and peptides to stimulate the repair of those neurons damaged by the injury.

When brain damage occurs,

> "...it triggers a complex cascade of processes that take place over potentially very long periods of time (days, weeks, months and perhaps even years) and produce changes throughout the entire nervous system which are not just limited to the injury site alone." (Stein & Glasier p.8)

In fact, and in spite of adverse publicity and the lack of government support for research using aborted fetuses, some experiments have been done using fetal brain tissue grafts to reduce the deficits caused by brain injuries and to enhance the Central Nervous System mending. While sensory, motor, and cognitive deficits have not been completely eliminated, the use of grafts, including those done with genetically engineered cells, have improved the recovery process to the extent that researchers have developed a much better understanding of how the human brain attempts to repair itself.

Which brings us to the subject of healing from brain injury, or what specialists prefer to call "recovery of function," since, once destroyed, brain tissue cannot be repaired, we are really only talking about behavioral, and not physiological, recovery. That behavioral recovery can take many forms. While some people resume their normal (or pre-brain injury) life, most patients with brain injuries appear to return to normal, but also report a wide range of disorders — from being tired all the time to an inability to concentrate.

Whatever the form the dislocation takes, a brain injury is almost certain to have an effect on personal relationships and job performance, no matter how well the person has initially returned to normal. This dislocation has often been termed a kind of "post-traumatic stress syndrome," with behavioral impairments similar to those of deprived children.

For while simple behaviors might be re-learned with relative ease, the complexity of dealing with real world situation might be unaffected by the apparent normality. Indeed, "who should decide what constitutes adequate functional recovery?" (Stein & Glasier p.10) Patients often learn new tricks in order to appear as normal as those around them.

An experiment done with rats trained to walk along a beam in order to get water, for example. After removal of their sensory-motor cortex, the rats initially kept falling off the beam. Within one week, however, their running along the beam looked very normal, to the naked eye. When films of their gait were analyzed closely, on the other hand, they clearly ran completely differently from "normal" rats, with a very abnormal pattern of hind leg movement.

The question arises, in other words, whether "recovery of function" following brain injury is truly a restitution of damaged brain functions at all, or simply the development of new alternative behaviors to replace those which were lost.

This consideration would appear to be relatively insignificant were it not for the fact that such theoretical ideas have an impact on therapy and rehabilitation following brain injury.

Training brain injury patients to develop simple compensatory strategies may, given the inclination of the human brain to undergo cerebral reorganization, and not simply at the site of the injury, have serious (and adverse?) effects on their eventual functional recovery. Do we want people in recovery from brain injury to become more normal, or more themselves?

2) So much for the brain in general. Moving on to aphasia in particular. Aphasia, they say, is not really a disease at all, but only a symptom of brain injury. Be that as it may, it would appear that those making such a claim have confined themselves to the study of left brain (mostly Broca's, due to a stroke) aphasia.

But rather than delve immediately into one of the many arguments concerning aphasia, let me begin with some statistics. More than 1 million American people have aphasia. Approximately 80,000 more a year develop aphasia, mostly from strokes and accidents.

Strokes, or cerebrovascular accidents (CVA), namely the obstruction or rupture of blood vessels in the brain, occurring at the rate of 300,000/year in America, are the third leading cause of death in the United States. A stroke in the left hemisphere causes numbness or paralysis on the right side of the body, and great interference with language abilities. A stroke in the right hemisphere, on the other hand, causes virtually identical numbness or paralysis, in this case on the left side of the body, but, of more significance to my situation, leaves the patient's language ability intact. Right hemisphere stroke victims do, however, have "a tendency to get lost, poor memory for nonverbal things, and a certain emotional flatness." (Blakeslee p.137)

Understanding the differences between left and right hemispheric damage from strokes can be very useful in understanding the relationship between brain damage and problems with language such as aphasia. Simply put, 97% of people suffering from permanent language disorders caused by brain injuries have been damaged on the left side of their brain. Damage to the right hemisphere, on the other hand, results in difficulty performing spatial tasks, such as drawing or whistling a tune. To quote Howard Gardner:

"An individual with a lesion in his right hemisphere may be unable to dress himself properly and may lose his way in the hospital while he can read and speak just as before." (Howard Gardner "Brain Damage: A Window on the Mind" <u>Saturday Review</u> (Aug.9, 1975), p.26)

I have concentrated on the significance of the 2 hemispheres in brain injuries because my aphasia was due to a right hemispheric lesion, not commonly connected with verbal dysfunction. And recent findings regarding right brain processes have shed a great deal of light on my research into right hemispheric brain damage.

Originally, the simplistic way of characterizing left brain as controlling verbal, and right brain spatial, tasks was sufficient, due to the obvious impairments resulting most often from brain injuries.

"It has been suggested more recently, though, that this difference simply reflects the way processes are organized in the right hemisphere: specific processes are distributed over larger regions of brain tissue in the right half of the brain than in the left half. The most likely reason for the slow recognition of the importance of the right hemisphere, however, is that disabilities caused by lesions in the right hemisphere were not so easy to analyze and fit into the traditional ideas about brain function. Most damage to the right hemisphere does not abolish any obvious human abilities in an all or none fashion; instead, it disturbs behavior in fairly subtle ways. Some of the problems occurring with right-brain damage are not as easy to label as the problems associated with left-hemisphere injury. They often went unnoticed or were masked by more obvious physical disabilities such as those found in most stroke victims." (Springer & Deutsch p.16)

Some of the ways in which my right hemisphere injury disturbed my <u>social</u> behavior are discussed in Chapter 5. In terms of my general behavior, however, and its relationship to my brain damage, it is worth noting that:

"...depression is more associated with left-hemisphere lesions, whereas patients with right hemisphere lesions are more frequently unconcerned with their condition." (Arnadottir p.203)

This lack of concern, or what is often termed emotional flatness of patients such as myself with injury to the right (or nondominant) hemisphere of the brain, of course also affects the way in which we often have indifference reactions and a tendency to joke." (Arnadottir p.203) Based on my experience with an injured brain, I would say that our inclination to tell jokes is virtually identical to the tendency of hard-of-hearing people to talk a lot. It's easier than listening, just as telling jokes is easier than conversing.

Allow me to quote for you the best brief synopsis I know for describing right brain injured patients:

> "People with nondominant brain injuries often are "flat," that is, they appear to be without strong or varied emotions. Sometimes, although the external appearance, facial expression and body language sends this message, people do not actually feel indifferent. Instead, they can feel sorrowful or moody and swiftly change from sadness to gaiety or silliness. They tend to be less cautious and anxious about their condition than people with dominant brain injuries. In fact they are often impulsive and indifferent to precarious situations because of the neglect or denial of their disabilities. Thus they may "wade" into sexual behaviors and activities without precautions. On the other hand, they may be indifferent to the point of having no interest in close relationships; they may be so distractible that they cannot attend to or concentrate on what a partner is trying to communicate." (Griffith and Lemberg p.47)

Which brings us, oddly enough, back to aphasia. My aphasia. I mostly experienced Crossed Aphasia — a very rare type of aphasia experienced by right-handed patients suffering injury to their right (nondominant) hemisphere. Other than language problems, there are usually movement difficulties due to spatial disorientation, some of these difficulties clearly being caused by disturbances in perception. Trouble with judging distances, or sizes of things, or the speed of moving objects, can result in loosing one's way, or clumsy movements, such as difficulty knowing how to put on clothing, or loosing one's balance and falling, or, as in my case, bumping into things.

Of far more significance to me than such minor spatial perception problems, however, was the rather severe impairment initially, of my language competence. For while linguistic ability is primarily a function of the left (dominant) hemisphere, non-dominant brain injury causes problems with the subtleties of language — of what is sometimes termed discourse. Injury to the parietal and occipital lobes of the left hemisphere causes linguistic dysfunctions with such things as possessives ('my boyfriend's mother'), prepositions ('right next to') and passives ('I was truck by a car'). Instead of damage to the basic grammatical, lexical and phonetic processes of language, right hemispheric aphasia affects such linguistic functions as idioms, discourse, and especially prosody, "the vocal inflection, stress, and melody of speech that can provide words and sentences with meanings that go beyond their basic dictionary definition. Consider, as an example, how the sentence "You are a bad boy" can have radically different meanings depending on whether the inflection reveals the speaker as irate or quietly concerned or as an ironic observer." (Damasio p.537)

Likewise, a phrase such as "too many cooks spoil the soup" can have absolutely nothing to do with food, and an aphasic knowledge of language may not be able to comprehend that at all. Woodrow Wilson's right hemisphere stroke, for example, did not affect his core language ability, but he definitely sounded differently, in that "his voice never regained the emotional inflections and resonance of his earlier years" (Wm. H. Calvin The Throwing Madonna: Essays on the Brain p.159).

So while literal meanings of words and phrases are understood, and with an apparently solid grasp of such things as morphology (phonetics), syntax (grammar) and semantics (vocabulary), there are still clear deficits in linguistic competence, given the more subtle and metaphorical aspects of a living language.

"Persons with nondominant brain injury may speak in a monotone, seemingly without emotion (aprosody). Their eye contact is often poor. They may be unaware of the rules of polite conversation, tending to stand too close, interrupt the other speaker, and not allow others "equal time." They may talk excessively, fail to come to the point, switch abruptly to other topics, and be disorganized in presenting their ideas. People with right brain injuries often fail to appreciate the subtleties of what others say. Frequently they are concrete in their interpretations. "The grass is always greener on the other side of the street" may mean just that to them. They may miss the meaning of facial expression, body movements and gestures, and the little variations of tone or voice or inflection that change the meaning of what is said, or are substituted for speech." (Griffith and Lemberg p.45)

It should be noted that such a pattern of communication is difficult to handle emotionally and is especially detrimental to social interaction. Most people have experienced a Freudian slip, or a temporary loss of a well-known person's name, or being at a loss for words. As an aphasic, however, I experienced such common events not only with amazing frequency and regularity, but with the feeling that I couldn't either control them or make them go away. And that's depressing. The give and take of true communication, rather than just listening and/or speaking, requires an active sensitivity to others in the world. Unfortunately,

> "the relationship between his capacity to express himself in language and his knowledge of the world is impaired. He resembles a kind of language machine, a talking computer that decodes literally what is said, and gives the most immediate (but not necessarily the implicitly called for) response, a rote rejoinder insensitive to the ideas behind the questions, the intentions or implications of the questioner." (Howard Gardner The Shattered Mind p.297)

Attempts to understand the remarkable difference in linguistic facility between the two hemispheres have tended to emphasize the right hemisphere's role in processing emotional, as well as phonetic, information connected with language. Thus, while the left brain analyzes linguistic input by means of a very intellectual approach, the right brain responds more intuitively, based on feelings. Children, for example, not yet as encumbered by the emotional baggage of adults, rarely develop aphasia as a consequence of right hemisphere damage. (Finger p.308) Adults with injured right hemispheres have a deficiency for interpreting the subtleties of language, due either to some dysfunction in their own emotional state, or due to the emotional aspects of the language.

3) OK. Enough on aphasia in general. Moving on to the particulars.

Many people have developed, and survived, aphasia. So much so, in fact, that the term aphasia has been used to describe a style of speaking, often called "aphasic speech":

> "The 68-year old [George Bush] president's mangled speech does in fact reveal a number of characteristics associated with a brain disorder called aphasia: frequent grammatical errors, talking around subjects, groping unsuccessfully for the right word, and substituting one word for another of close meaning or similar sound." (Jesse Furman "The Speech Thing: Is Bush brain-damaged?" The New Republic Aug.17 & 24, 1992, p.14)

There are many different types of aphasia, ranging from a to w: acoustic, ageusic, amnesic,...verbal, visual, Wernicke's, etc. Our knowledge concerning the varieties of aphasia derives, of course, from observation rather than experimentation, as with most language physiology, "because nature's accidents perform a messy experiment and we merely document the outcome and try to make some sense out of similar accumulated evidence." (Wm. H. Calvin <u>The Throwing Madonna: Essays on the Brain</u> (NY, 1983), p.168)

To make things somewhat easier to understand, these numerous varieties of aphasia can be organized into 4 broad categories, according to the National Institute of Health (NIH):

a) Expressive aphasias, such as motor, nonfluent, and Broca's aphasia, involve the difficulty in conveying thoughts, through either speech or writing.

b) Receptive (comprehensive) aphasias, such as sensory, fluent, and Wernicke's aphasia, involve a difficulty understanding spoken or written language. These patients cannot make sense of the words seen or heard. Speech for them is devoid of specific meaning. ("I like to do those things all the time with them, just like that.") These patients made abundant use of generic terms such as "thing" and "stuff." Also, words of similar associated meaning are often substituted for the appropriate word, as in "chair" for "table."

c) Anomic (or amnesic) aphasias are much milder aphasias, applying to such occasions as when a patient can't recall correct the precise word or name for something or somebody, so they talk around the object or person, until listeners understand to what or whom they are referring.

d) Global aphasias are very severe. The brain damage is extensive, whereby patients lose almost all their language functions. These patients cannot speak or understand speech, can neither read nor write.

My aphasia appears to have originally fit into the Receptive category, and then, as my year of recovery progressed, into the Anomic category of aphasia. The two most common types of aphasia — Broca's and Wernicke's — are not applicable to my experience, due to both Broca's area and Wernicke's area being situated in the left hemisphere. In particular, after reading descriptive summaries of most of the various types or symptoms of aphasia, I can identify most of all with the following:

— agraphia: the inability to write (early in my recovery).

— alexia: the inability to read (early in my recovery).

— anomia: difficulty recalling words and naming objects; the least localized disorder; patients not severely impaired (throughout my recovery, and, to a certain extent, still now).

— apraxia: the inability to perform an action, even though the muscles required are sound (early in my recovery).

— circumlocution: the ability to talk around the desired word, usually by means of descriptions and pointing, when unable to retrieve it (through my recovery year)

— paraphasia: the substitution of an incorrect word or phrase ("knife" for "fork") for the correct one (throughout my recovery year, with decreasing frequency).

— post traumatic amnesia: the disturbance of memory for events that occurred immediately following a head injury (still now).

— somatic: difficulty recalling the correct word for a concept, especially nouns, verbs and adjectives, often hesitating and using circumlocutions (throughout my recovery with decreasing frequency, and to a certain extent, still now).

Regarding my particular variety of aphasia, I would say that my mind operated somewhat like that of an infant, for whom information is continuously being processed. So much so, that the information, though received, is not able to be stored and filed away, due to the non-existence, as yet, of memory files such as "animal," "dog," and "puppy." Without such coding, by which to index incoming information, it falls out of one's mind just as quickly as it comes in, much like a sieve. Put another way, my ability to comprehend incoming information by bytes was intact, however the connections between the individual bytes, or the memory codes by which to file it away, had been disrupted.

> "Still others might not be able to name, say, a cat upon
> seeing it, but after making appropriate associations —
> it purrs and is furry to the touch — they manage to
> retrieve the animal's name by some alternate route."
> (Dobkin p.80)

Which brings me, at last, to the subject of recovery. The outlook for recuperation from aphasia is much better if the patient is younger and, obviously, with less extensive brain damage. In addition, again not surprisingly, recovery is easier for patients with better language comprehension, rich vocabularies, more creative ability and expressive/communication skills. More emotional balance, positive personal attitude, and strong family support before the injury all contribute to good treatment outcome.

First, a few comments regarding the impact of age on healing from brain injury. Normal aging of the mind involves an increase in the amount of information stored, but the percentage of memory recallable without difficulty stays the same. As a result, older people appear to forget more. With age, short term memory (STM) gets slower and long term memory (LTM) endures. Memory, after all, works better the more the connections. The more a memory is relived, the more permanent it becomes, and the more the depth of processing, (i.e. understanding, and not just memorizing), the better the retention.

Finally, for this appendix on brain injury in general, and aphasia in particular, perhaps the best descriptions, from my point of view, are those contained in fictional accounts written by authors Bernard Malamud and Paul Bowles. First, Malamud, in <u>Dubin's Lives</u> (NY, 1977):

"He wept because his memory was bad. He had at first almost not noticed, or tried not to notice. Recently, forgetting had laid hold hard. It didn't help that Dubin knew Montaigne had complained of a slow mind and incredible lack of memory, despite which he wrote works of genius. Emerson, at sixty-five, was closer to how Dubin felt at fifty-eight: the old man complained of a tied tongue; he said he was "wanting in command of imagery" to match his thought. You had this thing to say and the words would not come; butterflies appeared and flew around the thought. Dubin, against the will, actively forgot names, details, words. He was losing them as though they were coins dropping out of holes in his pockets; or out of his raddled brain. They fell like raindrops into a stream - go find them. Usually when he forgot words he would wait for them to seep back into consciousness like fish drawn up to the hungry surface of a stream. He would remember the initial letter of the forgotten word or sense sounds in it; soon the word reappeared in an illumination. Now words rarely returned when Dubin needed them. He concentrated, trying hard to conjure up a word he could not repossess. It had teased him with its closeness, then burst like a bubble. It was not his to have. He couldn't say what he wanted to; he remained silent…Where are the associations of yesteryear? It was a game of disappearances. Here's this man walking on the road but when you meet up it's his shadow; or it's another man or another road whom you don't remember or even want to know… Dubin forgot what he read as he was reading it, and / much of what he had recently read. Books fell apart in his head; or went up in smoke. He could not repeat, step by step, a long argument. He remembered only the bare bones of what he must know to keep working on his biography. He had notes in place of memory; had to reread often to recall what he had forgotten…When he reread what he had written about him, it seemed to Dubin that someone else had written it…Am I forgetting life, or is life forgetting me?" (pp.329-330)

Compare an equally insightful, if not more eloquent, description of a similar experience, by Paul Bowles, in <u>The Sheltering Sky</u> (NY, 1949):

"His mind was occupied with very different problems. Sometimes he spoke aloud, but it was not satisfying; it seemed rather to hold back the natural development of the ideas. They flowed out through his mouth, and he was never sure whether they had been resolved in the right words. Words were much more alive and more difficult to handle, now; so much so that Kit did not seem to understand them when he used them. They slipped into his head like the wind blowing into a room, and extinguished the frail flame of an idea forming there in the dark. Less and less he used them in his thinking. The process became more mobile; he followed the course of thoughts because he was tied on behind. Often the way was vertiginous, but he could not let go. There was no repetition in the lands ape; it was always new territory and the peril increased constantly. Slowly, pitilessly, the number of dimensions was lessening. There were fewer directions in which to move. It was not a clear process, there was nothing definite about it so that he could say: "now up is gone." Yet he had witnessed occasions when two different dimensions had deliberately, spitefully, merged their identities, as if to say to him: "Try and tell which is which." His reaction was always the same: a sensation in which the outer parts of his being rushed inward for protection, the same movement one sometimes sees in a kaleidoscope on turning it very slowly, when the parts of the design fall headlong into the center. But the center! Sometimes it was gigantic, painful, raw and false, it extended from one side of creation to the other, there was no telling where it was; it was everywhere. And / sometimes it would disappear, and the other center, the true one, the tiny burning black point, would be there in its place, unmoving and impossibly sharp, hard and distant. And each center he called "That." He knew one from the other, and which was the true, because when for a few minutes sometimes he actually came back to the room and saw it, and saw Kit, and said to himself: "I am in Sba," he could remember the two centers and distinguish between them, even though he hated them both, and he knew that the one which was only <u>there</u> was the true one, while the other was wrong, wrong, wrong. It was an existence of exile form the world. He never saw a human face or figure, nor even an animal; there were no familiar objects along the way, there was no ground below, nor sky above, yet the space was full of things. Sometimes he saw them, knowing at the same time that really they could only be heard. Sometimes they were absolutely still, like the printed page, and he was conscious of their terrible invisible motion underneath, and of its portent to him because he was alone. Sometimes he could touch them with his fingers, and at the same time they poured in through his mouth. It was all utterly familiar and wholly horrible — existence unmodifiable, not to be questioned, that must be borne. It would never occur to him to cry out." (pp.231—232)

Note: in my attempts to write regarding my encounter with aphasia, I have fallen into the trap of considering myself incapable of competing with the writings of true authors. Yet similar thoughts are in my head as well. They simply have remarkable difficulty getting out. And even when they do, they seem so very inferior to the experience they are attempting to describe.

==========

"Many aphasics come to feel incompetent even though their overall intelligence, as measured, say, by an intelligence quotient, does not decline. Those with insight into their impairment always anguish over their flubbed attempts to say what they mean. One of my patients, who could say only "yes, yes" a year after her stroke, once described her feelings to me by drawing a picture of herself as a mummy entombed in a bird's cage." (Dobkin p.80)

==========

4) OK. My attempt to approximate a medical scientist has run itself dry. But before I hand in the towel in this rather non-autobiographical section, let me take advantage of the opportunity to indulge myself in a few semi-philosophical suggestions (my brother the philosophy professor is going to <u>kill</u> me) on the relationship between language and thought.

I realize that I am not very well prepared to engage in discourse on this undoubtedly scholarly subject. Nor would some consider me very well equipped these days (since the accident) to ponder very deep thoughts. Nevertheless, I do feel slightly empowered to do so, due to my experiences during recovery, and I am encouraged to communicate some of my thoughts on the subject due to my work on this treatise — which has turned into an opus of substantial breadth, and hopefully depth.

To put the issue very simply: Is it possible to think without a language by which to do so?

Or, approached from the other direction: Are all the words (not sounds) that we say thoughts?

During my encounter with aphasia, I read a smattering of writings on the subject of the relationship between language and cognition, and I can tell you: opinions vary widely. The two opposing extreme positions are relatively simple to summarize, and just as simple to dismiss.

a) Language and cognition are two completely separate processes, so that our capacity to think is completely unimpaired by damage resulting from aphasia.

b) Language and cognition are two intimately connected processes, so that the occurrence of aphasia results in the virtual death of thought.

Given that aphasia is a disorder of linguistic processing, "the loss of the ability to make sense of language," (NIH <u>Aphasia: Hope through</u>

<u>Research</u> (#89-391) p.1) the mechanisms for translating thoughts into language are clearly disrupted. It is the extent to which the disruption of language affects the process of thought which is the question. And the question relates to the basic issue of what makes human thought distinct from that of animals.

We humans can do two things which animals cannot. We can think about things which are not real, and we can communicate our thoughts by means of language.

"Ultimately, it is our mental apparatus, or capacity to think, our capacity to deal with ideas, our capacity to find unities, coherences in variations, that's what makes us free, and that's what makes us human." (Dr. Joseph Kovach, The Menninger Foundation, quoted in PBS video "The Mind: Thinking" (episode 8), 1988.)

Communicating our thoughts by means of language is not only useful to our survival. It is also pleasurable, in that we create stories — a rich inner world of stories — which are no doubt useful to our survival as well. The two processes of language and thought are intensely connected, however I cannot believe that the second (thought) requires the first (language).

The three best analogies I can muster for this opinion are the languages of animals/infants, my experience in foreign lands, and the common problem of forgetting someone's name. Studies have shown that animals and infants clearly have thoughts without the words by which to express them, though language both facilitates the expression of those thoughts and facilitates their cognition. Similarly, when one can't recall someone's name, or is traveling in a foreign country and can't understand the language surrounding them, these people still know the person whose name they have forgotten, and they still have the thoughts, just not the means by which to express them. Concepts surely survive alterations in language, as anyone who has spent time with aphasic patients will tell you.

5) Looking back over my process of recovery from aphasia, I feel I must touch briefly on my life prior to my accident. I initiate this excursus because people rarely ask me what about my year-long healing from aphasia made the deepest impression upon me. If they did ask, however, my answer would entail a brief trip back into my pre-accident life, as I am suggesting an intimate relationship between my aphasia and the LSD trips I experienced over 20 years ago.

An aphasic, you must understand, experiences many realities. Unlike everyday reality, in which the world is encountered face-to-face in an overt kind of way, an aphasic perceives a world in which everything

— objects, dreams, fears, imaginings — is real. And as there remains little memory of everyday reality, everything thought, dreamed, or imagined, seems equally real. This abundance of realities is much like an LSD trip, or the morphing now seen in movies and music videos, however LSD is often alarming. It has been suggested that LSD trips are alarming "because the picture of the other, familiar everyday reality was still fully preserved in the memory for comparison." (Hofmann p.20) Those memories of everyday reality were, at least in my recovery, non-existent, with the result that there was nothing alarming about my realities. But it was overwhelming.

Any attempt, on the other hand, to describe this abundance of realities was as impossible as it is to get a person under the influence of LSD to describe, or even to draw, what they are sensing. Words don't seem sufficient, as they belong to another world. The whole idea of consciously describing the conscious, seems hilarious, even now, just thinking about it.

I do think, however, that I developed a new understanding of, I'll call it insight into, the unconscious, as a result of my year-long healing from aphasia. It has been suggested that:

> "Reality is inconceivable without an experiencing subject, without an ego. It is the product of the exterior world, of the sender and of a receiver, an ego in whose

deepest self the emanations of the exterior world, registered by the antennae of the sense organs, become conscious. If one of the two is lacking, no reality happens, no radio music plays, the picture screen remains blank." (Albert Hofmann <u>LSD, My Problem Child</u>: Reflections on Sacred Drugs, Mysticism, and Science, (trans. J. Olt), LA, 1983 (orig. 1979) p.196)

However one explains the difference between one's common awareness of everyday reality and the abnormal perception of many realities, there can be no doubt that the relationship between the conscious and the unconscious is different. "In the LSD state the boundaries between the experiencing self and the outer world more or less disappear, depending on the depth of the inebriation." (Albert Hofmann <u>LSD, My Problem Child</u> p.197) There is feedback between the complicated self and the complicated outer world. So much so (and this is my point) that one's appreciation of the world develops a different, and I would assert much deeper, meaning. Under the influence of LSD, that deeper meaning can be frightening to the point of terror, but under the influence of aphasia it constitutes more of a confusingly unconscious reality.

The boundary between real and unreal, between self and the other, ceases to exist. Those kinds of distinctions are simply far too simplistic for the complex world in which an aphasic lives.

Appendix II: Bibliography

Ahlsen, Elisabeth Discourse Patterns in Aphasia, Goteborg, 1985.

Albertson, E.T. "A glimpse into an aphasic's world," American Journal of Occupational Therapy, 1 (1947), 361-364.

Aphasia: Hope Through Research, N.I.H. Publication #89-391, U.S. Government Printing Office, Washington D.C., Reprinted Oct.1988.

Arnadottir, Gudrun The Brain and Behavior: Assessing cortical dysfunction through activities of daily living (ADL), St. Louis, 1990.

Bailey, Ronald H. The Role of the Brain (Time-Life), NY, 1975.

Beckett, Samuel "Comment Dire" (trans. "What Is the Word") in his Collected Poems, 1930-1978 (3rd ed.) London, 1984.

Begley, S. et al. "Memory," Newsweek (Sept.29, 1986), 48-54.

Blakeslee, Thomas R. The Right Brain: A new understanding of the unconscious mind and its creative powers, NY, 1980.

Brown, D.J. and Novick, R.M. "An Interview with Jerry Garcia" Magical Blend 41 (Jan. '94), 32-40, 88-89.

Bryden, M.P. & Ley, R.G. "Right Hemispheric Involvement in Imagery and Affect," Cognitive Processing in the Right Hemisphere, NY, 1983, 111-123.

Buck, M. "The language disorders: a personal and professional account of aphasia," Journal of Rehabilitation 29 (1963), 37-38.

Calvin, Wm. H. The Throwing Madonna: Essays on the Brain, New York, 1983.

_____ and Ojemann, George A. Inside the Brain: mapping the cortex, exploring the neuron, New York, 1980.

Chaikin, Joseph and Shephard, Sam (play) <u>The War in Heaven</u> (1987) in <u>A Lie of the Mind: a play in three acts</u> by Sam Shephard, New York, 1986.

_____ and Van Italie, Jean-Claude (play) <u>Struck Dumb</u>, NY, 1991.

Collett, Rosemary <u>Aphasia: My life in the Mists</u>, Duvall Media cassette, 1991. (Rev. by Gilmary Speirs, <u>Booklist</u> 88.16 (April 15, 1992), p.1546: "Rosemary Collett, who suffered a stroke in midlife, contrasts her previous life-style with the frustrations, anger, & grief of aphasiacs and outlines therapies and strategies that help her to cope.")

Critchley, M. "Dr. Samuel Johnson's aphasia," <u>Medical History</u> 6 (1962), 27-46.

Cousins, Norman <u>Anatomy of an Illness as Perceived by the Patient: Reflections on Healing and Regeneration</u>, NY, 1979.

Damasio, Antonio "Medical Progress: Aphasia" <u>New England J. of Medicine</u> 326.8 (1992), 531-539.

Dardick, Geeta "Prisoner of Silence," <u>Reader's Digest</u> (June 1991), 93-97.

Davis, G. A. Adult Aphasia Rehabilitation, San Diego, CA, 1985.

_____, A Survey of Adult Aphasia, Englewood Cliffs, N.J., 1983.

De Mille, Agnes Reprieve: A Memoir, NY, 1981.

De Reuck, A. and O'Connor, M. (eds.) Disorders of Language, Boston, 1964.

Dobkin, Bruce "Mechanic of the Mind," Discover 11.8 (August 1990), 78 -82.

Eisenson, J. Adult Aphasia: Assessment and Treatment, New York, 1973.

Finger, S., LeVere, T.E., Almli, C.R., and Stein, D.G. (eds.) Brain Injury and Recovery: Theoretical and Controversial Issues, NY, 1988.

Freud, Sigmund On Aphasia, NY, 1953, orig. 1891.

Furman, Jesse "The Speech Thing: Is Bush brain-damaged?," The New Republic (August 17 & 24, 1992), 14-15.

Gabbard, G.O., Twemlow, S.W., and Jones, F.C. "Do near-death experiences occur only near death?" J. Nerv. Ment. Dis. 169 (1981), 374 -378.

Gallup, G., Jr. Adventures in Immortality: A Look Beyond the Threshold of Death, NY, 1982.

Gardner, Howard "Brain Damage: A Window on the Mind," Saturday Review (Aug.9, 1975), 26-29.

_____, "The Shattered Mind: The person after brain damage, NY, 1974.

_____, Brownell, H., Wapner, W., & Michelow, D. "Missing the Point: The Role of the Right Hemisphere in the Processing of Complex Linguistic Materials," in Cognitive Processing in the Right Hemisphere, (ed. Ellen Perecman), NY, 1983, 169-191.

Geschwind, Norman "Language and the Brain," Scientific American 226.4 (April 1972), 76-83.

Gilman, Richard "Seeking the Words To Recapture a Past and Shape a Future (Joseph Chaikin's struggle to overcome aphasia)," The New York Times (May 19, 1991), sec.2 pp.H5 & H10.

Goldstein, K. Language and Language Disturbances, New York, 1948.

Grayson, B. and Flynn, C.P., eds. The Near-Death Experience: Problems, Prospects, Perspectives, Springfield, Ill., 1984 (BF789 D4 N42 1984): 21 articles on theories, clinical aspects, & consequences of NDEs, including an overview of the history of the field of near-death studies, which originated in the early 1970s with the work of Russell Noyes, Elisabeth Kübler-Ross, & Raymond Moody. Professional society founded 1981 called the International Association for Near-Death Studies (IANS); journal Anabiosis.

Griffith, Ernest K., and Lemberg, Sally Sexuality and the Person with Traumatic Brain Injury: A guide for families, Philadelphia, 1993.

Hall, W.A. "Return from silence: a personal experience," Journal of Speech and Hearing Disorders, 26 (1961), 174-176.

Han, Margaret & Foo, Sun-Hoo "Negative Evidence for Language Capacity in the Right Hemisphere: Reversed Lateralization of Cerebral Function," in Cognitive Processing in the Right Hemisphere (ed. Ellen Perecman), NY, 1983, 193-211.

Head, Henry Aphasia and Kindred Disorders of Speech, 2 vols., NY, 1963.

Hippocrates: on broken hip + bed-ridden for 50 days resulting in inability to use the leg.

Hodgins, E. Episode: report on the accident inside my skull, NY, 1964.

Hoff, H.E., Guilleman, R., and Geddes, L.A. "An 18th century scientist's observations of his own aphasia," Bulletin of Historical Medicine 32 (1958), 446-450.

Houchin, Thomas D. and DeLano, Phyllis J. How to Help Adults with Aphasia, Washington D.C., 1964.

Knox, D. R. Portrait of Aphasia, Detroit, 1971.

Kolb, Bryan "Mechanisms Underlying Recovery from Cortical Injury: Reflections on Progress and Directions for the Future" International School of Neuroscience 2 (1992), 1-13, in Recovery from Brain Damage: reflections and directions, ed. F. D. Rose and D. A. Johnson, London, 1992.

Kumin, Libby Aphasia, Lincoln, Nebraska, 1978.

Lerner, Max <u>Wrestling with the Angel: A Memoir of my Triumph over Illness</u>, NY, 1990.

Lesser, Ruth <u>Linguistics and Aphasia</u>, London, 1993.

Luria, A.R. <u>The Man with a Shattered World: The History of a Brain Wound</u>, NY, 1972.

McBride, Carmen <u>Silent Victory</u>, Chicago, 1969.

Moody, Raymond A., Jr. <u>Life After Life</u>, Covington, GA, 1975.

Moss, C. Scott <u>Recovery with Aphasia: The aftermath of my stroke</u>, Chicago, 1972.

Nolte, John <u>The Human Brain: An introduction to its Functional Anatomy</u>, 3rd Ed., St. Louis, 1993.

Ornstein, R. and Thompson, R.F. <u>The Amazing Brain</u>, Boston, 1984.

Osgood, C. and Miron, M. (eds.) <u>Approaches to the Study of Aphasia</u>, Baltimore, 1973.

Perecman, Ellen, ed. Cognitive Processing in the Right Hemisphere, NY, 1983.

Plato Republic 10, 614-621.

Primavera, A. and Bandini, F. "Crossed Aphasia: analysis of a case with special reference to the nature of the lesion," European Neurology 33 (1), (1993), 30-33.

Restak, Richard The Brain, New York, 1984.

Rife, Janet Miller Injured Mind, Shattered Dreams: Brian's Journey From Sever Head Injury to a New Dream, Cambridge, MA, 1994.

Ring, K. Life at Death: A Scientific Investigation of the Near-Death Experience, NY, 1980.

_____, Near-Death Studies: A New Area of Consciousness Research, Storrs, Conn., 1982.

Rolnich, M. and Hoops, H.R. "Aphasia as seen by the aphasic," Journal of Speech and Hearing Disorders, 34 (1970) 48-53.

Rose, F.D. and Johnson, D.A. Recovery from Brain Damage: reflections and directions, NY, 1992.

Rose, R.H. "A physician's account of his own aphasia," Journal of Speech and Hearing Disorders, 13 (1948), 294-305.

Rosenfield, Israel "Neural Darwinism: A New Approach to Memory and Perception" New York Review of Books 33.15 (9 Oct. 1986), pp.21-27.

Ruff, R.M., Levin, H.S. et al. "Recovery of Memory After Mild Head Injury: A Three-Center Study" in Levin, H.S., Eisenberg, H.M., Benton, A.L., eds. Mild Head Injury, Oxford, 1989, 176-188.

Sacks, Oliver Awakenings NY, 1976.

_____, A Leg to Stand On, NY, 1984.

_____, The Man Who Mistook His Wife for a Hat, and other clinical tales, NY, 1985.

Sarno, M. Aphasia: Selected Readings, New York, 1972.

Schuell, Hildred, Jenkins, James, & Jimenez-Pabon, Edward Aphasia in Adults: Diagnosis, Prognosis, and Treatment, NY, 1967.

Sies, L.F., and Butler, B. "A personal account of dysphasia," <u>Journal of Speech and Hearing Disorders</u> 28 (1963), 261-66.

Springer, Sally P. & Deutsch, Georg <u>Left Brain, Right Brain</u>, San Francisco, 1981.

Stein, Donald & Glasier, Marylou "An Overview of the Developments on Recovery from Brain Injury" in <u>Recovery from Brain Damage: reflections and directions</u>, ed. F. D. Rose and D. A. Johnson, New York, 1992, 1-22.

Van Italie, Jean-Claude (play) <u>The Traveler</u>, Los Angeles, 1987.

Wender, Dorothea "At the Edge of Silence," <u>Family Circle</u> (March 25, 1986), 62-69.

Wepman, Joseph M. <u>Recovery from Aphasia</u>, NY, 1951.

_____, <u>A Selected Bibliography on Brain Impairment, Aphasia, and Organic Psychodiagnosis</u>, Chicago, 1961.

Wilson, Jeanie "Bumped Your Head? Don't Laugh It Off," <u>Woman's Day</u> (Oct.15, 1985), 34-43.

Wulf, Helen H. <u>Aphasia, my world alone</u>, Detroit, 1973.

Yankowitz, Susan (play) <u>Night Sky</u>, New York, 1991.

Appendix III: Cast of Characters

Immediate Family:

Gayla — sister-in-law

Gene – younger brother

Jessie – niece

Bertha – Mom

Nancy – older sister

Sam – brother-in-law

Timothy – boyfriend at time of accident

Tom – lifetime-companion

Wesley – ex-husband

Others:

Anya – Timothy's daughter

Becky – OSU student

Bill – Kenyon Classics colleague

Bob – Kenyon colleague, died 1985

Collette – French friend in Greece

Fred – friend of Nancy's

Jerry – Robert's companion

Joan Straumanis – Kenyon Academic Dean in 1985

Kostas – Greek friend in Greece

Libby – Timothy's sister

Lisa – Timothy's daughter

Marianne – friend of Timothy's

Mark – Kenyon student

Marnie – Kenyon colleague

Pat – Bill's wife

Robert – Kenyon Classics colleague

Appendix IV: Timeline

1985:

May 21 – Accident

May 29 – Gene arrived in Greece

June 5 – New Bulletin to Kenyon College community

June 7 – Flight from Athens to Boston

June 10 – My mind woke up (Fell down trying to walk)

June 15 – Train from Boston to Charlottesville

June 19 – First walk

June 20 – Tried to run, but still too painful

June 26 – First dance

July 1 – First attempt to write

July 9 – First swim

July 12 – Did first load of laundry

July 18 – First cry

July 19 – First cup of coffee

July 20 – First run and first driving a car

July 23 – First played piano

August 8 – First awoke remembering a dream

August 12 – 17 – Trip by car to Epcot with Mom

September 10 – Ran without pain in my rear end

September 15 – Trip to Ohio

December 3 – UPI Interview

December 6 – Lecture at Stanford University

December 10 – Interview for Paul Harvey's "The Rest of the Story"

About the Author

Born in Japan and raised mostly in the American South, Harrianne Mills spent much of her childhood learning languages, playing the piano, and traveling abroad. After receiving a BA in history and doing graduate work in classics at Stanford, Harrianne spent 12 years teaching classical languages and history at Kenyon College in Ohio, working as an archaeologist on the Isthmia excavations in Greece, and publishing her research. After her accident, she worked for two Stanford research centers and the Carnegie Foundation for the Advancement of Teaching. She now works at the Pacific Graduate School of Psychology and is also editorial assistant for the Journal of Clinical Psychology. Harrianne has eclectic interests and enjoys traveling, reading and writing, and exploring new worlds of knowledge. She lives with her lifetime-companion, Tom Davidson, in Mountain View, California.

Made in the USA
San Bernardino, CA
09 January 2020